TREASURY OF
CROCHET
TECHNIQUES
& PATTERNS

TREASURY OF CROCHET TECHNIQUES & PATTERNS

Marshall Cavendish

Editor   Eleanor Van Zandt
House Editor   Elizabeth Longley
Designer   Heather Garioch

Published by
Marshall Cavendish Books Limited
58 Old Compton Street
London W1V 5PA

© Marshall Cavendish Limited 1985

ISBN 0 86307 333 6

Printed and bound in Italy by Sagdos SpA.
This volume is not to be sold in North America.

Contents

Introduction

Crochet is one of the most popular needle-crafts. Its versatility and adaptability, plus the wide range of garments for everyone in the family and the numerous – and beautiful – items for the home that can be created, make crochet a skill that is widely practiced, and one that is loved by its practitioners.

The TREASURY OF CROCHET TECHNIQUES AND PATTERNS contains more than a simple selection of projects to execute. For each project in the book, there are a number of variations of the stitch, or technique, used to make that item, and instructions for incorporating variations into that, or other, patterns to create a variety of totally different garments. It is a book for everyone who wants to improve their techniques and to explore lots of new ways of using crochet.

The TREASURY OF CROCHET TECHNIQUES AND PATTERNS is ideal for those who already enjoy crochet as well as those who are eager to learn. The main focus of the book is on the basic Techniques and Patterns in crochet. The first section deals with some of the textures, both simple and unusual, that can be created using crochet – from rice stitch and ridges to bobbles and shells, from Irish lace to extra-large patterns. Patterns and techniques using colour – jacquards, stripes, 'granny' squares, patchwork, and many more – make up the balance of Chapter One.

Each section of the chapter includes instructions for things to make using the skill described, plus ideas that can be adapted using the techniques learned. Each pattern, motif and variation is illustrated in full colour, and charts are provided wherever they are needed.

Crochet PLUS is next – Crochet PLUS Appliqué, Crochet PLUS Embroidery and Crochet PLUS Quilting are all skills which can be practiced by a relative beginner, but which offer tremendous scope for creating beautiful things with great flair. Projects include an embroidered outfit for a baby and jackets and waistcoats for children.

One of the prettiest ways to use crochet is as a trim on both clothes and household linen. The TREASURY OF CROCHET TECHNIQUES AND PATTERNS devotes a chapter to the subject, offering a beautiful selection of dainty lace edgings, insertions and buttons.

In addition, there is a handy reference section of Know How, including the basic stitches and techniques required for the projects.

Tools and Materials

Very little equipment is required for crochet. The basic tool is the crochet hook, which comes in a wide range of sizes, suitable for different yarns and stitch patterns. Very fine hooks are used for delicate lace fabrics and edgings, thick ones for working with heavy yarn or cord or to produce a very open fabric. Hooks are now sized metrically – from 0.60mm to 10mm in diameter. As they hold only one stitch at a time, they are approximately the same length. The fine ones are made of steel; the larger ones – often made of bone or ivory in the past – are now made of aluminium or plastic. The chart on page 168 gives the main metric sizes and their equivalents in the old British system of sizing, which divided hooks into the fine ones used with cotton and the larger ones used with wool. So if you have any old hooks, you can use them for modern patterns once you have determined their metric sizes.

For different types of crochet, such as Tunisian or hairpin crochet, you need special tools: a Tunisian, or afghan, hook, which holds many stitches at a time, and a hairpin fork, which holds loops that are crocheted together. But all the projects in this book are made with ordinary hooks.

Knitting needles are required for a few of the projects – for example, those with welts or cuffs of knitted rib. A tapestry needle in a fairly large size (15 to 13) is required for sewing seams. This type of needle has a blunt point, which will not snag the yarn, and a large eye for easy threading. It is also the type

of needle to use for any embroidery you may wish to work on crochet.

Stainless steel pins, with round heads, are used for pinning work out when blocking it into shape and for joining sections for seaming.

A ruler and tape measure are necessary for checking the tension and for measuring the work.

A small pair of scissors is also needed.

Yarns and threads

The range of materials suitable for crochet is enormous. In addition to the vast selection of knitting yarns, which include many different weights, fibres and styles – smooth, fluffy, silky and highly textured – you have a choice of numerous weights of crochet cotton, as well as linen and silk threads. Rug yarn and macramé cord can be used for household and personal accessories, from floor cushions to shopping bags. Ordinary parcel string, raffia, jute, and leather thonging are some unusual materials that can be used for crochet.

Yarns are classified in several ways – according to their weight or thickness, fibre content and construction.

Weight Shown at right are examples of the main weights of yarn. The word 'ply', used in describing some yarns, denotes the number of strands, or plies, twisted together to form the yarn. Although a ply may be of any thickness, terms such as 'three-ply yarn' and 'four-ply yarn' have a generally accepted meaning, so that a fuzzy yarn, for example,

might be described 'Knits as four-ply' to give an idea of its effective thickness.

This tightly-twisted two-ply yarn is equivalent to an ordinary three-ply and is suitable for lightweight garments.

This baby 'quickerknit' yarn is slightly thicker than a four-ply. Some baby yarns are finer; all come in pastel shades.

Made from cotton and rayon, this glossy fashion yarn (below) is about the same weight as a four-ply.

Double knitting yarn is about twice as thick as four-ply. It makes a warm garment, especially if spun of wool. This one has a noticeable twist, whereas other varieties have a smoother texture.

Chunky or double double yarns are used mainly for outer garments and for some furnishings. The example shown is a softly-spun wool of the Scandinavian type.

Fibre content Most knitting yarns today are spun either of wool, of a synthetic fibre such as acrylic, nylon or rayon or of a blend of wool and synthetic fibres. Mohair is another natural fibre that is often used, either by itself or combined with wool or a synthetic; it comes from the Angora goat and has a fluffy texture. Angora yarn, which is even softer, is made from the fur of the Angora rabbit. Alpaca is another soft fibre taken from a South American animal similar to a llama. It is often blended with wool. Cotton, silk and – less often – linen are other natural fibres used in knitting and crochet yarns.

Crochet cotton is a smooth yarn that comes in various types and thicknesses, graded by number, with the larger numbers designating finer threads. Among the types available are pearl cotton, or coton perlé (size 5), a shiny 2-ply thread that comes in a wide range of colours, six-cord cotton (sizes 20 and 30), which comes in white and ecru; and the finest tatting-crochet cotton (size 70), which comes in various colours. Some of these threads are sold by length, rather than weight. They are usually mercerized, a process that gives them greater strength and sheen.

Fibre content is an important consideration when buying yarn. Wool is the warmest and is the obvious choice for a garment intended for outdoor wear. It also has great resilience, holding its shape better than synthetics. Most wools can be hand-washed. Synthetic yarns, such as acrylics, are easy to care for – often machine-washable – which makes them a good choice for children's garments. The ball band normally gives information on the care of the yarn, often in symbolic form. A chart explaining these symbols is given on page 168.

Construction Most yarns have a smooth, or plain, texture, which may be loosely or tightly twisted. Some plain yarns have a noticeable 'cable' appearance; Aran and rug yarns fall into this category. Others, such as crêpe yarn, have a somewhat hard surface, which produces very clearly defined stitches. Still others, such as Shetland yarns, have a soft, slightly hairy texture. Smooth yarns are easy to handle and can be used for most projects.

Fashion yarns include a dazzling variety of textures that offer many possibilities for creating exciting designs. Mohair is perhaps the most popular fashion yarn. It is often combined with wool or acylic to produce a yarn that is less fuzzy than pure mohair. Bouclé is another popular yarn; its distinctive 'bumpy' texture contrasts effectively with a smooth yarn in a toning colour. Cotton bouclé yarns make summer garments with an attractive 'crunchy' look. Chenille yarn makes a velvety fabric. Metallic threads are popular for evening wear, and they may be combined with other threads to produce yarns in which the glittery effect has a pleasingly random quality.

A visit to a good yarn shop will reveal more exciting textures. Many patterns, including some in this book, are designed for fashion yarns. And if a pattern specifies a plain yarn, you can sometimes substitute a fashion yarn. However, if you want to do so, bear in mind this general rule: the more highly-textured the yarn, the simpler the stitch pattern should be; for these yarns tend to obscure the outlines of stitches. A mohair blend can often be used very successfully for bobbles or even some lace patterns, as it softens the outlines only slightly; however, a bouclé might ruin the effect. To make sure your choice of yarn is suitable, buy one ball to start with and make a sample of the stitch pattern. This will also enable you to see if you can achieve the correct tension (see page 10) with the substitute yarn.

When buying any yarn always buy enough for the whole project, making sure that all of the balls or skeins are from the same dye lot. This number is printed on the ball band. Colours do vary slightly from one dye lot to another, and this variation would be apparent in the finished project.

Another point to remember is that the length of yarn may vary from one ball to another, depending on the colour. Darker shades of dye add more weight to the yarn, so that 50 grams of black yarn will contain fewer metres than 50 grams of the same yarn in pink, for example.

Crochet Basics

From pages 12 to 138 you will find a selection of projects, along with alternative stitch patterns that can, in many cases, be substituted for the stitch pattern used in the project. Each project includes a special technique used in that design, which is explained and illustrated in detail.

Experienced crocheters will be able to follow the instructions for most projects with no further help. However, if you need help in other crochet techniques – including the most basic skills – you will find this in the special 'Know How' section, from page 146 to 165. Beginners should turn to this section first and learn the basic crochet stitches and techniques, such as joining yarn, increasing and decreasing. The section also includes helpful tips for left-handed crocheters (page 162).

Crochet patterns, like knitting patterns, are written in a kind of shorthand, which uses abbreviations and symbols to convey detailed information in relatively little space. Abbreviations are explained in the chart on this page.

Tension

This term refers to the number of stitches – and sometimes also the number of rows – that must be worked in a given measurement in order to obtain a piece of crochet of the correct size. It is vitally important that you work to the same tension as that established by the designer of the pattern; otherwise the measurements of the completed work will be either too large or too small. A difference of even half a stitch over 3 centimetres will produce a considerable difference over a width of, say, 45 centimetres. People differ naturally in the tension with which they work – some hold the yarn and hook much more loosely than others, producing a more open fabric. If the tension you produce differs from the one given for the pattern, adjust it by using a different size hook.

First, however, make a tension square using the hook specified. Work a sample containing a few more stitches and rows than given; for example, if the tension is 18 stitches and 20 rows to 10 cen-

timetres work about 22 stitches and 25 rows; this makes it easier to count the stitches. Lay the finished sample on a flat surface and mark off the specified number of stitches and rows with pins. Measure the distances between the pins; the measurements should be the same as those stated. If it is less, your tension is too small; change to a larger hook and work another sample. If it is more, change to a smaller hook. Make additional samples as necessary until you obtain the correct tension. Sometimes you will find it difficult to obtain the correct tension in both directions. Normally the stitch tension is more important than the row tension, particularly if little shaping is required. Concentrate on getting the stitch ten-

sion right; if the row tension is important (for example, on the top of a raglan sleeve, which contains a fixed number of rows), you should be able to adjust your method of working to correct it.

Making up

You should devote as much care to making up a crochet project as you give to working the stitches. 'Making up' generally includes: darning in the ends, blocking (sometimes pressing), and seaming.

To darn in ends, first thread them through a tapestry needle. Take the needle in and out of several stitches, either on the edge of the fabric or on the wrong side; work a backstitch once or twice as you go to secure the thread. Trim the end.

To block a piece of crochet, pin it to the correct shape on a flat surface – an ironing board or several thicknesses of turkish towel placed over a plastic sheet on the floor. If the work is highly textured, place it right side up. Lay a damp cloth over the work and leave it to dry thoroughly. Or spray it with water.

Pressing is seldom required, except on flat-textured work made of wool or cotton.

Use either a steam iron or a dry iron with a damp cloth. Hold the iron just above the work or so that it barely touches the surface – depending on the amount of texture. Do not slide the iron over the surface or let its weight rest on the work. Leave the crochet to dry thoroughly before unpinning it.

Different kinds of seams are used to join pieces of crochet, depending on the position of the seam and the type of work. A backstitch seam is often used on the underarm seam of a garment, for example, where a strong stitch is required. The edges are pinned together with right sides facing and the backstitch worked close to the edges, using a tapestry needle.

Other types of seam – both inconspicuous and decorative – are described on pages 86, 124, 162 and 165.

If a chunky or fashion yarn has been used, choose a lighter weight, plain yarn in a matching colour for the seaming to prevent excess bulk.

Abbreviations used in this book	
alt	alternate
approx	approximately
beg	begin(ning)
ch	chain
cm	centimetre(s)
cont	continu(e)(ing)
dc	double crochet
dec	decrease(e)(ing)
dtr	double treble
foll	follow(s)(ing)
g	gram(s)
gr(s)	group(s)
htr	half treble
inc	increase(e)(ing)
K	knit
LH	left hand
P	purl
patt	pattern
rem	remain(ing)
rep	repeat(ing)
qtr	quadruple treble
RH	right hand
RS	right side
sp(s)	space(s)
ss	slip stitch
st(s)	stitches
tog	together
tr	treble
tr tr	triple treble
WS	wrong side
yrh	yarn round hook

Other abbreviations are explained in the pattern in which they are used.

Chapter 1
Techniques and Patterns

Afghan squares

Use up scraps of old yarn and at the same time make beautiful garments or home furnishings; they're easily made from afghan squares, such as the granny square used for this colourful afghan.

The basic afghan rug

Size
The rug shown measures 110 x 84cm.

Materials
Each square requires a small amount of four-ply yarn in main colour A, and each of 5 contrast colours: B, C, D, E and F. 3.50mm crochet hook.

Tension
Each square measures 13 x 13cm, worked on a 3.50mm hook.

To save time, take time to check tension.

To make a square
Using 3.50mm hook and B, make 6ch, ss into first ch to form a circle.
1st round 3ch, 3tr into circle, * 3ch, 4tr into circle, rep from * twice, 3ch, join with a ss to 3rd of first 3ch. Fasten off.
2nd round Using C, join yarn to next 3ch sp, 3ch, 3tr, 3ch, 4tr all into 3ch sp. * 2ch, (4tr, 3ch, 4tr) into next 3ch sp, rep from * twice, 2ch, join with a ss to 3rd of first 3ch. Fasten off.
3rd round Using D, join yarn to next 3ch sp, 3ch, 3 tr, 3ch, 4tr all into 3ch sp, * 2ch, 4tr into next 2ch sp, 2ch, (4tr, 3ch, 4tr) into next 3ch sp, rep from * twice, 2ch, 4tr into next 2ch sp, 2ch, join with a ss to 3rd of first 3ch. Fasten off.
4th round Using E, join yarn to next 3ch sp, 3ch, 3tr, 3ch, 4tr all into next 3ch sp, * (2ch, 4tr into next 2 ch sp) twice, 2ch, (4tr, 3ch, 4tr) into next 3ch sp, rep from * twice, (2ch, 4tr into next 2ch sp) twice, 2ch, join with a ss to 3rd of first 3ch. Fasten off.
5th round Using F, join yarn to next 3ch sp, 3ch, 3tr, 3ch, 4tr all into 3ch sp, * (2ch, 4tr into next 2ch sp) 3 times, 2ch, (4tr, 3ch, 4tr) all into next 3ch sp, rep from * twice, (2ch, 4tr into next 2ch sp) 3 times, 2ch, join with a ss to 3rd of first 3ch. Fasten off.
6th round Using A, join yarn to next 3ch sp, 3ch, 3tr, 3ch, 4tr all into 3ch sp,* (2ch, 4tr into next 2ch sp) 4 times, 2ch, (4tr, 3ch, 4tr) into next 3ch sp, rep from * twice (2ch, 4tr into next 2ch sp) 4 times, 2ch, join with a ss to 3rd of first 3ch. Fasten off. Make a total of 48 squares.

To make up
Darn in all ends neatly on the WS. Press lightly according to instructions on ball band. Using A, with RS tog, join squares into 6 strips, each containing 8 squares, catch-stitching corresponding loops on the last rounds of squares. Sew long strips tog in the same way to form afghan.

Edging
Using 3.50mm hook and A, work 3 rounds in tr, working 1tr into each st and working 3tr into each sp and 8tr into outer corners on first round. Work one round in dc. Fasten off.

SPECIAL TECHNIQUE

simple edging

1 When working a corner in the simple treble and double crochet edging on the first round work along the edge to the 3 chain space at the corner of the afghan. Work 8 stitches into the space. On subsequent rounds, work 1 stitch into each of the 8 stitches at the corner.

2 To join rounds of crochet with a slip stitch, first work to the end of the round. Insert the hook into the top of the turning chain worked at the beginning of the round, take the yarn anti-clockwise over the hook and draw through all loops on the hook.

3 At the beginning of each round, work chain (3 chain for treble rounds, 1 chain for double crochet rounds) to count as the first stitch. Miss the first stitch and work treble or double crochet into each of the remaining corner stitches.

Adapting the afghan

Each of these squares can be used to make an afghan, or you could work several in one design.

Planning

Before beginning, sort the yarns into 'weights' – i.e. into double knitting, four-ply or three-ply yarn. Mixing different yarns could cause the afghan to become distorted. Afghans can be carefully planned like fabric patchwork, so that colours are used in groups of light, medium and dark shades. Colours can also be used randomly to produce a multicoloured fabric like the afghan on page 13, in which the final round of each square and the edging are worked in the main colour.

Tension

Tension is generally less important than in making a garment, although you should use a hook that produces a firm, even fabric.

However, if you want the finished fabric to be a particular size – perhaps to cover a cushion pad – you should check the tension carefully. If the motif is slightly too small or too large, change your hook size. If the size difference is large, try omitting the last round or adding another one.

Pattern Library: Afghan patterns

Circled square (1)

This square is worked in 2 colours, A and B.

Using A, make 6ch, ss into first ch to form a circle.

1st round 3ch, 15tr into circle, join with a ss to 3rd of first 3ch.

2nd round 5ch, (1tr into next tr, 2ch) 15 times, join with a ss to 3rd of 5ch.

3rd round Ss into first sp, 3ch, 1tr into same sp, (1ch, 2tr into next sp) 15 times, 1ch, join with a ss to 3rd of 3ch.

4th round Ss into next tr, ss into next sp, 1dc into same sp, * (3ch, 1dc into next sp) 3 times, 6ch, 1dc into next sp, rep from * 3 times omitting 1dc at end of last rep, join with a ss to first dc. Fasten off.

5th round Join B to first 3ch sp of any side, 3ch, 2tr into same sp, * 3tr into each 3ch sp to corner, (5tr, 2ch, 5tr) into corner 6ch sp, rep from * 3 times, join with a ss to 3rd of first 3ch. Fasten off.

Crossed square (2)

This square is worked in 4 colours, A, B, C and D.

Using A, make 6ch, ss to first ch to form a circle.

1st round 3ch, 3tr into circle, (3ch, 4tr) 3 times into circle, 3ch, join with a ss to 3rd of first 3ch. Fasten off and turn.

2nd round (RS) Join B to any 3ch sp, 3ch, 1tr into same sp, (1tr into each of next 4tr, 2tr into next 3ch sp, 1qtr into commencing circle between the 4tr groups, 2tr into same sp as last 2tr) 4 times omitting 2tr at end of last rep, join with a ss to 3rd of first 3ch. Fasten off and turn.

3rd round Join C to any qtr, 3ch, (1tr into each of next 8tr, 1tr, 3ch, 1tr into next qtr) 3 times, 1tr into each of last 8tr, 1tr into same place as join, 3ch, ss to 3rd of first 3ch. Fasten off and turn.

4th round Join D to any 3ch sp, 3ch, 1tr into same sp, (1tr into each of next 10tr, 2tr into next 3ch sp, 1qtr around stem of qtr worked on 2nd round inserting hook from right to left from front of work, 2tr into some sp as last 2tr) 4 times, omitting 2tr at end of last rep, join with ss to 3rd of first 3ch. Fasten off.

1

2

Five-colour square (3)

This square is worked in 5 colours, A, B, C, D and E. Using A, make 4ch, ss to first ch to form a circle.

1st round 4ch, 3dtr into circle, (2ch, 4dtr into circle) 3 times, 2ch, join with a ss to 4th of first 4ch. Fasten off and turn.

2nd round (RS) Join B to any 2ch sp, 2dc into same sp, (1dc into each of next 4 sts, 2dc, 2ch, 2dc into corner 2ch sp) 3 times, 1dc into each of next 4 sts, 2dc into same sp as join, 2ch, join with a ss to first dc. Fasten off and turn.

3rd round Join C to first dc after a 2ch sp, 3ch, 1tr into 2ch sp before join, * (miss next dc, 1tr into next dc, 1tr into missed dc) 3 times, miss 1dc, 1tr into next 2ch sp, 1tr into missed dc, 1tr into next dc, 1tr into 2ch sp before last tr, rep from * 3 times omitting last 2tr at end of last rep, join with a ss to 3rd of first 3ch. Fasten off and turn.

4th round Join D to same place as ss of last round, 3ch, 2tr into same sp. (1ch, 3tr into next tr. 1tr into each of next 8tr, 3tr into next tr) 4 times omitting 3tr at end of last rep, join with a ss to 3rd of first 3ch. Fasten off and turn.

5th round Join E to first tr after any 1ch sp, 1dc into same place as join, 1dc into next tr, * (1dtr into next tr, then bending dtr in half to form bobble on RS of square work 1dc into next tr, 1dc into next tr) 4 times, 3tr into corner 1ch sp, 1dc into each of next 2tr, rep from

* 3 times omitting 2dc at end of last rep, join with a ss to first dc. Fasten off and turn.

6th round Join A to first dc of any side, (1dc into each st to centre tr of 3tr at corner, 3dc into corner tr) 4 times, 1dc into next tr, join with a ss to first dc. Fasten off.

Sunburst square (4)

This square is worked in 3 colours, A, B and C. Using A, make 4ch, ss to first ch to form a circle.

1st Round 4ch, 1dtr into circle, 3ch, (leaving last loop of each dtr on hook work 2dtr into circle, yrh and draw through all 3 loops, 3ch) 7 times, join with a ss to 4th of first 4ch.

2nd round Ss into first ch of next 3ch sp, (1dc into centre ch of 3ch sp, 5ch) 8 times, join with a ss into first dc. Fasten off.

3rd round Join B to the centre ch of any 5ch sp, 1dc into same place as join, * (1tr tr, 1ch) 10 times, 1tr tr all into next 5ch sp, 1dc into next 5ch sp, rep from * 3 times, omitting 1dc at end of last rep, join with a ss to first dc. Fasten off.

4th round Join C to any 1ch sp, 2ch, 1tr into same sp, (1ch, leaving last loop of each tr on hook work 2tr into next 1ch sp, yrh and draw through all 3 loops) into each 1ch sp, 1ch, ss to top of first tr. Fasten off.

Pinwheel square (5)

This square is worked in 2 colours, A and B. Using A, make 6ch, join with a ss into a circle.

1st round 6ch, (1tr, 3ch into circle) 7 times, join with a ss to 3rd of first 6ch. Fasten off.

2nd round Join B to any 3ch sp, 3ch, 3tr, 2ch into 3ch sp, (4tr, 2ch into next 3ch sp) 7 times, join with a ss to 3rd of first 3ch. Fasten off.

3rd round Rejoin A to any 2ch sp, 3ch, 5tr, 1ch into 2ch sp, (6tr, 3ch into next sp, 6tr, 1ch into next sp) 3 times, 6tr, 3ch into next 3ch sp, join with a ss to 3rd of first 3ch. Fasten off.

4th round Rejoin B to any 3ch sp, 3ch, 1tr, 3ch, 2tr into 3ch sp, *3ch, 1dc between 3rd and 4th tr of next group, 3ch, 1dc into 1ch sp, 3ch, 1dc between 3rd and 4th tr of next group, 3ch, (2tr, 3ch, 2tr) into next 3ch sp, rep from * twice, 3ch, 1dc between 3rd and 4th tr of next group, 3ch, 1dc into 1ch sp, 3ch, 1dc between 3rd and 4th tr of next group, 3ch, join with a ss to 3rd to first 3ch. Fasten off.

5

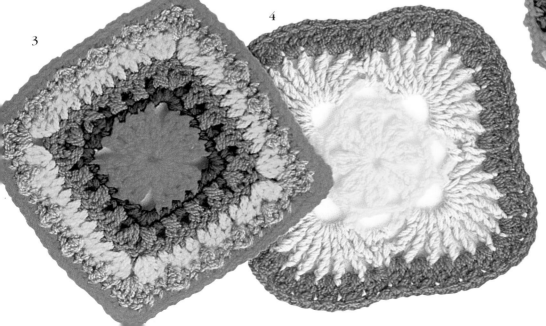

3

4

Double crochet variations

Basic double crochet can easily be varied to make firm fabrics that are ideal for hard-wearing garments such as these children's waistcoats

The basic double crochet waistcoat

Sizes
To fit 66 [71:76:81] cm chest
Length 43 [48:53:56] cm including border
Note: *Length is adjustable.*

Note: *Instructions for larger sizes are in square brackets [ ]; where there is only one set of figures it applies to all sizes.*

Materials
250 [300:400:450] g of a chunky yarn (A)
50 [50:100:100] g of a double knitting yarn (B)
4.00mm crochet hook
7.00mm crochet hook

Tension
10dc and 14 rows to 10cm over pattern worked on 7.00mm hook

To save time, take time to check tension.

Body (worked in one piece to armholes)
Using 7.00mm hook and A, make 65 [71:77:83] ch.
Base row 1dc into 3rd ch from hook, 1dc into each ch to end. Turn.
Pattern row 2ch, working into back loop only of each st, work 1dc into each dc to end. Turn. 64 [70:76:82] sts.
Rep Patt row until work measures 26 [29:32:34] cm from beg, ending with a WS row.
Divide for armholes
Next row Work in patt across first 13 [14:15:16] sts, turn.
Cont in patt for a further 10 [12:14:15] rows on these sts (until work measures 11 [14:17:19] cm from beg of armhole), ending at armhole edge.
Next row Work in patt across first 6 [7:7:8] sts, turn.
Leave 6 [7:7:8] sts unworked for neck. Work a further 6 [6:7:7] rows on these 6 [7:7:8] sts. Fasten off.

Back
Return to rem sts at armhole. With RS of work facing, leave 6 [7:8:9] sts unworked at armhole. Rejoin yarn to 7th [8th:9th:10th] st, 2ch, work in patt across first 25 [27:29:31] sts, turn, and leave rem sts unworked. Work a further 16 [18:21:22] rows on these sts. Fasten off.

Front
Return to rem sts at armhole. With RS of work facing, leave next 6 [7:8:9] sts unworked, rejoin yarn to 7th [8th:9th:10th] st, 2ch, work in patt across next 12 [13:14:15] sts. Turn.
Work a further 10 [12:14:15] rows in patt on these sts so that work measures 11 [14:17:19] cm from beg of armhole, ending at neck edge.
Shape neck
Next row Ss over first 8 [8:8:9] sts, 2ch, patt to end.
Work in patt on rem 6 [7:7:8] sts for a further 6 [6:7:7] rows. Fasten off.

To make up
Join shoulder seams.
Front, neck and lower borders
With RS of work facing and using 4.00mm hook and B, rejoin yarn to centre back neck. Work all round edge in dc, working 4dc for every 3 sts on main body at back neck, 1dc into each row end down front edges, 1dc into each st at front neck, 6dc for every 5 foundation sts along lower edge, and working 3dc into each right-angled corner. Join with a ss to centre back.
Work 4 more rounds dc on these sts, working 1 turning ch at beg of each round and remembering to work 3dc into each corner dc and dec 1dc at inner front neck corner shaping.
Next round Work in crab stitch (see Special Technique page 18) so that dc is worked from left to right rather than right to left. Join with a ss. Fasten off.
Armhole borders
Work as given for front, neck and lower edging, working 1dc into each dc at underarm and dec one st at underarm corners on each row. Work 1 round in crab stitch as before. Fasten off.

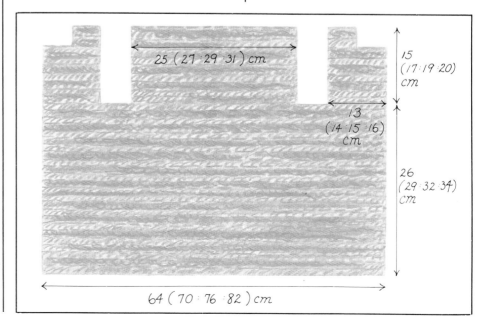

25 (27 :29 :31) cm

15 (17:19:20) cm

13 (14:15:16) cm

26 (29:32:34) cm

64 (70:76:82) cm

SPECIAL TECHNIQUE
working a crab stitch edging

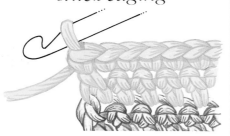

1 *Crab stitch is achieved by working double crochet from left to right instead of from right to left, usually on one or more foundation rows of double crochet, depending on how deep you would like the edging to be. End with the right side of the work facing.*

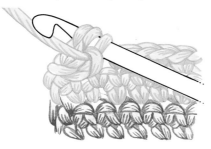

2 *Do not turn the work once the foundation rows have been completed. Keeping the yarn at left of work, work from left to right. Make one chain, then insert the hook from front to back into the next stitch. Hold the hook over the yarn before drawing yarn through from back to front.*

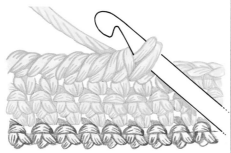

3 *Complete the double crochet in the usual way. Continue to work each stitch in the same way working from left to right instead of from right to left to the end of the row.*

Adapting the waistcoat

Any of the stitches on the following pages could be substituted for the ridge stitch used in the waistcoat to create a different texture.

Substituting a pattern

In order to substitute one of the alternative patterns you must first make a tension square in the pattern and yarn of your choice. If the tension obtained is the same as that given in the instructions you can proceed at once to make the garment from the original instructions. If, however, the tension is not the same, a certain amount of calculation will be needed before you can start.

Calculating from a tension square

In order to determine the number of stitches you will need to start your pattern, you must make a tension square approximately 10cm square in the yarn and stitch pattern of your choice, and then count the number of stitches and

Pattern Library: Double crochet variations

Double grain stitch (1)

Make a multiple of 2 plus 1ch with 3 extra ch.

Base row Insert hook into 4th ch from hook, yrh and draw through a loop, yrh and draw through 2 loops on hook – called 1 exdc –, *1ch, miss 1ch, 1exdc into next ch, rep from * to end. Turn.

Pattern row 2ch, *1exdc into next 1ch sp of previous row, 1ch, rep from * to end, 1 exdc into turning ch. Turn.

Rep patt row throughout.

1

rows obtained in your sample. You will see on the pattern diagram given with the instructions the width needed for your garment, and from your tension square you can calculate the number of stitches needed to obtain this measurement. For example, if the total width is 60cm and you obtain 12 stitches to 10cm, you will need 72 stitches to obtain the correct width. Row tension is not so important on a simple pattern.

Fitting in a pattern
Remember that when you calculate the number of stitches needed for the width of your garment, you must make allowances for the number of stitches needed to accommodate your stitch pattern. If, for example, your stitch pattern is divisible by 4, the number of stitches across the garment must either also be divisible by 4 or include edge stitches, to keep the pattern correct.

Shaping
If the shape of the garment is quite simple, requiring very little shaping at the armhole or neck – as in the waistcoat – it should be quite easy to calculate how many stitches need to be decreased, increased, or left unworked, using your tension square and measurement diagram once more. By working from the original instructions and tension you will see how many centimetres must be decreased to shape the armhole and can then calculate from your own sample the number of stitches you will need to decrease at that point, using your own pattern. For a garment entailing more complicated shaping or stitch patterns, more detailed calculations would be necessary, and you should work out the shape precisely on graph paper.

Albania stitch (2)
Make any number of ch.
Base row 1dc into 3rd ch from hook, 1dc into each ch to end. Turn.
Pattern row 1ch to count as first st, inserting hook into front loop only of each st work 1dc into each dc to end, 1dc into turning ch. Turn. Rep patt row throughout.

Crochet bobble stitch (3)
Make a multiple of 4 ch plus 3 extra ch.
Base row 1dc into 3rd ch from hook, 1dc into each ch to end. Turn.
1st row (RS) 1ch to count as first dc, *4ch, 1dc into each of next 4dc, rep from * ending 4ch, 1dc into turning ch. Turn.
2nd row Holding 4ch at back (RS) of work, work 1ch to count as first dc, 1dc into each dc to end, 1dc into turning ch. Turn.
3rd row 1ch to count as first dc, 1dc into each of next 2dc, *4ch, 1dc into each of next 4dc, rep from * to end, ending with 4ch, 1dc into each of last 2dc, 1dc into turning ch. Turn.
4th row As 2nd.
Rep first–4th rows throughout.

4

Daisy stitch (4)
Make an even number of ch plus 1.
Base row 1dc into 3rd ch from hook (1dc, 1ch, 1dc) into next ch – called 1dc group –, *miss 1ch, 1dc group into next ch, rep from * to last ch, 1dc into last ch. Turn.
1st row 2ch, *1dc group into centre 1ch sp of next 1dc group worked in previous row, rep from * to end, 1dc into top of turning ch. Turn. Rep patt row throughout.

2

3

Half treble variations

Half treble is one of the basic crochet stitches. On its own it produces a firm, fairly dense fabric; varied and combined with other basic stitches, it can form a surprising variety of stitch patterns, as shown in this cotton cardigan.

The basic half-treble cardigan

Sizes
To fit 71-76 [81-86] cm bust
Length (including welt) 55 [57] cm
Sleeve seam 19 [21] cm
Note: Instructions for larger sizes are in square brackets [ ] ; where there is only one set of figures it applies to all sizes.

Materials
350 [400] g of a size 3 crochet cotton in main colour A
50 [100] g in contrast colour B
50 [50] g in contrast colour C
4.00mm and 3.50mm crochet hooks
Pair of 3mm knitting needles
6 buttons

Tension
13 sts to 10cm on 4.00mm hook

To save time, take time to check tension.

Back and fronts (worked in one piece to armholes)
Using A and 4.00mm hook, make 100 [112] ch *loosely.*
Base row 1dc into 3rd ch from hook, 1dc into each ch to end. Turn. 99 [111] sts.
1st row 2ch, yrh, insert hook into first st, yrh and draw through a loop, yrh, insert hook into next st, yrh and draw through a loop, yrh and draw through all 5 loops on hook, 1ch, *yrh, insert hook into same st as 2nd loop of previous st, yrh and draw through a loop, yrh, insert a hook into next st, yrh and draw through a loop, yrh and draw through all 5 loops on hook – double half treble or dhtr worked –, 1ch, rep from * to turning ch, 1htr into turning ch. Turn.
2nd row (RS) 1ch, miss first st, 1dc into each 1ch sp to end, 1dc into top of turning ch. Turn.
1st and 2nd rows form one patt rep.
Work 2 more patts in A. Cont in stripe sequence as follows: one rep in B, 3 reps in A, one rep in C.
Cont in patt, working stripe sequence

as set until 17 patts in all have been worked.
Shape neck
Next row 2ch, miss first dc, work in dhtr to last 2 sts, 1dhtr into last dc. Turn. 2 dhtr dec.
Next row As 2nd row of patt.
Divide for armholes
Next row 2ch, work in dhtr across 15 [19] dc. Turn.
Left front
Next row As 2nd row of patt.
Next row 2ch, miss first dc, work in dhtr to end. 14 [17] dhtr.
Next row As 2nd row of patt.
Next row As first row of patt.
Next row As 2nd row of patt.
Next row As previous shaping row. 13 [16] dhtr.
Cont to dec one st at neck edge on alt dhtr rows until 9 [12] dhtr rem. Cont straight until work measures 50 [52] cm from beg ending with a 2nd row. Fasten off.

Back
With WS facing, miss next 10dc, and rejoin yarn to next st, 2ch, work in dhtr across 46 [52] dc. Turn. Cont in patt, until work measures same as left front to shoulder, ending with a 2nd row.
Next row 2ch, work in dhtr across 15 [17] dc, ss across 16 [18] dc, work in dhtr to end.
Fasten off.

Right front
With WS facing, miss next 10dc and rejoin yarn to next st, 2ch, work in dhtr across rem 16 [19] dc.
Next row As 2nd row of patt.
Next row 2ch, work in dhtr to last st. Turn. 15 [18] dhtr.
Next row As 2nd row of patt.
Next row As first row of patt.
Next row As previous shaping row. 14 [17] dhtr.

Complete to match left front.

Sleeves (both alike)
Using A and 4.00mm hook, make 45 [49] ch *loosely.*
Base row 1dc into 3rd ch from hook, 1dc into each ch to end. Turn. 43[47] sts.
Work 2 patt reps in A, one in C, 2 [3] in A.
Cont to work in stripe sequence as for back and fronts and at the same time:
Shape top
Next row Ss into first 7 sts, 2ch, work in dhtr to last 7dc, 1dhtr into next dc. Turn.
Next row As 2nd row of patt.
Next row 2ch, miss first dc, work in dhtr to last 2 sts, 1dhtr in last st. Turn. 2dhtr dec.
Next row As 2nd row of patt.
Next row As first row of patt.
Next row As 2nd row of patt. Rep last 4 rows twice more. 31 [35] sts.
Next row 2ch, miss first dc, dhtr to last 2 sts, 1dhtr into last st. Turn.
Next row As 2nd row of patt.
Rep last 2 rows 4 [5] times more. 21 [23] sts.
Next row 2ch, miss first dc, work in dhtr to last 2 sts, 1dhtr into last st. Turn.
Next row Ss into first 2 sts, 1ch, miss first st, work in dc to last 2 dhtr, turn.
Next row Ss into first 2 sts, 2ch, work in dhtr to last 2dc, ss into next dc.
Fasten off.

Lower welt
Using A, 3mm needles and with RS

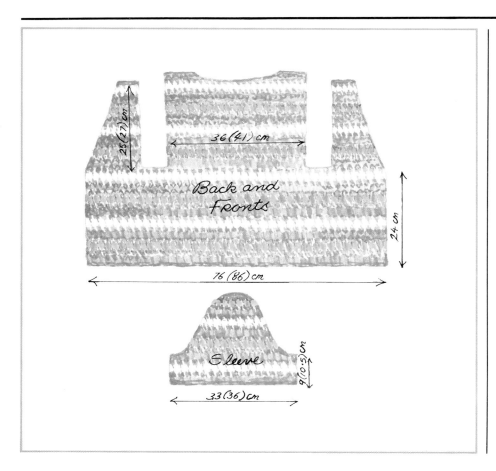

Back and Fronts

25 (27) cm

36 (41) cm

24 cm

76 (86) cm

Sleeve

9 (10.5) cm

33 (36) cm

facing, K up sts from free edge of foundation ch as follows: one st from first ch, *2 sts from next ch, one st from next ch, rep from * to end. 148 [166] sts. Work 5cm in K2, P2 rib. Cast off ribwise.

Cuffs (both alike)
Using A, 3mm needles and with RS facing, K up sts from free edge of foundation ch as for lower welt. 64 [70] sts. Work 10cm in K2, P2 rib. Cast off ribwise.

To make up
Join shoulder seams.
Front border
Using A, 3.50mm hook and with RS facing, beg at lower edge of centre front and work into front edge as follows: 1dc into each row end on right front, working 2dc into angle at beg of neck shaping, 1dc into each st across back neck, 1dc into each row end on left front, working 2dc as before. Turn.
Next row As for first row of patt rep.
Next row As 2nd row of patt.
Rep last 2 rows once more.
Next row As first row of patt.
On right front border, mark positions of 6 buttonholes, one 1cm from lower

---

SPECIAL TECHNIQUE
working double half treble

*1 Make two chain to begin the double half treble row. Take the yarn round the hook and insert the hook into the first stitch. * Yarn round hook and draw through a loop, yarn round hook and insert hook into next stitch, yarn round hook and draw through a loop.*

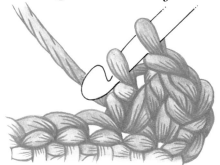

*2 Take the yarn round the hook and draw through all 5 loops on the hook * to form the first double half treble. Work one chain. To work the next double half treble, take yarn round hook and insert hook into the same stitch as the second loop of the previous stitch. Work from * to *. Work one chain.*

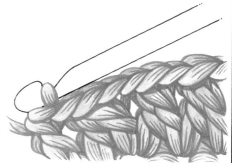

3 Continue to work double half treble and one chain alternately to the turning chain. Work one half treble into the last stitch. On the next row begin with one chain, miss the first stitch and work one double crochet into each one-chain space to the end, ending with one double crochet into the turning chain.

edge and one at beg of neck shaping and rem 4 spaced equally between.
Buttonhole row Using B, 1ch, 1dc into first 1ch sp, *2ch, miss next 1ch sp – buttonhole worked*, cont as for 2nd row of patt, working from * to * at markers until 6 buttonholes in all have been worked, then cont in dc to end. Turn.
Next row As for first row of patt, working 2dhtr into each 2ch sp. Turn.
Next row As for 2nd row of patt. Fasten off.
Join sleeve seams.
Set in sleeves, matching stripes.
Press work on WS with a warm iron over a damp cloth, omitting ribbing. Sew on buttons to correspond with buttonholes.

Adapting the basic cardigan

Use simple half-treble variations to create a variety of textured, firm and openwork fabrics.

Because of the tension of the double half-treble pattern used for the basic cardigan – in which the first and second pattern rows are of different depths – it is not possible to use any of the following half-treble variations as an alternative. These patterns do, however, show the range of effects that can be produced using the half-treble stitch in different combinations. To vary the cardigan, you could change the stripe sequence. Wider, narrower and random stripes are just three of the possibilities.

Matching stripes
The back and fronts of the cardigan on page 21 are worked in one piece to the armholes, so there is no difficulty in matching stripes at the side seams. However, whether you are working the basic cardigan or a variation of your own, take care to match stripes carefully at the armholes.
To do this, simply make sure that the shaping on both the body and the sleeves begins on the same row in the stripe sequence. For example, on the basic cardigan the armhole shaping begins on the third pattern worked in the main colour. When setting in the sleeves, ease the sleeve head so that the stripes match those on the body.

Pattern Library: Half-treble samples

Rug stitch (1)
Make a multiple of 2ch plus 3 extra.
Base row (RS) 1htr into 3rd ch from hook, 1htr into side of previous htr, * miss next ch, 1htr into next ch, 1htr into side of previous htr, rep from * to last 2ch, 1htr into last ch. Turn.
1st row 1ch, miss first st, 1dc into each st to end. Turn.
2nd row 2ch to count as first htr, miss first st, *1htr into next st, 1htr into edge of previous htr, miss next st, rep from * to turning ch, 1htr into top of turning ch. Turn.
Rep first and 2nd rows throughout.

Tulip stitch (2)
Use 2 colours, A and B. Using A, make a multiple of 3ch plus 3.
Base row (RS) (1htr, 1ch, 1htr) into 3rd ch from hook, *miss 2ch, (1htr, 1ch, 1htr) into next ch, rep from * to last 2ch, 1htr into last ch. Turn.
1st row 2ch to count as first htr, *(1htr, 1ch, 1htr) into next 1ch sp, rep from * to end, ending 1htr into top of turning ch. Turn.
2nd row Using B, 2ch to count as first htr, *3htr into next 1ch sp, rep from * to end, ending 1htr into top of turning ch. Return to beg of row.
3rd row Using A, 2ch, 1dc between turning ch and first group of 3htr, * 3ch, 1dc between next two groups of 3htr, rep from * to end, ending 3ch, 1dc into top of last st.
4th row 2ch to count as first htr, * (1htr, 1ch, 1htr) into next 3ch sp, rep from * to end, ending 1htr into top of turning ch. Turn. Rep first–4th rows throughout.

1

2

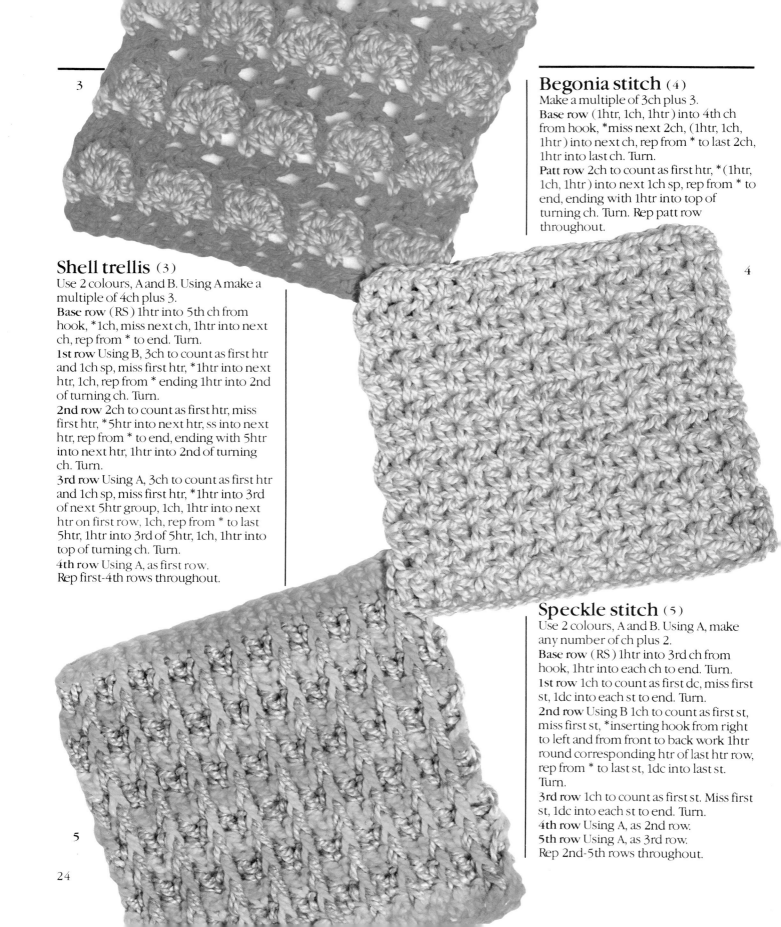

3

Begonia stitch (4)

Make a multiple of 3ch plus 3.
Base row (1htr, 1ch, 1htr) into 4th ch from hook, *miss next 2ch, (1htr, 1ch, 1htr) into next ch, rep from * to last 2ch, 1htr into last ch. Turn.
Patt row 2ch to count as first htr, *(1htr, 1ch, 1htr) into next 1ch sp, rep from * to end, ending with 1htr into top of turning ch. Turn. Rep patt row throughout.

Shell trellis (3)

Use 2 colours, A and B. Using A make a multiple of 4ch plus 3.
Base row (RS) 1htr into 5th ch from hook, *1ch, miss next ch, 1htr into next ch, rep from * to end. Turn.
1st row Using B, 3ch to count as first htr and 1ch sp, miss first htr, *1htr into next htr, 1ch, rep from * ending 1htr into 2nd of turning ch. Turn.
2nd row 2ch to count as first htr, miss first htr, *5htr into next htr, ss into next htr, rep from * to end, ending with 5htr into next htr, 1htr into 2nd of turning ch. Turn.
3rd row Using A, 3ch to count as first htr and 1ch sp, miss first htr, *1htr into 3rd of next 5htr group, 1ch, 1htr into next htr on first row, 1ch, rep from * to last 5htr, 1htr into 3rd of 5htr, 1ch, 1htr into top of turning ch. Turn.
4th row Using A, as first row.
Rep first-4th rows throughout.

4

Speckle stitch (5)

Use 2 colours, A and B. Using A, make any number of ch plus 2.
Base row (RS) 1htr into 3rd ch from hook, 1htr into each ch to end. Turn.
1st row 1ch to count as first dc, miss first st, 1dc into each st to end. Turn.
2nd row Using B 1ch to count as first st, miss first st, *inserting hook from right to left and from front to back work 1htr round corresponding htr of last htr row, rep from * to last st, 1dc into last st. Turn.
3rd row 1ch to count as first st. Miss first st, 1dc into each st to end. Turn.
4th row Using A, as 2nd row.
5th row Using A, as 3rd row.
Rep 2nd-5th rows throughout.

5

Ridged patterns

Three-dimensional ridges form beautifully tactile fabrics, especially when alternated with plain crochet stitches. Use these extremely versatile stitches as allover patterns – as in this handsome jacket – or to highlight particular features of a garment.

The basic ridged jacket

Sizes

To fit 96[101:106] cm chest
Length 70cm
Sleeve seam 48cm
Note: Instructions for larger sizes are in square brackets [ ]; *where there is only one set of figures it applies to all sizes.*

Materials

850 [900: 950]g of a Shetland-type double knitting yarn in main colour A
300[350:400]g in contrast colour B
3.00mm and 3.50mm crochet hooks
8 buttons

Tension

16tr to 10cm worked on 3.50mm crochet hook

To save time, take time to check tension.

Back and fronts (worked in one piece to armholes)

Using 3.00mm hook and A, make 48ch.
Base row 1dc into 2nd ch from hook, 1dc into each ch to end. Turn. 47dc.
Welt rib row 1ch to count as first dc, miss first st, 1dc into back loop only of each st to end. Turn.

Rep welt rib row until 160[168:176] rows have been worked from beg. Fasten off.
Change to 3.50mm hook.
Fold welt in half lengthways so that row ends meet.
Next row Using A, work a row of dc through both thicknesses of welt row ends. Turn.
160[168:176] sts.
Inc row Work in dc and inc 8 sts evenly across row. 168[176:184] sts.
Beg patt
* * **Next row** (WS) Using A, 2ch, miss first st, 1htr into front loop only of each st to turning ch, 1htr into top of turning ch. Turn.
Next row 2ch, miss first st, 1htr into each st to end, inserting hook under both loops of each st as normal. Fasten off and do not turn.
Return to loops unworked 2 rows previously and join A to free loop of first st.
Next row (RS) 3ch, miss first st, 1tr into each free loop to end. Turn.
Next row 3ch, miss first st, 1tr into each st to end. Turn.
Next row As last row. Turn. Fasten off.

With WS facing, insert hook into first htr and tr of the 2 layers. Join in B.
Next row Using B, 2ch, miss first st, inserting hook into corresponding htr and tr work in htr to end. Turn.
Next row 2ch, miss first st, 1htr into each st to end. Turn. Rep last row 3 times more. Change to A.
Next row Using A, 1ch to count as first dc, miss first st, 1dc into each st to end. Turn.* *
Rep from * * to * * until 8th ridge in A has been completed and work measures approx 52cm from lower edge, ending with a WS row.
Divide for back and fronts
Next row Patt 37[39:41]sts, ss across next 10 sts, patt 74[78:82]sts, ss across next 10 sts, patt last 37[39:41]sts. Turn.
Left front
Working on last set of sts, cont in patt without further shaping until work measures 66cm from beg, ending at front edge.
Shape neck
Next row Ss across first 5 sts, patt to end. Turn. 33[35:37] sts.
Dec one st at neck edge on next 2 rows and every foll alt row until 18[18:20] sts

---

SPECIAL TECHNIQUE
three-dimensional ridges

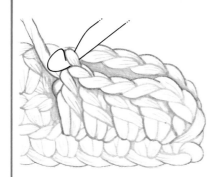

1 *Begin with a row of double crochet worked in the first colour. On the next row work in half treble crochet, inserting the hook into the front loop only of each stitch. Work a row of half treble as usual and fasten off, leaving a fairly long end. Return to the missed loops and rejoin the yarn to the first free loop. Work a row of treble into the missed loops.*

2 *Work two more rows of treble, inserting the hook under the two top loops of each stitch in the usual way. Fasten off, leaving a long end as before. With the wrong side facing, insert hook into the first half treble and treble at the side edge. Join in the second colour and work a row of half treble, inserting the hook through corresponding half treble and treble of the two layers.*

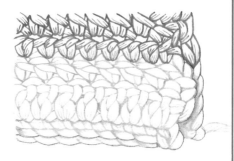

3 *Work three more rows of half treble as usual. Change back to the first colour and work a row of double crochet. Finish the side edges by working a row of double crochet into the row ends. Use the long ends left in steps 1 and 2 so that the colours match the pattern and leave the treble rows free on each individual ridge.*

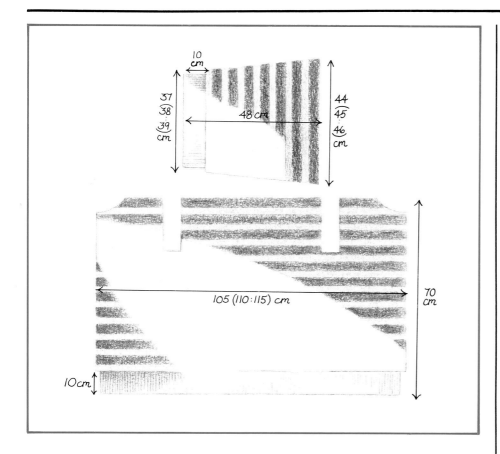

Right front band

Using 3.00mm hook and A, make 19ch.
Base row 1dc into 2nd ch from hook,
1dc into each ch to end. Turn. 18dc.
Next row 1ch to count as first dc, miss
first st, 1dc into each st to end. Turn.
Rep last row until band, when slightly
stretched, fits up right front from lower
edge of welt to beg of neck shaping.
Fasten off.

Left front band

Mark position of 7 buttonholes on left
front, the first 4cm from lower edge, the
last 3cm from neck shaping and the rem
5 evenly spaced in between.
Work left front band as for right front
band, work buttonholes as foll:
Next row 1ch to count as first dc, miss
first st, 1dc into next st, 3ch, miss next 3
sts, 1dc into each of next 8 sts, 3ch, miss
next 3 sts, 1dc into each of last 2sts.
Turn.
Next row 1ch to count as first dc, miss
first st, 1dc into next st, 3dc into next
3ch sp, 1dc into each of next 8 sts, 3dc
into next 3ch sp, 1dc into each of last
2sts. Turn.

To make up

Neaten all side edges with a row of dc,
using colours to match ridge patt (see
Special Technique, page 26). Fold
right-front band in half lengthways so
that row ends meet and sew neatly to
right front.
Using 3.00mm hook and A, work a row
of dc through both thicknesses at lower
edge.
Attach left-front band in the same way
and work buttonhole stitch over edges
of buttonholes.
Join shoulder seams.

Neckband

Using 3.00mm hook and A and with RS
facing, join A to first st on right front
band and work 87 [89:91]dc evenly all
round neck edge, ending at front edge
of left front band. Turn. Work in dc as
for right front band for 5cm, ending at
right front edge.
Buttonhole row Work in dc to last 6 sts,
3ch, miss next 3 sts, 1dc into each of last
3 sts. Turn.

rem.
Cont without further shaping until
work measures 69cm from beg, ending
at armhole edge.
Shape shoulder
Next row Ss across first 9[9:10] sts, patt
to end. Turn.
Next row Patt to end. Fasten off.

Back
With WS facing, return to sts left at
armholes, miss 10 slipped sts and
keeping patt correct, join yarn to next
st.
Next row Patt to end. Turn. 74[78:82]
sts.
Cont in patt without shaping until work
measures same as back to beg of
shoulder shaping.
Shape shoulders
Next row Ss across first 9[9:10] sts, patt
to last 9[9:10] sts, turn.
Next row As last row. Fasten off.

Right front
With WS facing, return to sts left at

armholes, miss 10 ss and keeping patt
correct, join yarn to next st.
Next row Patt to end. Turn. 37[39:41]
sts.
Complete to match left front, reversing
all shaping.

Sleeves (alike)
Using 3.00mm hook and A, make 30ch.
Work base row and welt rib row as for
welt until 51[53:55] rows have been
worked from beg.
Work next row and inc row as for welt
59[61:63] sts.
Using 3.50mm hook, rep from * * to * *
as for back and fronts until work
measures 11cm from beg, ending with a
WS row.
Shape sleeve
Inc one st at each end of next and every
foll 6th row until there are 71[73:75]
sts.
Cont without further shaping until
work measures 48cm from beg. Fasten
off.

Next row 1ch to count as first dc, miss first st, 1dc into each st to 3ch sp, 3dc into next 3ch sp, 1dc into each st to end. Turn.

Work in dc for 5cm more and then make a second buttonhole in the same way.

Work in dc for 5cm more.

Fasten off.

Fold neckband in half so that first and last rows meet and sew neatly into position on WS using matching yarn and an oversewn seam.

Neaten neckband buttonhole as before.

Work a row of dc through both thicknesses to close row ends of neckband.

Set in sleeves, matching centre of sleeve top to shoulder seam. Join side and underarm seams. Sew on buttons to correspond with buttonholes.

Adapting the basic ridged jacket

Use these variations from the Pattern Library to work several versions of the basic jacket. Whatever variation you choose, it's sure to please.

On the jacket the ridges are separated by four rows of half treble, worked in a contrast colour. The ridges could easily be spaced differently by working more or fewer rows in between.

An interesting, and more difficult, variation would be to work broken ridges. These could be left plain, or you could thread contrasting yarn through the tubes to accentuate them.

Altering the jacket

Men sometimes find sleeves restricting, and if you prefer you could easily use the jacket pattern to make a waistcoat instead. Work the back and fronts as instructed on pages 26-27. Omit the sleeves and substitute armbands, worked in the same way as the right front band.

The jacket can easily be made longer or shorter by working more ridged patterns on the back and fronts before dividing the stitches at the armholes. Sleeves could also be lengthened or shortened by working more rows in pattern. Remember always to end on a right or wrong side row as instructed.

Pattern Library: Ridged patterns

Crab stitch ridges (1)

Make any number of ch.

Base row 1dc into 2nd ch from hook, 1dc into each ch to end. Do not turn.

1st row (RS) 1ch, working into front loop only and working from left to right work 1dc into each st to end. Do not turn.

2nd row 1ch, 1dc into each unworked loop on first row. Turn.

3rd row 1ch to count as first dc, miss first st, 1dc into each st to end. Turn.

4th row As 3rd row. Do not turn. Rep first-4th rows throughout.

1

2

Cabled ridges (2)

Make a multiple of 3ch plus 3 extra.

Base row 1dc into 2nd ch from hook, 1dc into each ch to end. Turn.

1st row 1ch to count as first dc, miss first st, 1dc into each st to end. Turn.

2nd row (RS) 1ch, 1dc into first st, * 3ch, miss next 2 sts, 1dc into next st, turn, 1dc into each of 3ch just worked, turn, inserting hook behind 3ch work 1dc into each of 2 missed sts, rep from * to last st, 1dc into last st.

3rd row 1ch, 1dc into first st, * 2dc into next st behind cable, 1dc into next st behind cable, miss dc where 3ch was attached on last row, rep from * to last st, 1dc into last st.

4th row As first row.

Rep first-4th rows throughout.

Double crochet ridges (3)

Make any number of ch.

Base row 1dc into 2nd ch from hook, 1dc into each ch to end. Turn.

1st row (RS) 1ch to count as first dc, miss first st, 1dc into front loop only of each st to end. Turn.

2nd row 1ch to count as first dc, miss first st, 1dc into each unworked loop of 2nd row to end. Turn.

3rd row 1ch to count as first dc, miss first st, 1dc into each st to end. Turn.

4th row As 3rd row.

Rep first–4th rows throughout.

Popcorn ridges (4)

Make a multiple of 6ch plus 3.

Base row (RS) 1tr into 4th ch from hook, 1tr into each ch to end. Turn.

1st row 1ch, 1dc into first st, * 1ch, miss next st, 1dc into next st, rep from * to end. Turn.

2nd row 3ch, miss first st, * miss next 1ch sp, (5tr into next 1ch sp, remove hook from loop, insert into top of first of 5tr just worked and into loop just left, yrh and draw through all loops on hook – popcorn formed –, 1ch, 1tr, 1ch, popcorn; into next 1ch sp, miss next 1ch sp, 1tr into next dc, rep from * to end. Turn.

3rd row 1ch, 1dc into first st, * (1ch, 1dc into next 1ch sp) twice, 1ch, 1dc into next tr, rep from * to end, ending with 1dc into top of turning ch. Turn.

4th row 3ch, miss first st, * 1tr into next 1ch sp, 1tr into next dc, rep from * to end. Turn. Rep first–4th rows.

Puff-stitch ridges (5)

Make a multiple of 2ch plus 3 extra. Use 2 colours alternately.

Base row 1tr into 4th ch from hook, 1tr into each ch to end. Turn.

1st row (WS) 3ch, miss first st, * (yrh, insert hook into next st, draw through a loop) 4 times, yrh and draw through all 9 loops on hook – puff st formed –, 1tr into next st, rep from * to end. Turn.

2nd row 3ch, miss first st, 1tr into each unworked loop of first row to end. Turn. Rep first and 2nd rows throughout.

Multicolour ridges (6)

Work as for the basic jacket, omitting two of the half-treble rows worked between the ridges and using a different colour for each ridge.

Extra-large patterns

Extra-large stitches are shown off to their best when worked over a large area. The structure of each stitch produces a large-scale texture that is most striking worked in one colour, as in this attractive cover for a big floor cushion.

The basic panelled cushion

Size
To fit a cushion pad 90cm square

Materials
500g of a chunky yarn for back
700g for front
Cushion pad 90cm square
5.50mm crochet hook

Tension
14 sts and 10 rows to 12cm measured over patt of back

To save time, take time to check tension.

Back
Make 103 ch.
Base row 1dc into 2nd ch from hook, 1dc into each ch to end. Turn.
1st row 3ch, miss first st, 1tr into each st to end. Turn.
2nd row (RS) 1ch, 1dc into first tr, 1dc into each tr ending 1dc into top of turning ch. Turn.
Rep first and 2nd rows 43 times.
Fasten off.
With RS facing, work 112 dc evenly along row ends of each side edge.

Front
Note: *The measurement given in brackets at the end of each section of patt refers only to that section and not to the complete piece.*
Make 113 ch.
Base row 1dc into 2nd ch from hook, 1dc into each ch to end. Turn.
1st row 2ch, miss first st, 1tr into each st to end. Turn.

Raised treble boxes
1st row (RS) 2ch, miss first tr, 1tr into next tr, *inserting hook from front of work, from right to left, work 1tr around stem of next tr – 1tr front worked –, 1tr into each of next 2tr, rep from * to last 2 sts. 1tr front around stem of next tr, 1tr into top of turning ch. Turn.
2nd row 2ch, miss first tr, *1tr into next tr, 1tr front around stem of each of next 2tr, rep from * to last 3 sts, 1tr into next tr, 1tr front around stem of next st, 1tr into top of turning ch. Rep last 2 rows 3 times, then first row again. (8cm)
Next row 2ch, miss first tr, 1tr front around stem of each tr to last st, 1tr into top of turning ch. Turn.
Next row 2ch, miss first tr, inserting hook from back of work, from right to left work 1tr around stem of each tr to last st, 1tr into top of turning ch. Turn.

Raised crosses
1st row 2ch, miss first st, 1tr into each st to end, 1tr into top of turning ch. Turn.
2nd row (RS) 1ch, 1dc into first st, 1dc into next st, *miss next 2tr, 1dtr front around stem of next tr, working behind dtr work 1dc into each of 2 missed sts, miss next st, 1dc into each of next 2 sts, 1dtr front around stem of missed st, rep from * to last 2 sts, 1dc into next st, 1dc into top of turning ch. Turn.
3rd row As first row.
4th row 1ch, 1dc into first tr, 1dc into next tr, *miss next tr, 1dc into each of next 2tr, 1dtr front around stem of missed tr, miss next 2tr, 1dtr front around stem of next tr, working behind dtr work 1dc into each of 2 missed tr, rep from * to last 2 sts, 1dc into next st, 1dc into top of turning ch. Turn.
Rep last 4 rows twice. (12cm)
Next row 2ch, miss first dc, 1tr into each st to end. Turn.
Next row 2ch, miss first tr, 1tr back around stem of each tr, 1tr into top of turning ch. Turn.
Next row 2ch, miss first tr, 1tr front around stem of each tr, 1tr into top of turning ch. Turn.

Basket stitch
1st row (RS) 2ch, miss first tr, 1tr front around stem of each of next 3 tr, *1tr back around stem of each of next 4tr, 1tr front around stem of each of next 4tr, rep from * to last 4 sts, 1tr back around stem of each of next 3tr, 1tr into top of turning ch. Turn.
2nd to 4th rows Rep first row 3 times.
5th row 2ch, miss first tr, 1tr back around stem of each of next 3 tr, *1tr front around stem of each of next 4tr, 1tr back around stem of each of next 4tr, rep from * to last 4 sts, 1tr front around stem of each of next 3tr, 1tr into top of turning ch. Turn.
6th to 8th rows Rep 5th row 3 times.
Rep first to 4th rows once. (11cm)
Next row 2ch, miss first tr, 1tr back around stem of each tr to end, 1tr into top of turning ch. Turn.
Next row 2ch, miss first tr, 1tr front around stem of each tr to end, 1tr into top of turning ch. Turn.

Large diamond pattern
1st row (RS) 1ch, 1dc into first tr, 1dc into each tr to end, 1dc into top of turning ch. Turn.
2nd row 2ch, miss first st, 1tr into each of next 7 sts, *leaving last loop of each st on hook work 4tr into next st, yrh and draw through all 5 loops – cluster worked –, 1tr into each of next 15 sts, rep from * omitting 8tr at end of last rep. Turn.
3rd row 1ch, 1dc into first st, 1dc into each of next 4 sts, **1tr tr front around stem of st 3 rows below and 2 sts to the left, miss next st of last row, 1dc into

next st, inserting hook from front of work, from right to left, work 1dc around top of cluster – 1dc front worked –, 1dc into next st, 1tr tr front around same st as last tr tr, miss next st, 1dc into each of next 4 sts *, 1tr tr front around stem of st 3 rows below and 1st to left, miss next st, 1dc into next st, 1tr tr front around same st as last tr tr, miss next st, 1dc into each of next 4 sts **, rep from ** to ** to last 11 sts, rep from ** to *, 1dc into next st, 1dc into top of turning ch. Turn.

4th row 2ch, miss first st, 1tr into each of next 5 sts, *cluster into next st, 1tr into each of next 3 sts, cluster into next st, 1tr into each of next 11 sts, rep from * to end omitting 6 tr at end of last rep. Turn.

5th row 1ch, 1dc into first st, 1dc into each of next 2 sts, **1tr tr front around stem of next tr tr 2 rows below, miss next st, 1dc into next st, 1dc front around top of next cluster, 1dc into each of next 3 sts, 1dc front around top of next cluster, 1dc into next st, 1tr tr front around stem of next tr tr 2 rows below, miss next st, 1dc into each of next 3 sts*, leaving last loop of each st on hook

work 1tr tr front around stem of each of next 2 tr tr 2 rows below, yrh and draw through all 3 loops, miss next st, 1dc into each of next 3 sts**, rep from ** to ** to last 13 sts, rep from ** to *, 1dc into top of turning ch. Turn.

6th row 2ch, miss first dc, 1tr into each of next 3 sts, *(cluster into next st, 1tr into each of next 3 sts) twice, cluster into next st, 1tr into each of next 7 sts, rep from * to end omitting 4tr at end of last rep. Turn.

7th row 1ch, 1dc into first st, *1tr tr front around stem of next tr tr 2 rows below, miss next st of last row, 1dc into next st, (1dc front around top of next cluster, 1dc into each of next 3 sts) twice, 1dc front around top of next cluster, 1dc into next dc, 1tr tr front around stem of next tr tr 2 rows below, miss next st, 1dc into each of next 3 sts, rep from * to end omitting 1dc at end of last rep and working last dc into top of turning ch. Turn.

8th row As 4th row.

9th row 1ch, 1dc into first st, 1dc into each of next 2 sts, *1tr tr front around tr tr to right 2 rows below, miss next st, 1dc into next st, 1dc front around top of

next cluster, 1dc into each of next 3 sts, 1dc front around top of next cluster, 1dc into next st, 1tr tr front around stem of next tr tr to left 2 rows below, miss next st, 1dc into each of next 7 sts, rep from * to end omitting 3dc at end of last rep and working last dc into top of turning ch. Turn.

10th row As 2nd row.

11th row 1ch, 1dc into first dc, 1dc into each of next 4 sts, **1tr tr front around tr tr to right 2 rows below, miss next st, 1dc into next st, 1dc front around top of cluster, 1dc into next st, 1tr tr front around tr tr to left 2 rows below, miss next st, 1dc into each of next 4 sts*, 1tr tr front around stem of tr 1 st to left 3 rows below, miss next st, 1dc into next st, 1tr tr front around same tr as last tr tr, miss next st, 1dc into each of next 4 sts**, rep from ** to ** to last 11 sts, rep from ** to *, 1dc into next st, 1dc into top of turning ch. Turn.

12th row 2ch, miss first st, 1tr into each st to end. Turn.

13th row 1ch, 1dc into first st, 1dc into each of next 6 sts, *leaving last loop of each st on hook work 1tr tr front around each of next 2tr tr 2 rows below, yrh

---

1 Articles made up of panels of different stitches look most effective when the patterns and textures are divided by horizontal ridges. The double ridges on the cushion on page 31 are formed from trebles worked round the stem.

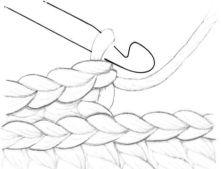

2 Work the first ridge row with the wrong side facing. Make two chain to count as the first stitch. Inserting the hook from the front of the work, work one treble round the stem of the next and every following treble to the last stitch. Work one treble into the turning chain. Turn.

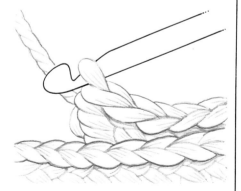

*3 Begin and end the following, right side, row as in step 2, but when working the treble round the stem of each stitch, insert the hook from the back of the work. As before, this forms a ridge on the right side.
(See page 159 for more on working round the stem.)*

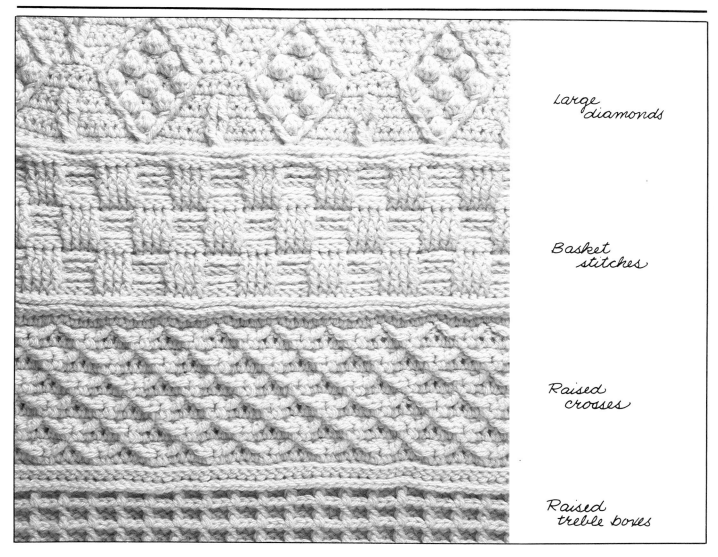

Large diamonds

Basket stitches

Raised crosses

Raised treble boxes

and draw through all 3 loops, miss next st, 1dc into each of next 7 sts, rep from * to last st, 1dc into top of turning ch. Turn.

14th row As 12th row.

Next row 2ch, miss first st, 1tr back around stem of each st to end working 1tr into top of turning ch. Turn.

Next row 2ch, miss first st, 1tr front around stem of each st to last st, 1tr into top of turning ch. Turn.

Work the 12 rows of basket stitch section.

Next row 2ch, miss first st, 1tr back around stem of each st to last st, 1tr into top of turning ch. Turn.

Next row 2ch, miss first st, 1tr front around stem of each st to last st, 1tr into top of turning ch. Turn.

Next row 1ch, 1dc into first st, 1dc into each st, 1dc into top of turning ch. Turn. Work the 12 rows of raised crosses section.

Next row 2ch, miss first st, 1tr into each st to end. Turn.

Next row 2ch, miss first st, 1tr back around stem of each st to last st, 1tr into top of turning ch. Turn.

Next row 2ch, miss first st, 1tr front around stem of each st to last st, 1tr into top of turning ch. Turn.

Work the 9 rows of raised treble box section.

Next row 1ch, 1dc into first st, 1dc into

each st to end. Fasten off.
With RS facing work 102 dc evenly along row ends of each side.

To make up

With WS tog place front on top of back with the row ends of the front to the commencing ch and the last row of the back. (Placing the pieces at a right-angle to each other helps to maintain the shape.) Leaving an opening to insert pad, join back and front with dc, working 2dc at each corner.
Insert pad into cover and sew opening edges tog.

Adapting the panelled cushion

Crochet a multi-textured cushion to display your repertoire of stitch patterns.

Most of these extra-large patterns could be crocheted in a chunky yarn to make a textured cushion, but for successful results some calculations are necessary.

Checking tension

First, carefully measure your cushion pad. The finished cover should be slightly smaller than the cushion to ensure a neat fit, so subtract 2cm from both the height and width of the cush-ion. The result will be the measurements of the finished cover. Work a tension square, using your yarn and the stitch you intend to use for the back of the cover. Count the number of stitches in 10cm of your sample. Multiply this number by the finished width of the cover. Then divide by 10 to obtain the number of stitches required to go across the width of the cover.

The pattern repeat

Make sure that each extra-large pattern can be worked *exactly* on the number of stitches across the width of the cush-ion. Count the stitches between the first asterisk (*) in the pattern rows and the words 'rep from . . .'; this will give you the number of stitches in the pattern repeat. Count the stitches at each side of the repeat; these are the edge stitches.

Divide the total number of stitches by the pattern repeat. For the pattern to fit exactly, the result should be a whole number, plus the number of edge stitches. Because of this, you may need to alter slightly the total number of stitches to accommodate the pattern repeat and edge stitches.

Pattern Library: Extra-large patterns

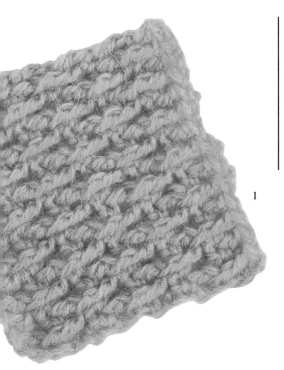

1

Alternating raised trebles (1)

Make an odd number of ch.
Base row 1tr into 4th ch from hook, 1tr into each ch to end. Turn.
1st row 1ch, 1dc into first tr, 1dc into each st to end working last dc into top of turning ch. Turn.
2nd row (RS) 3ch, miss first dc, *miss next dc of last row and inserting hook from front of work, from right to left, work 1dtr around stem of corresponding tr on row below – 1dtr front worked –, 1tr into next dc, rep from * to end. Turn.
3rd row As first row.
4th row 3ch, miss first dc, *1tr into next dc, miss next dc of last row and work 1dtr front around stem of corresponding tr on row below, rep from * to last 2dc, 1tr into each of last 2dc. Turn.
Rep first-4th rows throughout.

2

3

Raised treble cables (2)
Make 19ch.

Base row 1tr into 4th ch from hook, 1tr into each ch to end. Turn.

1st and every alt row 1ch, 1dc into first st, 1dc into each st to end working last dc into top of turning ch. Turn.

2nd row (RS) 3ch, miss first dc, *(miss next dc of last row and inserting hook from front of work, from right to left, work 1dtr around stem of corresponding st of row below – 1dtr below worked) 4 times*, 1tr into each of next 7dc, rep from * to * once, 1tr into last dc. Turn.

4th row 3ch, miss first dc, 1tr into next dc, rep from * to * of 2nd row, 1tr into each of next 5dc, rep from * to * of 2nd row, 1tr into each of last 2 dc. Turn.

6th row 3ch, miss first dc, 1tr into each of next 2dc, rep from * to * of 2nd row, 1tr into each of next 3dc, rep from * to * of 2nd row, 1tr into each of last 3dc. Turn.

8th row 3ch, miss first dc, 1tr into each of next 3dc, rep from * to * of 2nd row, 1tr into next dc, rep from * to * of 2nd row, 1tr into each of last 4 dc. Turn.

10th row As 6th row.

12th row As 4th row.

14th row As 2nd row.

15th row As first row.

Rep 4th-15th rows throughout.

Basket stitch (3)
Make a multiple of 8ch plus 4 extra.

Base row 1tr into 4th ch from hook, 1tr into each ch to end. Turn.

1st row 2ch, miss first tr, *(inserting hook from front of work, from right to left, work 1tr around stem of next tr – 1tr front worked) twice, (inserting hook from back of work, from right to left, work 1tr around stem of next tr – 1tr back worked) 4 times, 1tr front around stem of each of next 2tr, rep from * to last st, 1tr into top of turning ch. Turn.

2nd row 2ch, miss first tr, *1tr back around stem of each of next 2tr, 1tr front around stem of each of next 4 tr, 1tr back around stem of each of next 2tr, rep from * to last st, 1tr into top of turning ch.

3rd row As first row.

4th row As 2nd row.

5th row As 2nd row.

6th row As first row.

7th row As 2nd row.

8th row As first row.

Rep first-8th rows throughout.

Bobbles

Bobbles are fun to work and look great on most kinds of garment, so either make our dazzling sweater or use one of our bobble patterns to create your own original design.

The basic bobble sweater

Sizes

To fit **82**[87:92:97]cm bust
Length 57[59:61:63]cm
Sleeve seam 47[49:50:52]cm
Note: *Instructions for larger sizes are in square brackets* [ ]; *where there is only one set of figures it applies to all sizes*

Materials

200[250:250:300]g of a medium weight wool/mohair blend in main colour A
200 [200:250:250] g in colour B
4.50mm and 6.00mm crochet hooks

Tension

7tr and 3 rows to 5cm worked on 6.00mm hook.

Back and front (alike)

Note: *Work the 2 sts at each end of every row at a slightly looser tension to keep work flat.*
Using 6.00mm hook and A, make 4ch.
Base row 4tr into 4th ch from hook. Turn.
1st inc row 3ch, 2tr into first tr, 1tr into each of next 3tr, 3tr into top of turning ch. Turn. 9 sts.
2nd inc row 3ch, 2tr into first tr, 1tr into each st to last st, 3tr into top of turning ch. Turn. 4 sts inc.
Rep last row 17[18:19:20] times. 81[85:89:93] sts.
Next row (RS) 3ch, 2tr into first tr, 1tr into next tr, change to B, 5tr into next tr, remove loop from hook, insert hook from front to back in top of first tr,

replace loop on hook and draw through the tr – 1 bobble formed on RS of work –, * change to A, 1tr into each of next 3tr, change to B, 1 bobble into next tr, rep from * to last 2 sts, 1tr into next tr, 3tr into top of turning ch. Turn. Fasten off B. Rep 2nd inc row once.
89[93:97:101] sts. Fasten off A. Join in B.
1st dec row 3ch, miss first tr, leaving last loop of each st on hook work 1tr into each of next 3 sts, yrh and draw through all 4 loops – 2tr dec –, 1tr into each st to within last 4 sts, dec 2tr over next 3 sts, 1tr into top of turning ch. Turn. 4 sts dec.
2nd dec row (WS) 3ch, miss first tr, dec 2tr over next 3 sts, * change to A, work 1 bobble in next tr but insert hook from back to front in top of first of 5tr to make the bobble at the back (RS) of work, change to B, 1tr into each of next 3tr, rep from * to last 5 sts, 1 bobble in next tr, dec 2tr over next 3 sts, 1 tr into top of turning ch. Turn. Fasten off A.
Rep first dec row until 5 sts rem.
Next row 3ch, miss first tr, leaving last loop of each st on hook work 1tr into each of next 3 sts, 1tr into top of turning ch, yrh and draw through all 5 loops. Fasten off.

Sleeves

Make one sleeve in A and one sleeve in B.
With 6.00mm hook make 52[56:60:64] ch.
Base row 1tr into 4th ch from hook, 1tr into each ch to end. Turn. 50[54:58:62] sts.
1st row 3ch, miss first tr, 1tr into each st,

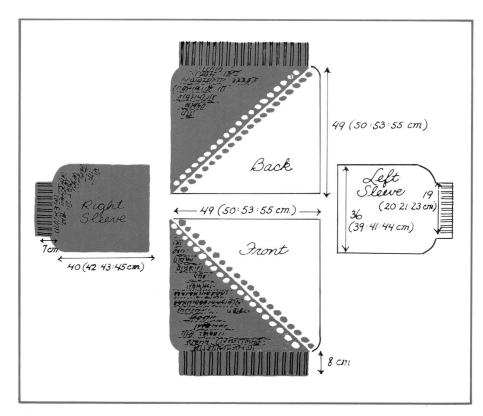

crochet rib

1 A crochet rib with 'knit' and 'purl' stitches can be formed by working round the stems of the stitches on the previous row. Work the turning chain. Take the yarn round the hook and insert the hook from front to back between the stems of the first and second treble. Bring the hook to the front between the second and third treble. Complete the treble as usual.

2 To form the 'purl' stitches of the rib, take the yarn round the hook and insert the hook from back to front between the stems of the second and third treble. Then bring the hook from front to back between the stems of the third and fourth treble. Complete the treble.

3 Continue in this way along the row, working the last stitch around the stem of the turning chain. On following rows, keep the rib correct by working from front to back around the stems of the treble that form the 'knit' ribs and from back to front around the stems of the 'purl' treble.

ending 1tr into top of turning ch. Turn. Rep first row 20 [21:22:23] times.

Dec row 3ch, miss first tr, * leaving last loop of each st on hook, work 1tr into each of next 2tr, yrh and draw through all 3 loops, rep from * to last st, 1tr into top of turning ch. Turn. 26[28:30:32] sts.

Rep first row once more.

Cuff
Change to 4.50mm hook.

Next row 2ch, miss first tr, * work 1tr around stem of next tr inserting hook from front from right to left – 1tr front worked –, work 1tr around stem of next tr inserting hook from back, from right to left – 1tr back worked –, rep from * to end, ending 1tr front around stem of turning ch. Turn.

Rep last row 6 times.

Fasten off.

Welt
With WS tog place back and front top with A sections tog and with B sections tog. Join side seams for 13 rows and shoulder seams for 7 rows. With 4.50mm hook join A to side seam, work 104[108:112:116] dc evenly around lower edge, ss to first dc.

Next round 3ch, miss first dc, 1tr into each dc to end, ss to top of 3ch.

Next round 2ch, * 1tr front around next tr, 1tr back around next tr, rep from * ending 1tr front around last tr, ss to top of 2ch.

Rep last round 6 times. Fasten off.

To make up
Join sleeve seams. Matching colours, set in sleeves. With 4.50mm hook and B, work 1 round of dc evenly around neck, ss to first dc.

Fasten off.

Adapting the basic sweater pattern

Vary the basic sweater shown here, or add bobbles to your favourite simple crochet pattern.

The front and back of the sweater on page 37 are worked on the diagonal, beginning and ending at a corner, with the colours changing at the widest point. The bobbles are in contrast colours to emphasize the diagonal styling.

Varying the pattern
The basic sweater could easily be crocheted in one background colour, with bobbles worked every few rows, either in the same or in a contrast colour and placed on the sleeves, as well as on the front and back, to produce a highly-textured fabric. Randomly-scattered bobbles, crocheted along with the main fabric or added to the background after it has been completed, could be worked in contrast colours; or the diagonal lines could be emphasized by working the fabric, including the bobbles, in narrow or broad bands.

More experienced workers could, after working a tension square, use the measurement diagram as a guide to the basic shape and work the back and front vertically, in the usual way, beginning at the lower edge and including bands of horizontally-placed bobbles.

Adding bobbles
It is easy to add bobbles to a pattern worked in treble or double crochet.

Use the smaller, double treble bobbles with a double crochet fabric and the larger, treble crochet bobbles with trebles.

Large bobbles, like those in the basic sweater pattern, can be added to other stitch patterns after the main fabric is completed by working into the free loops at the top of the stitches on the right side of the fabric.

Buying yarn
Both large- and small-bobbled fabrics need more yarn than plain fabrics, so if you add more bobbles to the basic sweater or to any other crochet pattern, remember to buy more yarn than quoted by the pattern, so that you have enough to complete the garment.

Pattern Library: Bobble patterns

Tufted bobbles (1)

This pattern can be used to make the sweater on page 37. Use three colours, A, B and C.

Background Using A make any number of ch.

Base row 1tr into 4th ch from hook, 1tr into each ch to end. Turn.

1st row (RS) 3ch, miss first tr, working into back loops only work 1tr into each tr, 1tr into top of turning ch. Turn.

2nd row 3ch, miss first tr, working into front loops only work 1tr into each tr, 1tr into top of turning ch. Turn.

Rep first-2nd rows throughout.

Bobbles Join B to any free loop on RS of work, 3ch, 4tr into same place as join, remove loop from hook, insert hook through the top of the 3ch, replace loop on hook and draw loop through the ch, ss to corresponding loop of row above. Fasten off. Secure ends on WS. Using 3 strands of C tog, knot a small tassel into the base of each bobble.

Scattered bobbles (2)

This pattern can be used to make the sweater on page 37. Work the bobbles in oddments of yarn.

Background Make any number of ch.

Base row 1tr into 4th ch from hook, 1tr into each ch to end. Turn.

1st row (RS) 3ch, miss first tr, working into back loops only work 1tr into each tr, 1tr into top of turning ch. Turn.

2nd row 3ch, miss first tr, working into front loops only work 1tr into each tr, 1tr into top of turning ch. Turn.

Rep first-2nd rows throughout.

Bobbles Join yarn to any free loop on RS of work, 3ch, 4tr into same place as join, remove loop from hook, insert hook through the top of the 3ch, replace loop on hook and draw loop through the ch, ss to corresponding loop of row above. Fasten off. Secure ends on WS.

Large bobble pattern (3)

This pattern can be used to make the sweater on page 37. Make a multiple of 4ch plus 1 extra.

Base row (RS) 5tr into 4th ch from hook, remove loop from hook, insert hook in top of first of 5tr, replace loop on hook and draw loop through tr – 1 bobble worked –, * 1tr into each of next 3ch, 1 bobble in next ch, rep from * to end, ending 1tr into last ch. Turn.

1st row 1ch, 1dc into first tr, 1dc into each st to end. Turn.

2nd row 3ch, miss first dc, 1tr into each of next 2dc, * 1 bobble into next dc, 1tr into each of next 3dc, rep from * to end. Turn.

3rd row As first row.

4th row 3ch, miss first dc, * 1 bobble into next dc, 1tr into each of next 3dc, rep from * to end, ending 1 bobble into next dc, 1tr into last dc. Turn.

Rep first-4th rows throughout.

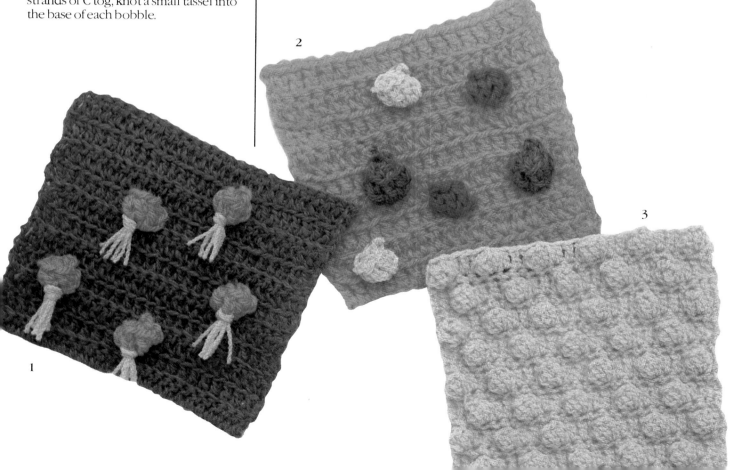

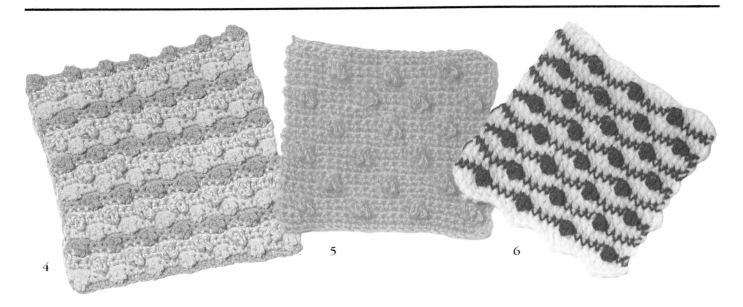

4

5

6

Three-colour alternating bobbles (4)

Use 3 colours, A, B and C. Using A make a multiple of 4ch.

Base row (RS) With A, 1dc into 2nd ch from hook, 1dc into each ch to end. Turn.

1st row With B, 1ch, miss first dc, 1dc into first dc, * leaving last loop of each st on hook work 2dtr into next dc, yrh and draw through all 3 loops, bend the 2dtr in half to back (RS) of work, 1dc into each of next 3dc*, rep from * to * to end, omitting 2dc at end of last rep. Turn.

2nd row With B, 1ch, 1dc into first dc, 1dc into each st to end. Turn.

3rd row With C, 1ch, 1dc into first dc, 1dc into each of next 2dc, rep from * to * of first row to end. Turn.

4th row With C, as 2nd row.

5th row With A, as first row.

6th row With A, as 2nd row.

7th row With B, as 3rd row.

8th row As 2nd row.

9th row With C, as first row.

10th row With C, as 2nd row.

11th row With A, as 3rd row.

12th row With A, as 2nd row.

Rep first-12th rows throughout.

Bobbles on double crochet (5)

Make a multiple of 6ch.

Base row (RS) 1dc into 2nd ch from hook, 1dc into each ch to end. Turn.

1st row 1ch, 1dc into first dc, 1dc into each dc to end. Turn.

2nd row As first row.

3rd row 1ch, 1dc into first dc, 1dc into next dc, * leaving last loop of each st on hook work 3dtr into next dc, yrh and draw through all 4 loops, bend the 3dtr to back (RS) of work to form a bobble, 1dc into each of next 5dc*, rep from * to * to end, omitting 3dc at end of last rep. Turn.

4th row 1ch, 1dc into first dc, 1dc into each st to end. Turn.

5th and 6th rows As first row.

7th row 1ch, 1dc into first dc, 1dc into each of next 4dc, work from * to * of 3rd row to end. Turn.

8th row As 4th row.

Rep first-8th rows throughout.

Wavy bobbles (6)

Use 2 colours, A and B. With A make a multiple of 6ch plus 2 extra.

Base row (RS) With A, 1dc into 2nd ch from hook, * 1htr into next ch, 1tr into next ch, 1dtr into next ch, 1tr into next ch, 1htr into next ch, 1dc into next ch, rep from * to end. Turn.

1st row With B, 1ch, 1dc into first dc, 1dc into each of next 2 sts, * 1dtr into next st, bend dtr in half to back (RS) of work, 1dc into each of next 5 sts, rep from * to end, omitting 2dc at end of last rep. Turn.

2nd row With A, 4ch, miss first dc, * 1tr into next st, 1htr into next st, 1dc into next st, 1htr into next st, 1tr into next st, 1dtr into next st, rep from * to end. Turn.

3rd row With B, 1ch, 1dc into first dtr, * 1dc into each of next 5 sts, 1dtr into next st, bend dtr in half to back (RS) of work, rep from * to last 6 sts, 1dc into each of last 5 sts, 1dc into top of turning ch. Turn.

4th row With A, 1ch, 1dc into first dc, * 1htr into next st, 1tr into next st, 1dtr into next st, 1tr into next st, 1htr into next st, 1dc into next st, rep from * to end. Turn.

Rep first-4th rows throughout.

Graduated patterns

Graduated patterns are made by working stitches of different heights in the same row – as illustrated by this ice-cream colour top.

The basic graduated-stitch top

Size
To fit 81-86cm bust
Length 46cm, including edging
Sleeve seam 7cm, including edging

Materials
75g of a four-ply cotton yarn in main
colour A
75g in contrast colour B
100g in contrast colour C
75g in contrast colour D
4.50mm crochet hook
Note: *Introduce new colour while
working last stitch in old colour.*

Tension
12 sts and 5 rows to 10cm, worked in dtr
using 4.50mm hook

To save time, take time to check
tension.

Back
Using 4.50mm hook and A, make 53ch.
Base row (RS) 1dtr into 5th ch from
hook, 1dtr into each ch to end. Turn. 50
sts.
1st row 1ch to count as first dc, miss first
st, 1dc into each of next 13 sts, 1tr into
each of next 7 sts, 1dtr into each of next
29 sts. Turn.
2nd row 4ch, miss first st, 1dtr into each
of next 15 sts, 1tr into each of next 9 sts,
ss into each of next 25 sts. Turn.
3rd row Using B, 4ch, miss first st, 1dtr
into each of next 20 sts, 1tr into each of
next 5 sts, 1dc into each of next 24 sts.
Turn.
4th row 2ch, miss first st, 1htr into each
of next 21 sts, 1tr into each of next 13
sts, 1dtr into each of next 15 sts. Turn.
5th row 4ch, miss first st, 1dtr into each
of next 23 sts, 1tr into each of next 6 sts,
1htr into next st, ss into each of next 19
sts. Turn.
6th row 1ch to count as first dc, miss
first st, 1dc into each of next 21 sts, 1htr
into each of next 6 sts, 1tr into each of
next 4 sts, 1dtr into each of next 18 sts.
Turn.
7th row Using C, 1ch to count as first dc,
miss first st, 1dc into each of next 16 sts,
1htr into each of next 6 sts, 1tr into each
of next 7 sts, 1dtr into each of next
20sts. Turn.

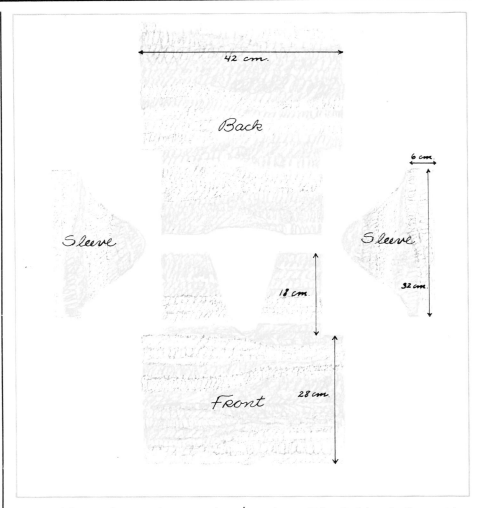

8th row 4ch, miss first st, 1dtr into each
of next 19 sts, 1tr into each of next 6 sts,
1htr into each of next 24 sts. Turn.
9th row 1ch to count as first dc, miss
first dc, 1dc into each of next 17 sts, 1htr
into each of next 7 sts, 1tr into each of
next 6 sts, 1dtr into each of next 19 sts.
Turn.
10th row 4ch, miss first st, 1dtr into each
of next 19 sts, 1tr into each of next 6 sts,
1htr into each of next 24 sts. Turn.
11th row 1ch to count as first dc, miss
first st, 1dc into each of next 17 sts, 1tr
into each of next 6 sts, 1dtr into each of
next 26 sts. Turn.
12th row Using D, 1ch to count as first
dc, miss first st, 1dc into each of next 14
sts, 1htr into each of next 3 sts, 1tr into
each of next 8 sts, 1dtr into each of next
24 sts. Turn.

13th row Using B, 4ch, miss first st, 1dtr
into each of next 12 sts, 1tr into each of
next 4 sts, 1htr into each of next 4 sts,
1dc into each of next 29 sts. Turn.
14th row Using A, 1ch to count as first
dc, miss first st, 1dc into each of next 15
sts, 1htr into each of next 15 sts, 1tr into
each of next 7 sts, 1dtr into each of next
12 sts. Turn.
15th row 4ch, miss first st, 1dtr into each
of next 16 sts, 1tr into each of next 8 sts,
1htr into each of next 25 sts. Turn.
16th row 2ch, miss first st, 1htr into each
of next 22 sts, 1tr into each of next 11
sts, 1dtr into each of next 16 sts.
Shape armholes
17th row Join C to 5th st from beg, 1ch
to count as first dc, miss first st, 1dc into
each of next 12 sts, 1htr into each of
next 4 sts, 1tr into each of next 4 sts,

1dtr into each of next 25 sts. Turn.
18th row Ss into first 5 sts, 4ch, miss first st, 1dtr into each of next 20 sts, 1tr into each of next 3 sts, 1htr into each of next 18 sts. Turn. 42 sts.
19th row 3ch, miss first st, 1tr into each of next 19 sts, 1dtr into each of next 22 sts. Turn.
20th row Using A, 4ch, miss first st, 1dtr into each of next 18 sts, 1tr into each of next 3 sts, 1htr into each of next 2 sts, 1dc into each of next 18 sts. Turn.
21st row Using D, 4ch, miss first st, 1dtr into each of next 16 sts, 1tr into each of next 8 sts, 1htr into each of next 17 sts. Turn.
22nd row 2ch, miss first st, 1htr into each of next 16 sts, 1tr into each of next 8 sts, 1dtr into each of next 17 sts. Turn.
23rd row 4ch, miss first st, 1dtr into each of next 16 sts, 1tr into each of next 2 sts, 1htr into each of next 23 sts. Turn.
24th row Using B, 4ch, miss first st, 1dtr into each of next 16 sts, 1tr into each of next 7 sts, 1htr into each of next 18 sts. Turn.
25th row 2ch, miss first st, 1htr into each of next 19 sts, 1tr into each of next 3 sts, 1dtr into each of next 19 sts. Turn.
26th row 4ch, miss first st, 1dtr into each of next 16 sts, 1tr into each of next 4 sts, 1htr into each of next 6 sts, 1dc into each of next 15 sts. Turn.

27th row 2ch, miss first st, 1htr into each of next 18 sts, 1tr into each of next 7 sts, 1dtr into each of next 16 sts. Turn.
28th row Using C, 1ch to count as first dc, miss first st, 1dc into each of next 16 sts, 1htr into each of next 5 sts, 1tr into each of next 2 sts, 1dtr into each of next 18 sts. Turn.
29th row 4ch, miss first st, 1dtr into each of next 18 sts, 1tr into next st, 1htr into next st, 1dc into each of next 21 sts. Turn.
Shape neck
30th row 3ch, miss first st, 1tr into each of next 10 sts. Fasten off.
Miss next 20 sts and rejoin C to next st, 3ch, miss first st, 1tr into each of next 10 sts. Fasten off.

Front
Using 4.50mm hook and A, make 53ch.
Base row 1dtr into 5th ch from hook, 1dtr into each ch to end. Turn.
50 sts. Cont as for back, but match side seams by reversing patt thus:
1st row 4ch to count as first dtr, miss first st, 1dtr into each of next 28 sts, 1tr into each of next 7 sts, 1dc into each of next 14 sts. Cont reversing patt in this way to the end of 16th row.
Shape right armhole
17th row Using C, 4ch, miss first st, 1dtr into each of next 24 sts, 1tr into each of

next 4 sts, 1htr into each of next 4 sts, 1dc into each of next 12 sts, turn. 46 sts.
Shape right neck
18th row 2ch, miss first st, 1htr into each of next 11 sts, 1tr into each of next 4 sts, 1htr into next st, 1dc into next st, turn. 18 sts.
19th row 1ch to count as first dc, miss first st, work 2dc tog, 1htr into each of next 2 sts, 1tr into each of next 4 sts, 1htr into each of next 9 sts. Turn. 17 sts.
20th row Using A, 1ch to count as first dc, miss first st, 1dc into each of next 8 sts, 1htr into each of next 4 sts, 1tr into each of next 2 sts, work 2htr tog. Turn. 16 sts.
21st row Using D, 4ch, miss first st, work 2dtr tog, 1dtr into each of next 13 sts. Turn. 15 sts.
22nd row 4ch, miss first st, 1dtr into each of next 12 sts, work 2dtr tog. Turn. 14 sts.
23rd row 4ch, miss first st, work 2dtr tog, 1dtr into each of next 10 sts, 1tr into next st. Turn. 13 sts.
24th row Using B, 1ch to count as first dc, miss first st, 1dc into each of next 10 sts, work 2dc tog. Turn. 12 sts.
25th row 1ch to count as first dc, miss first st, work 2dc tog, 1dc into each of next 9dc. Turn. 11 sts.
26th row 2ch, miss first st, 1htr into each st to end. Turn.

SPECIAL TECHNIQUE
working a graduated edging

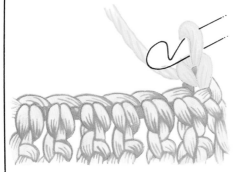

1 Graduated stitches can be used to form a curved edging. With right side facing, join the yarn to the first stitch on the free side of the foundation chain. Make one chain to count as the first stitch.

2 Work a slip stitch into the next stitch, one half treble into the next stitch, one treble into each of the next three stitches, and one half treble into the next stitch.

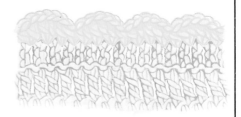

3 Repeat the six stitches in step 2 to the end of the foundation chain. Work one slip stitch into the last stitch and fasten off.

27th row 3ch, miss first st, 1tr into each st to end. Turn.

28th row Using C, 4ch, miss first st, 1dtr into each st to end. Turn.

29th-30th rows As 28th row. Fasten off.

Shape left armhole and neck

18th row With WS facing, miss next 6 sts at centre front and rejoin C to next st, 2ch, miss first st, 1tr into each of next 3tr, 1dtr into each of next 14 sts. Turn. 18 sts.

19th row 3ch, miss first st, 1dtr into each of next 14 sts, 1tr into next tr, work 2htr tog. Turn. 17 sts.

20th row Using A, 3ch, miss first st, work 2tr tog, 1dtr into each of next 14 sts. Turn. 16 sts.

21st row Using D, 2ch, miss first st, 1htr into each of next 11 sts, 1tr into each of next 2 sts, work 2tr tog. Turn. 15 sts.

22nd row 2ch, miss first st, work 2htr tog, 1htr into each of next 8 sts, 1tr into each of next 4 sts. Turn. 14 sts.

23rd row 1ch to count as first dc, miss first st, 1dc into each of next 11 sts, work 2dc tog. Turn. 13 sts.

24th row Using B, 4ch, miss first st, work 2dtr tog, 1dtr into each of next 10 sts. Turn. 12 sts.

25th row 4ch, miss first st, work 2dtr tog, 1dtr into each of next 9 sts. Turn. 11 sts.

26th row 4ch, miss first st, 1dtr into each st to end. Turn.

27th row As 26th row.

28th row Using C, 1ch to count as first st, miss first st, 1dc into each st to end.

29th row As 28th row.

30th row 2ch, miss first st, 1htr into each st to end. Turn. Fasten off.

Sleeves (alike)

Using 4.50mm hook and A, make 41ch.

Base row 1dtr into 5th ch from hook, 1dtr into each ch to end. 38 sts.

1st row 4ch, miss first st, 1dtr into each of next 6 sts, 1tr into each of next 2 sts, 1htr into each of next 9 sts, 1dc into each of next 20dc. Turn.

2nd row 1ch to count as first dc, miss first st, 1dc into each of next 13 sts, 1htr into each of next 4 sts, 1tr into each of next 3 sts, 1dtr into each of next 17 sts. Turn.

3rd row Using C, 1ch to count as first dc, miss first st, 1dc into each of next 16 sts, 1htr into each of next 4 sts, 1tr into each of next 3 sts, 1dtr into each of next 14 sts. Turn.

Shape sleeve top

4th row Ss into first 3 sts, 4ch, miss first st, 1dtr into each of next 12 sts, 1tr into each of next 5 sts, 1htr into each of next 16 sts. Turn. 34 sts.

5th row 2ch, miss first st, 1htr into each of next 15 sts, 1tr into each of next 4 sts, 1dtr into each of next 11 sts, 1tr into next st. Turn. 32 sts.

6th row Using A, 4ch, miss first st, 1dtr into each of next 11 sts, 1tr into each of next 3 sts, 1htr into each of next 6 sts, 1dc into each of next 11 sts. Turn. 32 sts.

7th row Using D, 4ch, miss first st, 1dtr into each of next 12 sts, 1tr into each of next 5 sts, 1htr into each of next 14 sts. Turn. 32 sts.

8th row Ss into each of first 2 sts, 2ch, miss first st, 1htr into each of next 12 sts, 1tr into each of next 7 sts, 1dtr into each of next 8 sts, 1tr into each of next 2 sts. Turn. 30 sts.

9th row Ss into each of first 2 sts, 4ch, miss first st, 1dtr into each of next 10 sts, 1tr into each of next 4 sts, 1htr into each of next 13 sts. Turn. 28 sts.

10th row Using B, 4ch, miss first st, 1dtr into each of next 13 sts, 1tr into each of next 5 sts, 1htr into each of next 9 sts. Turn.

11th row Ss into first 2 sts, 1ch to count as first dc, miss first st, 1dc into each of next 8 sts, 1htr into each of next 4 sts, 1tr into each of next 3tr, 1dtr into each of next 10 sts. Turn.

12th row Ss into first 3 sts, 4ch, miss first st, 1dtr into each of next 5 sts, 1tr into each of next 4 sts, 1htr into each of next 5 sts, 1dc into next 7 sts. Turn. 22 sts.

13th row Ss into first 2 sts, 3ch, miss first st, 1tr into each of next 11 sts, 1dtr into each of next 4 sts, 1tr into each of next 2 sts, 1htr into next st, 1dc into next st. Turn. 20 sts.

14th row Using C, ss into first 3 sts, 1ch to count as first dc, miss first st, 1dc into each of next 5 sts, 1htr into each of next 3 sts, 1tr into each of next 4 sts, 1dtr into each of next 2 sts, 1tr into next st. Turn. 16 sts.

15th row Ss into first 2 sts, 3ch, miss first st, 1tr into each of next 5 sts, 1htr into each of next 8 sts. Turn. 14 sts.

16th row Ss into each of first 5 sts, 2ch, miss first st, 1htr into each of next 5 sts. Fasten off.

To make up

Join shoulder seams.

Work in dc all round neck opening, working 1 st in dc and htr row ends, 2 sts into tr row ends and 3 sts into dtr row ends.

Work 1 round of htr. Fasten off.

Set in sleeves, easing sleeve top to fit, and matching patt with front.

Sleeve edging

With RS facing, join yarn to lower edge of sleeve, 1ch, miss first st, *ss into next st, 1htr into next st, 1tr into each of next 3 sts, 1htr into next st, rep from * to last st, ss into last st. Fasten off.

Lower edging

With RS facing, join yarn to lower edge and work as for sleeve edging. Join side and sleeve seams. Press seams lightly under a damp cloth.

Adapting the graduated top

Graduated patterns are fascinating to work and look good when used for either lightweight or heavy garments.

Because the pattern for the top on page 41 is fairly complex, it is not possible to substitute another stitch pattern for the one used. However, different effects could be obtained by the clever use of different yarn or colours.

Yarn manufacturers often produce both plain and textured yarns of the same weight. You could combine two such yarns – both four-ply – and perhaps add others to create intriguing variations in texture and appearance.

If you prefer to use only one yarn, using a different colour for each row would produce a marvellously marbled effect.

Designing

Of course, when substituting yarn, you must check your tension very carefully before you begin and change your hook size as necessary to obtain the specified tension.

Tension is especially important when creating your own design; unless you are very experienced, avoid shaping if at all possible and work with simple T-shaped patterns.

Pattern Library: Graduated patterns

Millstone stitch (2)

Use 2 colours, A and B. Using A, make a multiple of 10ch plus 2 extra.
Base row 1dc into 2nd ch from hook, 1dc into each ch to end. Turn.

2

1st row (RS) Using B, 1ch, miss first st, *1dc into next st, 1htr into next st, 1tr into each of next 5 sts, 1htr into next st, 1dc into next st, 1ch, miss next st, rep from * to end, omitting 1ch at end of last rep and working 1dc into last st. Turn.
2nd row As first row.
3rd row Using A, 1ch, miss first st, *1dc into each of next 9 sts, 1tr into missed st of 2 rows previous, rep from * to end, omitting 1tr at end of last rep and working 1dc into last st.
4th row 1ch, miss first st, 1dc into each st to end. Turn.
5th row Using B, 3ch, miss first st, *1tr into each of next 2 sts, 1htr into next st, 1dc into next st, 1ch, miss next st, 1dc into next st, 1htr into next st, 1tr into each of next 3 sts, rep from * to end. Turn.
6th row As 5th row.
7th row Using A, 1ch, miss first st, *1dc into each of next 4 sts, 1tr into missed st on 3rd row, 1dc into each of next 5 sts, rep from * to end. Turn.
8th row 1ch, miss first st, 1dc into each st to end. Turn.
Rep first-8th rows throughout.

Diamond pattern (1)

Use 2 colours, A and B. Using A, make a multiple of 6ch plus 2 extra.
Base row (RS) 1dc into 2nd ch from hook, 1dc into each ch to end. Turn.
1st row 4ch, miss first st, 1tr into next st, 1htr into next st, 1dc into next st, *1htr into next st, 1tr into next st, 1dtr into next st, 1tr into next st, 1htr into next st, 1dc into next st, rep from * to last 3 sts, 1htr into next st, 1tr into next st, 1dtr into last st. Turn.
2nd row Using B, 1ch, miss first st, 1htr into next st, 1tr into next st, *1dtr into next st, 1tr into next st, 1htr into next st, 1dc into next st, 1htr into next st, 1tr into next st, rep from * to last 4 sts, 1dtr into next st, 1tr into next st, 1htr into

next st, 1dc into top of turning ch.
3rd row As 2nd row.
4th row Using A, as first row.
Rep first-4th rows throughout.

1

Jacquard patterns

Jacquard patterns can easily be crocheted using bright colours and simple stitches. Work small, repeating patterns for a 'Fair Isle' effect, as on this boy's pullover, or scatter individual motifs as your fancy takes you.

The basic jacquard pullover

Sizes
To fit 71 [76:82:87] cm chest
Length 57 [58:61:62] cm
Sleeve seam 41 [41:43:43] cm
Note: *Instructions for larger sizes are in square brackets [ ]; where there is only one set of figures it applies to all sizes.*

Materials
150 [150:200:200] g of a four-ply yarn in main colour A
100g each in contrast colours B, C and D
50g each in contrast colours E and F
3.00mm crochet hook
Pair of 2¾mm knitting needles
Set of four 2¾mm knitting needles, pointed at both ends

Note: *Strand yarn not in use loosely on the wrong side of the work.*

Tension
24 sts and 30 ows to 10cm over jacquard patt worked on 3.00mm hook.

To save time, take time to check tension.

Back
Using 2¾mm knitting needles and A, cast on 99 [103:107:111] sts.
Work in K1, P1 rib, beg alt rows P1, K1, until work measures 5cm from beg.
Cast off ribwise until one loop rem.
Transfer loop to 3.00mm hook.
Next row (RS) 1ch to count as first dc, miss first st, 1dc into top of each cast-off st to end. Turn.
99 [103:107:111] sts.
Next row 1ch to count as first dc, miss first st, 1dc into each st to end. Cont to work in dc, commence jacquard patt from chart.
Work 36 rows of jacquard patt 3 times in all.
3rd and 4th sizes only
Work 5 more rows in jacquard patt.
All sizes
Fasten off at end of last row.
Shape armholes
Keeping jacquard patt correct, miss first 7 sts and rejoin yarn to next st.
Next row 1ch to count as first dc, miss first st, patt to last 7 sts, turn.
85 [89:93:97] sts.
Next row 1ch to count as first dc, miss first st, work next 2dc tog, patt to last 3 sts, work 2dc tog, 1dc into last st. Turn.
Next row 1ch to count as first dc, miss first dc, 1dc into each st to end.
Turn.
Rep last 2 rows until 75 [79:83:87] sts rem.
Cont without further shaping until 18th [18th:24th:24th] row of jacquard patt is complete.
Break off yarn. Join in B.
Next 2 rows Using B, 1ch to count as first dc, miss first st, 1dc into each st to end. Turn.
Break off B. Join in A.

SPECIAL TECHNIQUE
working into knitted rib

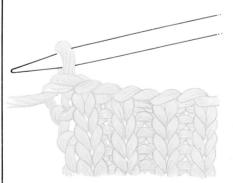

1 Being more elastic, knitted ribs are often preferable to crocheted ribs, especially if the garment will receive hard wear. The knitting can be worked after the crochet is completed, or, as in the basic sweater, the crochet can be worked into the top of the knitting. Cast off in rib until only one loop remains on the needle.

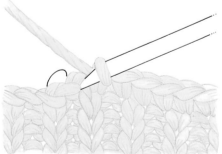

2 Transfer the loop to a crochet hook. Work one chain to count as the first double crochet and miss the first stitch. Inserting the hook under both horizontal loops, work one double crochet into each cast-off stitch to the end of the row. Work following rows in double crochet as usual.

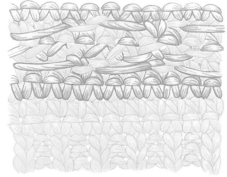

3 This method can be used whenever you want a knitted rib on a crochet garment. It not only prevents a hard ridge on the wrong side (as shown above), but also avoids the need to work into the other side of the foundation chain, which can be difficult, especially when using textured yarns.

Yoke

Using A only, work in dc for 29 [32:29:32] rows.

Shape neck and shoulders

Next row 1ch to count as first dc, miss first dc, 1dc into each of next 17 [19:20:22] sts, turn.

Next row 1ch to count as first dc, miss first dc, work next 2dc tog, 1dc into each st to end. Turn.

Next row Ss over first 5 [6:6:7] sts, 1ch to count as first dc, miss first st, 1dc into each st to end. Turn.

Next row 1ch to count as first dc, miss first st, 1dc into each of next 5 [6:6:6] sts.

Fasten off.

Miss next 39 [39:41:41] sts on back neck and rejoin A to next st.

Next row 1ch to count as first dc, miss first st, 1dc into each st to end. Turn.

Next row 1ch to count as first dc, miss first st, 1dc into each st to last 3 sts, work next 2dc tog, 1dc into last st. Turn.

Next row 1ch to count as first dc, miss first st, 1dc into each of next 11 [12:13:13] sts, turn.

Next row Ss across first 5 [6:7:7] sts, 1ch

47

to count as first dc, miss first st, 1dc into each st to end. Fasten off.

Front
Work as for back until 21 [24:21:24] rows of yoke have been completed.
Shape left neck
Next row 1ch to count as first dc, miss first st, 1dc into each of next 22 [24:25:27] sts, turn.
Next row Ss across first 4 sts, 1ch to count as first dc, miss first st, 1dc into each st to end. Turn.
Next row 1ch to count as first dc, miss first st, 1dc into each of next 16 [18:19:20] sts, turn.
Work 7 more rows without further shaping.
Shape left shoulder
Next row Ss across first 5 [6:6:7] sts, 1ch to count as first dc, miss first st, 1dc into each st to end. Turn.
Next row 1ch to count as first dc, miss first st, 1dc into each of next 5 [6:6:7] sts. Fasten off.
Miss next 29 [29:31:31] sts on front neck and rejoin A to next st.
Complete right neck and shoulder to match left side, reversing all shaping.

Sleeves (both alike)
Using 2¾mm knitting needles and A, cast on 67 [67:75:75] sts.
Work in K1, P1 rib as given for back until work measures 5cm from beg. Cast off ribwise until one loop rem. Transfer loop to 3.00mm crochet hook.
Next row (RS) 1ch to count as first dc, miss first st, 1dc into top of each cast-off st to end. Turn.
67 [67:75:75] sts.
Next row 1ch to count as first dc, miss first st, 1dc into each st to end. Turn.
Cont to work in dc, work first 9 rows of jacquard patt from chart.
Next row 1ch to count as first dc, miss first st, 2dc into next st, 1dc into each st to last 2 sts, 2dc into next st, 1dc into last st. Turn.
Keeping jacquard patt correct, cont to inc one st at each end of every foll 10th row 6 [6:4:4] times in all.
79 [79:83:83] sts.
Cont in patt without further shaping until 3 reps of jacquard patt have been

worked. Work 1 [1:5:5] more rows in patt. Fasten off.
Shape top
Keeping jacquard patt correct, miss first 6 sts and rejoin yarn to next st.
Next row 1ch to count as first dc, miss first st, patt to last 6 sts, turn.
Next row 1ch to count as first dc, miss first st, work next 2dc tog, patt to last 3 sts, work next 2dc tog, 1dc into last st. Turn.
Keeping jacquard patt correct, cont to dec one st at each end of every foll alt row until 43 [43:47:47] sts rem.
Cont to dec one st at each end of next 12 rows. 19 [19:23:23] sts.
Break off yarn. Join in B.
Next row Using B only, ss across first 4 [4:5:5] sts, 1ch to count as first dc, miss first st, 1dc into each of next 10 [10:12:12] sts, turn.
Next row Ss across first 4 sts, 1ch to count as first dc, miss first st, 1dc into

each of next 3 [3:5:5] sts. Fasten off.

To make up
Press each piece as recommended on ball band. Join shoulder seams. Join side and sleeve seams.
Armhole borders (both alike)
Using 3.00mm crochet hook and with RS facing, join B to underarm seam. Work 80 [84:86:90] dc evenly round armhole, joining last st to first st with a ss. Work one more round in dc, ending with a ss to first st. Fasten off.
Set in sleeves.
Neckband
Using A and set of 4 double-pointed knitting needles, K up 112 [112:120:120] sts evenly round neck. Work in rounds of K1, P1 rib for 5cm. Cast off.
Turn rib to WS and sew to base of rib on WS to form a crew neck.
Press all seams.

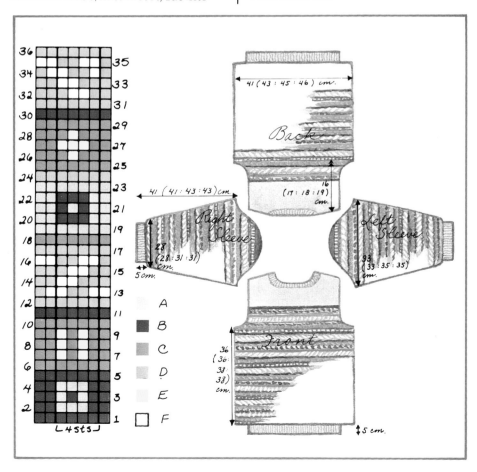

Adapting the basic jacquard sweater

Jacquard is fun to do and the results are very impressive.

The simple pattern repeat on the teenager's sweater on page 47 is worked by stranding the yarn not in use loosely across the back of the work.

The pattern is a simple repeat of four stitches plus three edge stitches; a number of the double crochet patterns on this page and on page 51 can be substituted for the original one.

Using large motifs

The repeating 'Fair Isle' pattern could be omitted and the basic shape of the sweater could provide a plain background for a large motif. When working larger motifs, you should not, of course, strand the yarn but use separate balls of yarn for each section of colour in the design.

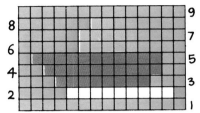

Pattern Library: Jacquard patterns

Seascape

These double crochet charts can be used either for repeating patterns, as here, or for separate motifs. Use a separate ball of yarn for each section of colour.

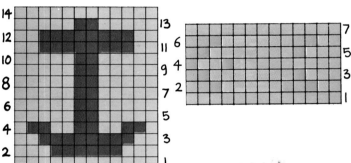

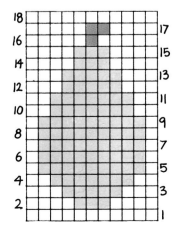

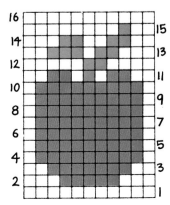

Fruit salad

Work these charts in double crochet, using a separate ball of yarn for each colour. Use either as a repeating pattern or as motifs.

Child's jacquard sweater

Two basic shapes – one for the back and front and the other for the sleeves – make this warm, bright-coloured sweater.

Size
To fit 66cm chest
Length 43cm
Sleeve seam 29cm

Tension
18 sts and 10 rows to 10cm over patt worked on 4.00mm hook

To save time, take time to check tension.

Materials
200g of a double knitting yarn in main colour A
50g in each of contrast colours B, C, D and E
3.50mm and 4.00mm crochet hooks

Front and Back (alike)
Using A and 3.50mm hook, make 64ch.
Base row 1tr into 4th ch from hook, 1tr into each ch to end. Turn. 62 sts.
1st row (RS) Using 4.00mm hook, work from checks chart (see page 51) to end. Cont in patt for a further 38 rows.
40th row Using A only, 3ch, 1tr into next 17sts, turn.
41st row 3ch, 1tr into each st to end. Fasten off.
Return to 39th row. Miss next 27 sts across neck and rejoin A with ss to next st.
Next row As 41st row. Fasten off.

Sleeves (both alike)
Using A and 3.50mm hook, make 52ch.
Work as given for back until 27 rows are complete. Fasten off.

To make up
Press each piece carefully. Join shoulder and sleeve seams. Join side seams leaving 5cm unjoined at lower edge. Set in sleeves. With RS facing, using 3.50mm hook, join A with ss to neck edge of shoulder seam. Work 3 rows dc all round neck edge. Fasten off. Using 3.50mm hook, join A with ss to lower edge of sweater. Work 1 row dc all round edge including unsewn sides. Fasten off. Using 4.00mm hook, join A with ss to sleeve seam and work 8 rows dc all round sleeve. Fasten off. Turn up cuffs.

Geometric trebles

Work these patterns in treble, stranding yarn as necessary.

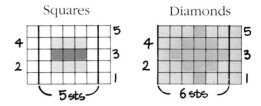

Squares   Diamonds

Terrific trebles

Trebles are best suited to simple repeating patterns, as shown here, in which the yarn is stranded loosely on the wrong side of the work.

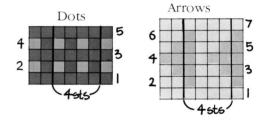

Dots   Arrows

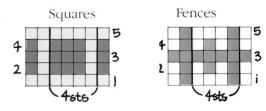

Squares   Fences

Dazzling double crochet

All these repeating patterns, in which the yarn is stranded on the wrong side of the work, could be used in the basic sweater on page 47.

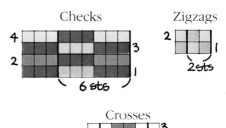

Checks   Zigzags

Crosses

Picture jacquard

Pictures sweaters worked in crochet are fascinating to make and are always great fun to wear. Either make the winter or summer sweaters shown here or choose your own subject, collect yarns in beautiful colours and start to create your own work of art.

The basic picture sweaters

Sizes
To fit 86-91 [96-101] cm bust/chest
Length 62[66]cm

Long sleeve seam 41[46]cm
Short sleeve seam 25[29]cm

Note: *Instructions for the larger size are in square brackets [ ]; where there is only one set of figures it applies to all sizes.*

Materials
Winter sweater
450[500]g of a double knitting yarn in main colour A
100g in contrast colour B
50g in each of four contrast colours,

C, D, E and F
100g in contrast colour G

Summer sweater
400[450]g of a double knitting yarn in main colour A
100g in contrast colour B
50g in each of contrast colours C, D, E and F
50[100]g in contrast colour G
50g in contrast colour H
3.50mm and 4.00mm crochet hooks

Tension
18dc and 19 rows to 10cm worked on 4.00mm hook
18htr and 14 rows to 10cm worked on 4.00mm hook
To save time, take time to check tension.

Winter sweater
Back
Using 4.00mm hook and A, make 84[93]ch.
Base row 1htr into 3rd ch from hook, 1htr into each ch to end. Turn. 83[92]sts.
Patt row 2ch to count as first htr, miss first st, 1htr into each st to end. Turn.
Rep patt row 74[78] times more.
Shape neck
Next row 2ch to count as first htr, miss first st, 1htr into each of next 24[27] htr, work next 3htr tog, turn. 26[29] sts.
Next row 2ch to count as first htr, miss first st, work next 3htr tog, 1htr into each st to end. Turn. 24[27] sts.
Next row 2ch to count as first htr, miss first st, 1htr into each htr to last 3 sts, work last 3 sts tog. Turn. 22[25] sts.
Fasten off.
Return to sts left at beg of neck shaping, miss next 27[30] sts and rejoin A to next st.
Next row 2ch to count as first htr, miss first st, work next 3htr tog, 1htr into each st to end. Turn. 27[29] sts.
Complete to match other side of neck.

Sleeves (both alike)
Using a 3.50mm hook and A, make 38[44]ch.
Base row 1tr into 4th ch from hook, 1tr into each ch to end. Turn. 36[42] sts.
Rib row 3ch to count as first tr, miss first st, * inserting hook from front to back work 1tr round stem of next tr – 1tr front worked –, inserting hook from back to front work 1tr round stem of next tr – 1tr back worked –, rep from * to turning ch, 1tr into top of turning ch. Turn.
Rep rib row 8 times more.
Change to 4.00mm hook.
Inc row 2ch to count as first htr, miss first st, * 2htr into next st, 1htr into next st, rep from * to turning ch, 1htr into top

of turning ch. Turn. 53[62] sts.
Work 5 more rows of htr.

Shape sleeve
Inc row 2ch to count as first htr, miss
first st, 2htr into next st, 1htr into each
st to last 2 sts, 2htr into next st, 1htr into
last st. Turn. 55[64] sts. Work 6 more
rows of htr. Work one inc row. 57[66]
sts. Rep last 7 rows 5[6] times more,
ending with an inc row. 67[78] sts.
Fasten off.

Note: *Use new colour to complete last
st in old colour and use small separate
balls of yarn for each area of colour.
(See Special Technique below.)*

Front
Using 4.00mm hook and B, make
84[93]ch.

Base row (RS) 1dc into 2nd ch from
hook, 1dc into each ch to end. Turn.
83[92]dc.

1st row 1ch to count as first dc, miss first
st, 1dc into each st to end. Turn. Cont in
dc and foll 'winter' chart, beg at
appropriate arrow on RH edge and
working rem 89 rows of chart.
Using A only, work 10[14] more rows of
dc.

Shape neck
Next row 1ch to count as first dc, miss

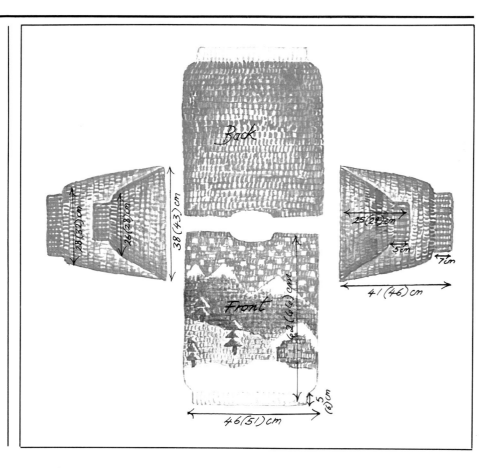

SPECIAL TECHNIQUE
working picture jacquard

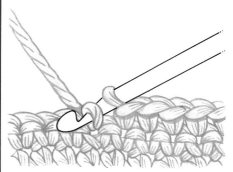

*1 When changing colour, always
introduce the new colour when
completing the last stitch in the old
colour. When working double crochet,
insert the hook into the last stitch, wind
the old colour round the hook and draw
through a loop.*

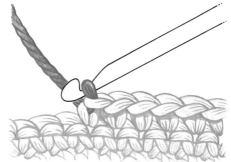

*2 Drop the old colour and wind the new
colour round the hook. Draw the new
colour through both loops on the hook to
complete the stitch. Continue as
appropriate in the new colour.*

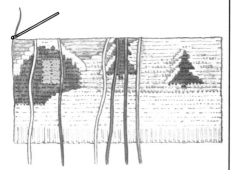

*3 Stranding yarn across the back of the
work would be very wasteful in
picture jacquard, so use separate balls of
yarn for each colour, and leave them on
the wrong side of the work when not in
use. Either wind small amounts of yarn
onto bobbins or use long, loose strands.*

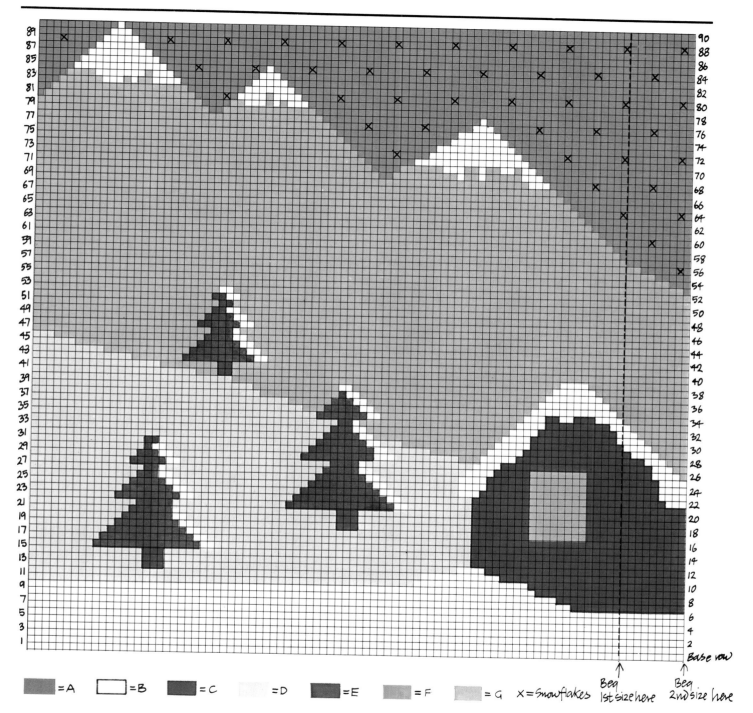

Row numbers on left (bottom to top): 1, 3, 5, 7, 9, 11, 13, 15, 17, 19, 21, 23, 25, 27, 29, 31, 33, 35, 37, 39, 41, 43, 45, 47, 49, 51, 53, 55, 57, 59, 61, 63, 65, 67, 69, 71, 73, 75, 77, 79, 81, 83, 85, 87, 89

Row numbers on right (bottom to top): 2, 4, 6, 8, 10, 12, 14, 16, 18, 20, 22, 24, 26, 28, 30, 32, 34, 36, 38, 40, 42, 44, 46, 48, 50, 52, 54, 56, 58, 60, 62, 64, 66, 68, 70, 72, 74, 76, 78, 80, 82, 84, 86, 88, 90

Base row

Bea 1st size here   Bea 2nd size here

■ = A   □ = B   ■ = C   ▨ = D   ■ = E   ▨ = F   ▨ = G   X = Snowflakes

first st, 1dc into each of next 26[29]dc, work next 2dc tog, turn. 28[31] sts.
Next row 1ch, miss first st, work next 2dc tog, 1dc into each st to end. Turn. 27[30] sts. Turn.
Rep last 2 rows until 22[25] sts rem.

Fasten off.
Return to sts left at beg of neck shaping, miss next 25[28] sts and rejoin A to next st.
Next row 1ch to count as first dc, miss first st, work next 2dc tog, 1dc into each

st to end. Turn. 28[31] sts. Complete to match first side of neck.

To make up
Using B and foll 'winter' chart, embroider snowflakes on front using

55

French knots.
Using C, embroider window frame on cottage in chain stitch .

Neckband
Join shoulder seams.
With RS facing and using 3.50mm hook, join A to left shoulder seam and work 10tr down left front, 25[28]tr across front neck, 10tr up right front and 27[30]tr across back neck, ss to first st. 72[78] sts.

Rib round 3ch to count as first tr, miss first st, * 1tr front into next st, 1tr back into next st, rep from * to last st, 1tr front into last st, ss to top of first 3ch. Rep rib round once more. Fasten off.
Set in sleeves, matching centre of sleeve top with shoulder seam. Join side and sleeve seams.

Welt
With RS facing and using 3.50mm hook,

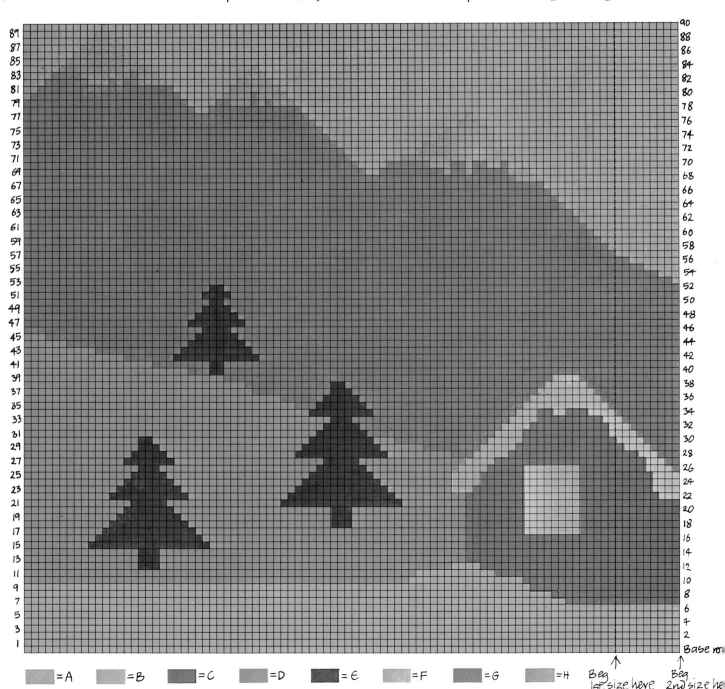

=A   =B   =C   =D   =E   =F   =G   =H

Beg 1st size here   Beg 2nd size here

join A to left side seam and work 166[184]tr into lower edge of front and back.
Rep rib round as for neckband 5[6] times more. Fasten off.

Summer sweater

Back
Work as for back of Winter Sweater.

Sleeves (both alike)
Using 3.50mm hook and A, make 44[48]ch.

Base row 1tr into 4th ch from hook, 1tr into each ch to end. 42[46] sts. Work rib row as for Winter Sweater sleeve 7 times in all.
Change to 4.00mm hook.

Shape sleeve
Inc row 2ch to count as first htr, miss first st, 2htr into next st, 1htr into each st to last 2sts, 2htr into next st, 1htr into top of turning ch. Turn. 44[48] sts.
Rep inc row twice more. 48[52] sts.
Next row Work in htr.
Next row Work inc row. 50[54] sts. Rep last 2 rows 10[12] times more. 70[78] sts.
Work 3[5] rows of htr without further shaping. Fasten off.

Front
Working in dc and foll 'summer' chart (see page 56) work as given for Winter Sweater.

To make up
Using H, embroider window frame on cottage using chain stitch .
Complete as given for Winter Sweater, omitting snowflakes.

Adapting the basic picture sweaters

Create your own original design by adapting one of these sweaters.

The basic sweaters can easily be varied if you use equivalent textured yarns instead of plain yarns. For example, the snow could be worked in white mohair or the trees could be worked in green bouclé yarn to suggest leaves.
The Pattern Library gives two motifs which could also be added to the sweaters. Draw the motif on the appropriate chart on page 55 or 56 and use suitable colours to work the motif as part of the picture.

Pattern Library: Picture jacquard patterns

Sheep
Use this motif on the summer sweater. Work the body of the sheep in white bouclé yarn and the legs in black plain yarn.

Small cottage
Place several small cottages in the background of either sweater. Change the colours, depending on whether it is summer or winter.

Random jacquard

Random jacquard is a fascinating technique which presents the ideal opportunity to use your own imagination to work multicoloured fabrics. Here, the technique is used for a charming outfit for a baby.

The basic random jacquard outfit

Jacket and dungarees

Size
To fit 51cm chest (9-12 months)
Jacket length 24cm
Sleeve seam 18cm
Dungarees
Length from waist to ankle 44cm
Inside leg to ankle 21cm

Materials
Jacket 60g of a four-ply yarn in main colour A
20g in each of contrast colours B, C and D
3 small toggles
Dungarees
150g of a four-ply yarn in main colour A

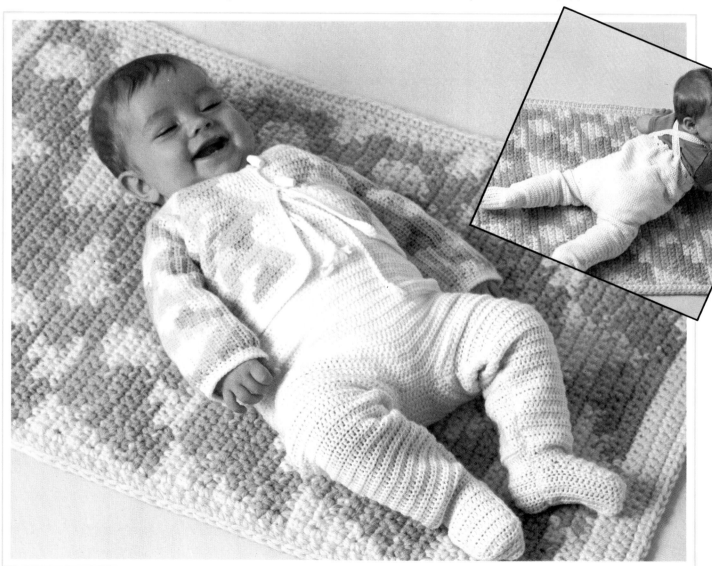

2 small buttons
3.00mm crochet hook
Note: *When working jacquard pattern on the jacket and rug, use a small ball of yarn for each area of colour.*

Tension

22htr and 18 rows to 10cm using 3.00mm hook

To save time, take time to check tension.

Jacket

Note: *Jacket is worked in one piece, beg at lower back edge.*
Using 3.00mm hook and A, make 63ch.
Base row (WS) Using A, 1htr into 3rd ch from hook, 1htr into each ch to end. Turn. 62 sts.
1st row Using A, 2ch to count as first htr, miss first st, foll chart on page 61, work 1htr into each st to end. Turn.
Cont in htr, working jacquard patt from chart until work measures approx 14cm from beg and 12th row of chart has been completed.
Shape sleeve
Using 2nd ball of A, make 41ch.
Fasten off.
Return to main piece, join in A at beg of next row and make 41ch.
Next row Using D, 1htr into 3rd ch from hook, miss first st, 1htr into each of next 5 sts, using B, 1htr into each of next 3 sts, work 13th row of chart across next 30 sts and across first 41 sts of back, using B, yrh, insert hook into last st of back and into first of separate 41ch, yrh and draw through first ch and last st of back, yrh and draw through 3 loops on hook – left-sleeve sts joined to back –, patt across rem 40ch. Turn. 142 sts.
Cont in jacquard patt until work measures 24cm from beg, ending with a WS row.
Shape right neck
Next row 2ch, miss first st, patt across next 60 sts, turn. 61 sts.
Patt 2 rows without further shaping.
Keeping jacquard patt correct, inc one st at neck edge on foll 4 rows, ending at neck edge. 65 sts.
Next row Using A make 5ch, keeping

jacquard patt correct work 1htr into 3rd ch from hook, 1htr into each of next 2ch, patt to end. 69 sts.
Shape right front
Cont in jacquard patt without further shaping until sleeve measures 20cm from underarm, ending at centre front edge.
Next row 2ch, miss first st, patt across next 28 sts, turn. 29 sts.
Cont in jacquard patt on these sts until work measures 48cm from beg.
Using A, work one row of htr.
Fasten off.
Shape left neck and front
With RS facing, return to back neck sts, miss next 20 sts, keeping jacquard patt correct rejoin yarn to next st.
Next row 2ch, miss first st, patt to end. 61 sts.
Complete to match other side of neck and front, reversing all shaping.

To make up
Do not press.
Join underarm and side seams.
Outer edging
With RS facing and using 3.00mm hook, join A to lower edge at right side seam. Work a round of dc along right front, up right front edge, around neck, down left front edge, along left front and back, working 1dc into each st and row end and 3dc into corners.
Work 3 more rounds of dc.
Fasten off.
Sleeve edging (both alike)
With RS facing and using 3.00mm hook, join A to sleeve seam. Work a round of dc, working 1dc into each st.
Work 3 more rounds of dc.
Fasten off.
Button loops (make 3)
Sew toggles into position on left front (for girls) or right front (for boys) placing one toggle 1cm from neck edge, one 12cm from lower edge and one evenly spaced in between.
Make button loop on opposite front edge as foll:
With RS facing and using 3.00mm hook, join A to edge st directly opposite toggle, ss into same place as join, 8ch, ss into same place as join.
Fasten off.

Dungarees

Front
Beg at waist and using 3.00mm hook, make 62ch.
Base row (RS) 1htr into 3rd ch from hook, 1htr into each ch to end. Turn. 61 sts.
Next row 2ch to count as first htr, miss first st, 1htr into each st to end. Turn.
Cont in htr until work measures 20cm from beg, ending with a WS row.
Shape crotch
1st row 2ch, miss first st, 1htr into each of next 28 sts, 2htr into next st, 1htr into next st, 2htr into next st, 1htr into each of last 29 sts. Turn. 63 sts.
2nd, 4th and 6th rows Work in htr.
3rd row 2ch, miss first st, 1htr into each of next 28 sts, 2htr into next st, 1htr into each of next 3 sts, 2htr into each of last 29 sts. Turn. 65 sts.
5th row 2ch, miss first st, 1htr into each of next 28htr, 2htr into next st, 1htr into each of next 5 sts, 2htr into next st, 1htr into each of last 29htr.
Turn. 67 sts.
**Divide for legs
Next row 2ch, miss first st, 1htr into each of next 28 sts, turn. 29 sts.
Work in htr on these sts for 3 more rows.
Dec one st at inside leg edge on next and every foll 6th row until 23 sts rem.
Cont in htr without further shaping until work measures 44cm from beg.
Fasten off.
With RS facing, return to missed sts on front, miss next 9 sts, rejoin yarn to next st.
Next row 2ch, miss first st, 1htr into each st to end. 29 sts.
Complete as for first leg, reversing all shaping.**

Back
Work base row and 9 rows of htr as given for back, ending with a WS row.
Shape back
Next row 2ch, miss first st, 1htr into each of next 53 sts, turn.
Next row 2ch, miss first st, 1htr into each of next 46 sts, turn.
Next row 2ch, miss first st, 1htr into each of next 39 sts, turn.

Next row 2ch, miss first st, 1htr into each of next 32 sts, turn.

Next row 2ch, miss first st, 1htr into each of next 32 sts just worked, 1htr into 14 sts missed at side edge. Turn.

Next row 2ch, miss first st, 1htr into each of next 46 sts, 1htr into 14 sts missed at side edge. Turn. 61 sts.

Cont in htr without further shaping until back measures same as front at side edges.

Work from ** to ** as for front.

Feet

Do not press. Join outside leg seams. With RS facing, rejoin yarn to first st on left leg.

Next row 1ch to count as first dc, miss first st, *1dc into each of next 2 sts, work next 2dc tog, rep from * to last st, 1dc into last st. 35 sts.

Work 3 more rows in dc without further shaping.

Next row Ss across first 4dc, 2ch, miss ss at base of 2ch, 1htr into each of next 11 sts, turn. 12 sts.

Work 10 more rows in htr on these sts without further shaping.

Fasten off.

With RS facing, rejoin yarn to first ss.

Next row 2ch, miss first st, 1htr into each of next 2ss, 1htr into each of next 10 row ends, 1htr into each of next 12 sts, 1htr into each of next 10 row ends, 1htr into each of next 20 sts. Turn. 55sts.

Next row 2ch, miss first st, 1htr into each of next 29 sts, (work next 2htr tog) 4 times, 1htr into each of next 15 sts. Turn. 51 sts.

Work 4 more rows of htr without further shaping.

Next row 2ch, miss first st, 1htr into each of next 15 sts, (work next 2htr tog) twice, 1htr into each of next 21 sts, (work next 2htr tog) twice, 1htr into each of next 6 sts. Turn. 47 sts.

Next row 2ch, miss first st, 1htr into each of next 5 sts, (work next 2htr tog) twice, 1htr into each of next 19 sts, (work next 2htr tog) twice, 1htr into each of next 14 sts. 43 sts. Fasten off.

Work 2nd foot in the same way reversing all shaping.

Front bib

** With RS facing and using 3.00mm hook, rejoin yarn to first st on front.

Next row 1ch to count as first dc, miss first 2 sts, 1dc into each st to last 2 sts, work last 2dc tog. Turn. 59 sts. Work 4 more rows of dc without shaping.

Next row 3ch, miss first st, 1tr into each of next 2 sts, *1ch, miss next st, 1tr into each of next 3 sts, rep from * to end. Turn.

Next row 1ch to count as first dc, miss first st, 1dc into each of next 2 sts, *1dc into next 1ch sp, 1dc into each of next 3 sts, rep from * to end.

Work one more row in dc.

Fasten off. **

With RS facing, miss first 12 sts on bib and rejoin yarn to next st.

Next row 2ch, miss first st, 1htr into each of next 34 sts, turn. 35 sts.

Work one more row of htr.

Cont in htr, dec one st at each end of next and every foll 3rd row until 25 sts rem.

Work one more row in htr.

Work 2 rows of dc.

Buttonhole row 1ch to count as first dc, miss first st, 1dc into next st, 3ch, miss next 3 sts, 1dc into each of next 15 sts,

---

SPECIAL TECHNIQUE

increasing for the sleeves

  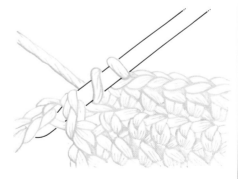

1 The basic jacket is worked in one piece, beginning at the lower back edge, and so stitches must be increased to form the sleeves. Work as given until the back is the required length to the underarms, ending with a wrong side row. Remove the hook from the loop on the back. Using another ball of main colour, work 41 chain and fasten off.

2 Return to the loop on the back that was left in step 1. Join in the main colour at the beginning of the row and work 41 chain. Pattern across these in double crochet — 40 sleeve stitches. Pattern across the first 61 stitches of the back.

3 To join the 41 chain worked separately (which will form the left sleeve stitches), wind the yarn round the hook and insert the hook into the last stitch on the back and into the first of the 41 chain. Wind the yarn round the hook and draw a loop through the chain and last stitch. Wind the yarn round the hook and draw through the remaining 3 loops on the hook. Patt the next 40 stitches — 142 stitches have been worked.

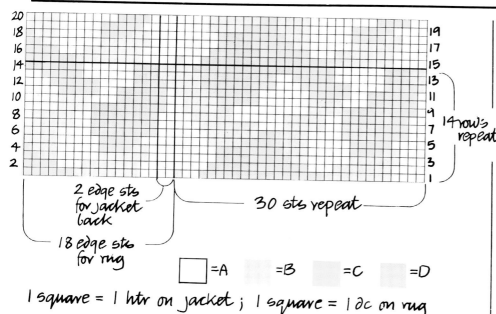

20
18
16
14
12
10
8
6
4
2

19
17
15
13
11
9
7
5
3
1

14 rows repeat

2 edge sts
for jacket
back

18 edge sts
for rug

30 sts repeat

☐ =A   =B   =C   =D

1 square = 1 htr on jacket ; 1 square = 1 dc on rug

and D
7.00mm crochet hook

Tension
9dc and 9 rows to 10cm worked on
7.00mm hook

To make
Using 7.00mm hook and A, make 49ch.
Base row (WS) 1dc into 2nd ch from
hook, 1dc into each ch to end. Turn.
48 sts.
1st row Using A, 1ch to count as first dc,
miss first st, foll chart shown above,
work 1dc into each st to end.
Turn.
Cont in dc, working jacquard patt from
chart until work measures 83cm from
beg. Using A, work one row of htr.
Fasten off.

Edging
Do not press.
With RS facing and using 7.00mm hook,
rejoin A to first st on foundation ch.
1st round 1ch to count as first dc, miss
first st, (1dc into each st to corner st, 3dc
into corner st, 1dc into each row end to
corner st, 3dc into corner st) twice,
ending last rep with 2dc, ss to first ch.
Rep last round twice more.
Fasten off.

3ch, miss next 3 sts, 1dc into each of last
2 sts. Turn.
Next row 1ch to count as first dc, miss
first st, 1dc into next st, 3dc into next
3ch sp, 1dc into each of next 15 sts, 3dc
into next 3ch sp, 1dc into each of last 2
sts. Turn. Fasten off.
With RS facing and using 3.00mm hook,
rejoin yarn to first row end of bib and
work 1dc into each row end up left side,
into each st across top and into each
row end down right side. Fasten off.

Back bib
Work from ** to ** as for front bib.

Straps (make 2)
Using 3.00mm hook, make 61ch.
Base row 1htr into 3rd ch from hook,
1htr into each ch to end. Turn.
60 sts.
Work 3 more rows of htr. Fasten off.

To make up
Do not press.
Join inside leg and foot seams.
Stitch straps into place at back and sew
buttons on to straps as required to
correspond with buttonholes.
Make a twisted cord (see page 164)
100cm long and thread it through eyelet
holes.

Rug
Size
Rug measures approx 91cm × 61cm.

Materials
650g of a rug yarn in main colour A
250g in each of contrast colours B, C

28 cm
14 cm
18 cm
20 cm
13 cm

Adapting the jacquard outfit

Use the Pattern Library to make an original outfit for a baby.

Many of the Pattern Library samples can be used to make the basic jacket and blanket, since, unlike conventional jacquard patterns, random jacquard does not have obvious pattern repeats. There is therefore no need to worry about balancing the pattern at the side edges. You can either work a totally random pattern, inventing the design as you go, or work a random-style repeating pattern as on the jacket and rug.

Work the stitch repeat as often as possible within the stitches for the garment. Then work as much of the repeat as required for the remaining stitches. For example, on the chart shown on page 61, the 18 edge stitches on the blanket are the last 18 stitches of the stitch repeat, whereas the jacket uses only the last two stitches of the repeat (the first two at the right) as edge stitches.

Pattern Library: Random jacquard patterns

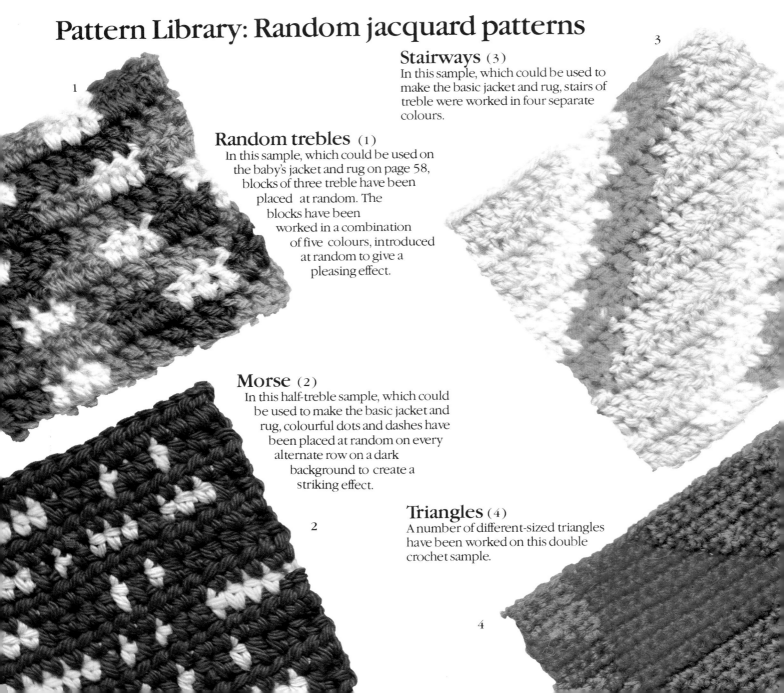

Stairways (3)
In this sample, which could be used to make the basic jacket and rug, stairs of treble were worked in four separate colours.

Random trebles (1)
In this sample, which could be used on the baby's jacket and rug on page 58, blocks of three treble have been placed at random. The blocks have been worked in a combination of five colours, introduced at random to give a pleasing effect.

Morse (2)
In this half-treble sample, which could be used to make the basic jacket and rug, colourful dots and dashes have been placed at random on every alternate row on a dark background to create a striking effect.

Triangles (4)
A number of different-sized triangles have been worked on this double crochet sample.

Puffs and popcorns

Puffs and popcorns are two kinds of large crochet bobble that can be worked either by themselves or in combination with other stitches. Use them to make highly textured fabrics, as for this attractive pullover and cardigan, or scatter them on a plain background.

The basic textured sweater and cardigan

Sizes

To fit 86-91 [96-101]cm chest/bust
Length 52[58]cm excluding knitted rib welt
Sleeve seam 46[50]cm excluding knitted rib cuffs
Note: *Instructions for larger sizes are in square brackets [ ]; where there is only one set of figures it applies to both sides.*

Materials

Pullover or cardigan
1100 [1400] g of a medium-weight crochet cotton
4.50mm crochet hook
Pair of 3¼mm knitting needles
Cardigan only
3.50mm crochet hook

Tension

14 sts and 10 rows to 10cm measured over patt worked on 4.50mm hook

To save time, take time to check tension.

Special abbreviations

Br – berry st: (yrh, insert hook into st and draw through a loose loop, yrh and draw through first loop on hook) twice, yrh and draw through first 4 loops on hook, yrh and draw through rem 2 loops on hook.

Cb – cluster bobble: leaving last loop of each st on hook work 4tr into next st, yrh and draw through first 4 loops on hook, yrh and draw through rem 2 loops on hook.

Pc – popcorn st: 4tr into next st, remove hook from loop and insert into first tr just worked and into loop just left, yrh and draw through all loops on hook.

Pf – puff st: (yrh, insert hook into st and draw through a loose loop) 4 times, yrh and draw through first 8 loops on hook, yrh and draw through rem 2 loops.

Panel 1 (worked over 20 sts)

1st row (RS) 1tr into each of next 8 sts, pc into next st, 1tr into each of next 2 sts, pc into next st, 1tr into each of next 8 sts.
2nd row 1dc into each of next 5 sts, pf into next st, 1dc into each of next 8 sts, pf into next st, 1dc into next 5 sts.
3rd row 1tr into each of next 3 sts, * miss next st, inserting hook from front to back work 1tr tr round stem – called 1tr tr front – of tr 2 sts to left and 2 rows below, 1tr into each of next 3 sts, miss next st, 1tr tr front round tr 2 rows below and now 2 sts to right * *, 1 tr into next tr, pc into each of next 2 sts,

1tr into next st, rep from * to * * once more, 1tr into each of next 3 sts.
4th row 1dc into each of next 4 sts, pf into next st, 1dc into next st, pf into next st, 1dc into each of next 6dc, pf into next st, 1dc into next st, pf into next st, 1dc into each of next 4 sts.
5th row 1tr into next st, * miss next st, 1tr tr round tr tr to left 2 rows below, 1tr into each of next 7 sts, miss next st, 1tr tr round tr tr to right 2 rows below * *, rep from * to * * once more, 1tr into next st.
6th row 1dc into each of next 4 sts, pf into next st, 1dc into next st, pf into next st, 1dc into each of next 6 sts, pf into next st, 1dc into next st, pf into next st, 1dc into each of next 4 sts.
7th row 1tr into each of next 3 sts, * miss next st, 1tr tr front round tr tr to right 2 rows below, 1tr into each of next 3 sts, miss next st, 1tr tr front round tr tr to left 2 rows below *, 1tr into next st, pc into each of next 2 sts, 1tr into next st, rep from * to * * once more, 1tr into each of next 3 sts.
8th row 1dc into each of next 5 sts, pf into next st, 1dc into each of next 8 sts, pf into next st, 1dc into each of next 5 sts.
9th row 1tr into each of next 5 sts, * miss next st, leaving last loop of each

---

working puff stitch

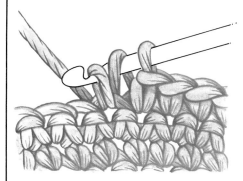

1 Puff stitches can be worked with either the right or the wrong side facing. Work to the position of the puff stitch. Wind the yarn round the hook, insert the hook into the next stitch and draw through a loose loop — three loops on the hook.

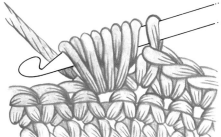

2 * Wind the yarn round the hook, insert the hook into the same stitch and draw through a loose loop — five loops on the hook. Rep from * twice more — nine loops on the hook — making sure that all loops are sufficiently loose.

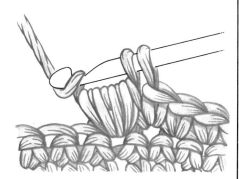

3 Wind the yarn round the hook and draw through the first eight loops on the hook. (This would be very difficult if the loops had been worked tightly.) Wind the yarn round the hook and draw through the remaining two loops on to the hook to complete the puff stitch.

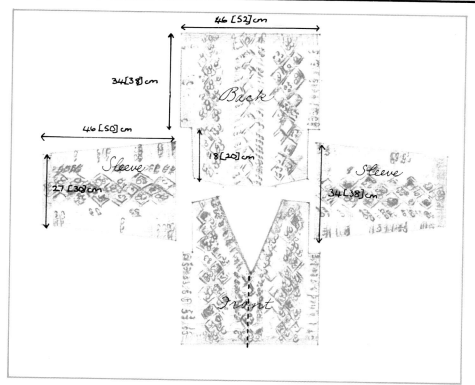

st on hook work 1tr tr front round tr tr to right 2 rows below and 1 tr tr front round tr tr to left 2 rows below, yrh, and draw through rem 3 loops on hook **, 1tr into each of next 2 sts, (pc into next st, 1tr into each of next 2 sts) twice, rep from * to ** once more, 1tr into each of next 5 sts.

10th row 1dc into each of next 5 sts, pf into next st, 1dc into each of next 8 sts, pf into next st, 1dc into each of next 5 sts.

11th row 1tr into each of next 3 sts, * miss next st, 1tr tr round tr tr to left 2 rows below, 1tr into each of next 3 sts, miss next st, 1tr tr round tr tr to right 2 rows below **, 1tr into next st, pc into each of next 2 sts, 1tr into next st, rep from * to ** once more, 1tr into each of next 3 sts.

4th-11th rows form patt of Panel 1. Rep them as required.

Panel 2 (worked over 3 sts)

1st row (RS) 1tr into next st, pc into next st, 1tr into next st.

2nd row Pf into next st, 1tr into next st, pf into next st.

First and 2nd rows form patt of Panel 2. Rep them as required.

Panel 3 (worked over 9 sts)

1st row 1tr into next st, pc into next st, 1tr into each of next 5 sts, pc into next st, 1tr into next st.

2nd row 1dc into each of next 2 sts, cb into next st, 1dc into each of next 3 sts, cb into next st, 1dc into each of next 2 sts.

3rd row 1tr into each of next 3 sts, pc into next st, 1tr into next st, pc into next st, 1tr into each of next 3 sts.

4th row 1dc into each of next 4 sts, cb into next st, 1dc into each of next 4 sts.

5th row 1tr into each of next 4 sts, pc into next st, 1tr into each of next 4 sts.

6th row As 4th row.

7th row As 3rd row.

8th row As 2nd row.

First-8th rows form patt of Panel 3. Rep them as required.

Pullover

Back

Using 4.50mm hook, make 66[74] ch.

Base row (WS) Ss into 3rd ch from hook, 2ch, br into next ch, (ss into next ch, 2ch, br into next ch) 1[3] times, 1dc into each of next 55ch, (2ch, br into next ch, ss into next ch) 2[4] times, 1dc into last ch. Turn. 65[73] sts.

1st row (RS) 3ch, miss first st, (1tr into next ss, 1dc into next br) 2[4] times, work first rows of panels as foll:
Panel 1, Panel 2, Panel 3, Panel 2, Panel 1, (1dc into next br, 1tr into next ss) 2[4] times, 1tr into top of turning ch. Turn.

2nd row (2ch, br into next tr, ss into next dc) 2[4] times, work 2nd rows of panels as foll: Panel 1, Panel 2, Panel 3, Panel 2, Panel 1, (ss into next dc, 2ch, br into next tr) 2[4] times, 1dc into top of turning ch. Turn.

3rd row 3ch, miss first st, (1dc into next br, 1tr into next ss) 2[4] times, work next rows of panels as set, (1tr into next ss, 1dc into next br) 2[4] times, 1tr into first of 2ch. Turn.

4th row 1ch, miss first st, (ss into next dc, 2ch, 1br into next tr) 2[4] times, work next rows of panels as set, (2ch, br into next tr, ss into next dc) 2[4] times, 1dc into top of turning ch. Turn.

Cont working border of br and panels as set, rep panel patts as previously instructed, until 34[38] rows in all have been worked from the foundation ch.

Shape armholes

Next row Ss across first 6[8] sts, 1ch, miss ss at base of first ch, 1dc into each of next 0[2] sts, work panels as set, 1dc into each of next 1[3] sts, turn. 55[59] sts.

3ch, miss first st, 1tr into each of next 0[2] sts, work panels as set, 1tr into each of next 1[3] sts. Turn.

Cont to work panels and edge sts as set until 18[20] rows have been worked from beg of armhole.

Shape shoulders

Next row Ss across first 7 sts, 1dc into each of next 7 sts, 1tr into each of next 27[31] sts, 1dc into each of next 7 sts. Fasten off.

Front

Work as for back until 26[34] rows have been worked from beg.

Shape neck

Next row Patt across 28[32] sts, 1dc into each of next 4dc, turn. 32[36] sts.

Next row 3ch, miss first st, 1tr into each of next 3 sts, patt to end. Turn.
* * **Next row** Patt across 28[32] sts, 1dc into next st, work next 2dc tog, 1dc into last st. Turn. 31[35] sts.
Next row 3ch, miss first st, 1tr into each of next 2 sts, patt to end. Turn.
2nd size only. Shape armhole
Next row Ss across first 8 sts, 1ch, miss ss at base of first ch, patt to last 3 sts, work next 2dc tog, 1dc into last st. Turn. 27 sts.
1st size only
Next row Patt across 28 sts, work next 2dc tog, 1dc into last st. Turn. 30 sts.
Both sizes
Next row 3ch, miss first st, 1tr into next st, patt to end. Turn.
Next row Patt across 24[21] sts, pf into next st, 1dc into next st, pf into next st, work next 2dc tog, 1dc into last st. Turn. 29[26] sts.
Next row 3ch, miss first st, 1tr into each of next 2 sts, pc into next st, patt to end. Turn.
1st size only. Shape armhole
Next row Ss across first 6 sts, 1ch, miss ss at base of first ch, patt across 18 sts, pf into next st, 1dc into next st, pf into next st, work next 2dc tog, 1dc into last st. Turn. 23 sts.
2nd size only
Next row Patt across 20 sts, pf into next st, 1dc into next st, pf into next st, work next 2dc tog, 1dc into last st. Turn. 25 sts.
Both sizes
Next row 3ch, miss first st, 1tr into each of next 2 sts, pc into next st, patt to end. Turn.
Next row Patt across 17[19] sts, pf into next st, 1dc into next st, pf into next st, work next 2dc tog, 1dc into last st. Turn. 22[24] sts.
Next row 3ch, miss first st, 1tr into each of next 2 sts, pc into next st, patt to end. Turn.
Keeping panel and neck edge patts correct, cont to dec one st at neck edge on next and every foll alt row until 16[18] sts rem.
Next row 3ch, miss first st, 1tr into each of next 2 sts, pc into next st, patt to end. Turn.
2nd size only Shape shoulder

Next row Ss across first 7 sts, 1dc into each of next 7 sts, 1tr into each of next 4tr. Fasten off.
1st size only
Next row Patt across 9 sts, 1dc into next st, pf into next st, 1dc into next st, pf into next st, work next 2dc tog, 1dc into last st. Turn. 15 sts.
Next row 3ch, miss first st, 1tr into each of next 2 sts, pc into next st, 1tr into next st, patt to end. Turn.
Shape shoulder
Next row Ss across first 7 sts, 1dc into each of next 7 sts, 1tr into next st. Fasten off. * *
Both sizes
Return to first row of neck shaping, miss next st and rejoin yarn to next st, 1ch,

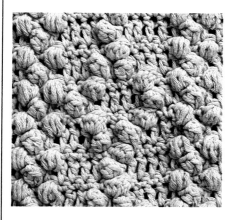

miss first st, patt to end. 32[36] sts.
Complete to match other side of neck, reversing all shaping.

Sleeves (both alike)
Using 4.50mm hook, make 39[43] ch.
Base row (WS) Ss into 3rd ch from hook, 2ch, br into next ch, (ss into next ch, 2ch, br into next ch) 1[2] times, 1dc into each of next 28ch, (2ch, br into next ch, ss into next ch) 2[3] times, 1dc into last ch. Turn. 38[42] sts.
1st row 3ch, miss first st, (1tr into next ss, 1dc into next br) 2[3] times, 1tr into next st, work first rows of panels as foll: Panel 2, Panel 1, Panel 2, 1tr into next st, (1dc into next br, 1tr into next ss) 2[3] times, 1tr into top of turning ch. Turn.
2nd row (2ch, br into next tr, ss into next dc) 2[3] times, 1dc into next st, work 2nd rows of panels as foll: Panel 2,

Panel 1, Panel 2, 1dc into next st, (ss into next dc, 2ch, br into next tr) 2[3] times, 1dc into last st. Turn.
3rd row 3ch, miss first st, (1dc into next br, 1tr into next ss) 2[3] times, 1tr into next st, work next row of panels as set, 1tr into next st, (1tr into next ss, 1dc into next br) 2[3] times, 1tr into top of turning ch. Turn.
Shape sleeve
4th row 1ch, 1dc into first st at base of first ch, (ss into next dc, 2ch, br into next tr) 2[3] times, 1dc into next st, work next row of panels as set, (1dc into next tr) 2[3] times, 1dc into next st, work next row of panels as set, 1dc.
Cont to rep panels as previously instructed, while *at the same time* inc one st at each end of every foll 4th row until there are 48[54] sts.
Cont in patt without further shaping until 46[50] rows have been worked from beg. Fasten off.

To make up
Do not press. Pin out all pieces to size. Spray lightly with water and leave to dry naturally.
Welts (both alike)
With RS facing and using 3¼mm needles, K up 65[73] sts from foundation ch.
1st rib row K1, (P1, K1) to end.
2nd rib row P1, (K1, P1) to end. Rep first and 2nd rib rows 6 times more.
Cast off loosely in rib.
Cuffs (alike)
With RS facing and using 3¼mm needles, K up 37[41] sts from foundation ch.
Rep first and 2nd rib rows 7 times. Cast off loosely in rib.
Using leftover yarn split in half, join shoulder and side seams. Join sleeve seam, leaving open approx 5[7]cm at top edge. Set in sleeve, joining open edges to underarm edges.
Neck border
With RS facing and using 4.50mm hook, join yarn to left shoulder seam.
Next row 1ch, working 1dc into each st and into each dc row end and 2dc into each tr row end, work in dc across back neck and down right front, work 1dc into missed st at front neck marking this

st with a contrasting thread, work in dc up left front, ss to first ch.

Next row 1ch, work in dc to right shoulder seam, miss next st, work in dc to 2 sts before marked st, work next 2dc tog, 1dc into marked st, work next 2dc tog, work in dc to last st, miss last st, ss to first ch.

Rep last row once more. Fasten off.

Cardigan

Back and sleeves

Work as for Pullover.

Left front

Using 4.50mm hook, make 33[37]ch.
Base row (WS) Ss into 3rd ch from hook, 2ch, br into next ch, (ss into next ch, 2ch, br into next ch) 1[3] times, 1dc into each ch to end. Turn. 32[36] sts.
1st row 3ch, miss first st, 1tr into each of next 3 sts, work first rows of panels as foll: Panel 2, Panel 1, (1dc into next br, 1tr into next ss) 2[4] times, 1tr into top of turning ch. Turn.
2nd row (2ch, br into next st, ss into next st) 2[4] times, work 2nd rows of panels as foll: Panel 1, Panel 2, 1dc into each of last 4 sts. Turn.
3rd row 3ch, miss first st, 1tr into each of next 3 sts, work next row of panels as set, (1tr into next ss, 1dc into next br) 2[4] times, 1tr into top of turning ch.

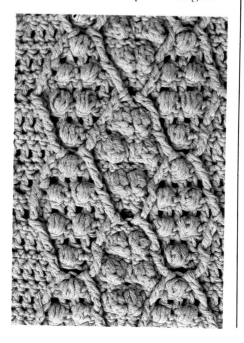

Turn.
4th row 1ch, miss first st, (ss into next st, 2ch, br into next st) 2[4] times, work next row of panels as set, 1dc into each of last 4 sts. Turn.
Cont working borders and panels as set, rep panel patts as previously instructed, until 28[36] rows have been worked. Work from * * to * * as for Pullover front.

Right front

Using 4.50mm hook, make 33[37] ch.
Base row (WS) 1dc into 3rd ch from hook, 1dc into each of next 26ch, (2ch, br into next ch, ss into next ch) 2[4] times, 1dc into last ch. Turn. 32[36] sts.
1st row 3ch, miss first st, (1tr into next ss, 1dc into next br) 2[4] times, work first rows of panels as foll: Panel 1, Panel 2, 1tr into each of last 4 sts. Turn.
2nd row 1ch, miss first st, 1dc into each of next 3 sts, work 2nd rows of panels as foll: Panel 2, Panel 1, (ss into next dc, 2ch, br into next tr) 2[4] times, 1dc into top of turning ch. Turn.
Complete as for left front, reversing all shaping.

To make up

Work back welt and cuffs as for Pullover.
Front welts (both alike)
With RS facing and using 3¼mm needles, K up 31[35] sts from foundation ch. Rep first and 2nd rib rows 7 times. Cast off loosely in rib. Join shoulder, side and sleeve seams and set in sleeves as for Pullover.

Front band

Woman's version Mark position of 4 buttonholes on right front. With RS facing and using 4.50mm hook, join yarn to first row end on lower R H edge.
Next row Working 1dc into each st, into each rib row end and into each dc row end and 2dc into each tr row end, work in dc up right front, across back neck and down left front. Turn.
Next row Work in dc. Turn.
Next row (Work in dc to marker, 2ch, miss next 2dc) 4 times, work in dc to end. Turn.
Next row Work in dc to first 2ch sp, (2dc into next 2ch sp, work in dc to next 2ch sp) 4 times, work in dc to end. Turn.
Man's version Mark position of 4 buttonholes on left front, and complete front band as for woman's version, reversing position of buttonholes.

Buttons (make 4)
Wind off a little yarn to stuff button. Using 3.50mm hook, make 5ch, join with a ss to form a circle.
1st round 3ch, leaving last loop of each st on hook work 2tr into circle, yrh and draw through all 3 loops on hook, (leaving last loop of each st on hook, work 3tr into circle, yrh and draw through all 4 loops on hook) 3 times, ss into 3rd of first 3ch.
2nd round 1ch, (work next 2dc tog) twice, inserting spare yarn as button closes, ss to first ch. Fasten off firmly. Sew on buttons to front band to correspond with buttonholes.

Adapting the pullover and cardigan

Combine puff and popcorn stitches with other crochet bobbles to create a highly textured fabric.

Intricately patterned garments such as the basic pullover and cardigan are very difficult to adapt radically; it is much safer, if you wish to vary their appearance, to introduce contrast colours when working the bobbles. Remember to introduce the new colour when completing the last stitch in the old colour.

Using puffs and popcorns

Puffs and popcorns can be incorpo-
rated into plain crochet fabrics; puffs are usually worked in a double crochet fabric and popcorns in a treble fabric. These bobble stitches, however, may alter the tension, so change hook size accordingly. Estimate carefully the amount of yarn you will need. Use up a ball of yarn patterning across the width of the back. Divide the area of the garment by the area of the sample; the result is the number of balls needed.

Pattern Library: Puff and popcorn patterns

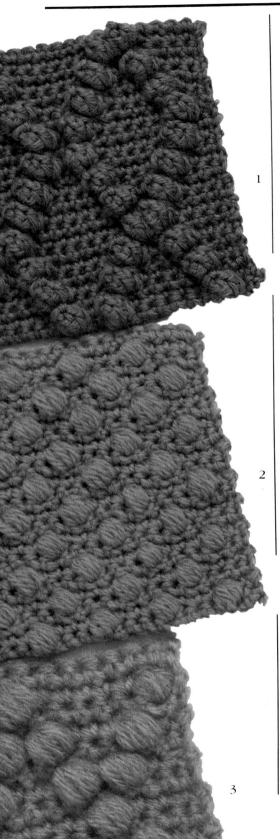

Popcorn lattice (1)

Make a multiple of 10ch plus 3 extra.
Base row 1dc into 2nd ch from hook, 2dc into each ch to end. Turn.
1st row (RS) 1ch to count as first dc, miss first st, 1dc into next st, * 4tr into next st, remove hook from loop and insert into first tr just worked and into loop just left, yrh and draw through all loops on hook – popcorn st or pc formed –, 1dc into each of next 6 sts, pc into next st, 1dc into each of next 2 sts, rep from * to end. Turn.
2nd and every alt row 1ch to count as first dc, miss first st, 1dc into each st to end. Turn.
3rd row 1ch to count as first dc, miss first st, 1dc into each of next 2 sts, * (pc into next st, 1dc into each of next 4 sts)
twice, rep from * ending last rep with 3dc. Turn.
5th row 1ch to count as first dc, miss first st, 1dc into each of next 3 sts, * pc into next st, 1dc into each of next 2 sts, pc into next st, 1dc into each of next 6 sts, rep from * ending last rep with 4dc. Turn.
7th row 1ch to count as first dc, miss first st, 1dc into each of next 4 sts, * pc into each of next 2 sts, 1dc into each of next 8 sts, rep from * ending last rep with 5dc. Turn.
9th row As 5th row.
11th row As 3rd row.
13th row As first row.
14th row As 2nd row.
Rep first-14th rows throughout.

Puff stitch (2)

Make a multiple of 4ch plus 2 extra.
Base row 1dc into 2nd ch from hook, 1dc into each ch to end. Turn.
1st row (WS) 1ch to count as first dc, miss first st, 1dc into next st, * (yrh, insert hook into next st and draw through a loose loop) 4 times, yrh and draw through first 8 loops on hook, yrh and draw through rem 2 loops on hook – puff st or pf formed –, 1dc into each of
next 3 sts, rep from * ending last rep with 2dc. Turn.
2nd row 1ch to count as first dc, miss first st, 1dc into each st to end. Turn.
3rd row 1ch to count as first dc, miss first st, * 1dc into each of next 3 sts, pf into next st, rep from * to last 4 sts, 1dc into each of last 4 sts. Turn.
4th row As 2nd row.
Rep first-4th rows throughout.

Puff-stitch crosses (3)

Make a multiple of 6ch plus 4 extra.
Base row 1dc into 2nd ch from hook, 1dc into each ch to end. Turn.
1st row (RS) 1ch to count as first dc, miss first st, * (yrh, insert hook into next st and draw through a loose loop) 5 times, yrh and draw through first 10 loops on hook, yrh and draw through rem 2 loops on hook – puff st or pf formed –, 1dc into each of next 5 sts, rep from * to last 2 sts, pf into next st, 1dc into last st. Turn.
2nd and every alt row 1ch to count as first dc, miss first st, 1dc into each st to end. Turn.
3rd row 1ch to count as first dc, miss first st, 1dc into next st, * pf into next st,
1dc into each of next 3 sts, pf into next st, 1dc into next st, rep from * to last st, 1dc into last st. Turn.
5th row 1ch to count as first dc, miss first st, * 1dc into each of next 2 sts, pf into next st, 1dc into next st, pf into next st, 1dc into next st, rep from * to last 2 sts, 1dc into each of last 2 sts. Turn.
7th row 1ch to count as first dc, miss first st, 1dc into each of next 3 sts, * pf into next st, 1dc into each of next 5 sts, rep from * ending last rep with 4dc. Turn.
9th row As 5th row.
11th row As 3rd row.
12th row As 2nd row.
Rep first-12th rows throughout.

Floral patterns

Of all natural forms, flowers have most often served as inspiration for needlework. Blossoms and petals worked on crochet add a new dimension to garments – such as this beach robe – and accessories.

The basic floral beach robe

Sizes

To fit 61-66 [71-76:81-86:91-97] cm
chest/bust
Length 50 [54:72:76] cm
Sleeve seam 32 [38:45:46] cm
Note: *Instructions for larger sizes are
in square brackets* [ ] ; where there is
only one set of figures it applies to all
sizes.

Materials

300 [400:500:600] g of a three-ply
crepe yarn
2.50mm crochet hook

Tension

22htr and 20 rows to 10cm worked on
2.50mm hook

To save time, take time to check
tension.

Back and fronts

(worked in one piece to armholes)
Using 2.50mm hook, make 143
[164:185:206] ch *loosely.*
Base row (RS) 1htr into 3rd ch from
hook, 1htr into each ch to end. Turn. 142
[163:184:205] sts.
1st row 2ch, 1htr into sp between htr to
end, working last htr in top of 2ch. Turn.
Rep last row twice more.
4th row 2ch, 1htr into sp between htr 3
times, *6tr round stem of next htr on
previous row, turn, 6tr round stem of
next htr on previous row, join with a ss
to first tr, turn – flower worked –, 1htr
into sp between htr 6 times, rep from *
to last 5 sts, work 1 flower, 1htr into sp
between htr to end. Turn.
5th row 2ch, 1htr into each sp between
htr and each ss to end. Turn.
6th-9th rows As first row.
10th row 2ch, 1htr into sp between htr
7 times, *work flower, 1htr into sp
between htr 6 times, rep from * to last 8
htr, work flower, 1htr into sp between
htr to end. Turn.
11th row As 5th row.
12th row As 2nd row.
These 12 rows form patt. Cont in patt
until work measures 23 [26:34:36] cm
from beg, ending with a WS row.

Shape fronts

Note: *Keep patt correct throughout.*
Dec row Ss into top of first htr, 2ch, patt
to within last 2 sts. Turn. 2 sts dec.
Keeping continuity of patt correct, dec
1 st at each end of every foll alt
[alt:3rd:3rd] row until 16 [16:16:17]
decs have been worked at both ends of
the row.
At the same time when work measures
34 [35:50:50] cm from beg, divide
work for back and fronts thus:
Leave centre 82 [97:114:127] sts for
back and cont on end sts only for fronts.
Right and left fronts
Keeping armhole edge straight, cont to
dec at front edge as set until 14
[17:19:22] sts rem.
Cont without further shaping until
work measures 48 [54:72:76] cm from
beg. Fasten off.

Back

With WS facing, miss next 14 [17:21:24]
sts and rejoin yarn to next htr. 2ch, patt
into next 53 [61:71:77] htr, turn. 54
[62:72:73] sts.
Keeping patt correct, cont on these sts
until armholes measure same as left
front armhole. Fasten off.

Sleeves (both alike)

Using 2.50mm hook, make 74
[86:100:114] ch *loosely.*
Base row 1htr into 3rd ch from hook,
1htr into each ch to end. Turn. 71
[85:99:103] sts.

SPECIAL TECHNIQUE
working raised flowers

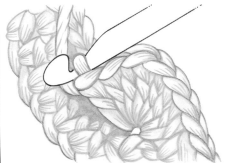

1 On the flower row, begin with two
chain followed by (one half treble
into the space between the next two half
treble) three times. To work the first half of
the flower, work six treble round the stem
of the next half treble on the previous row,
inserting the hook from front to back.

2 To work the second half of the flower,
turn, and work six treble round the
stem of the next half treble on the previous
row. Insert the hook from front to back as
before. You will find this easier if you hold
the work upside down as shown. Join with
a slip stitch to the first treble.

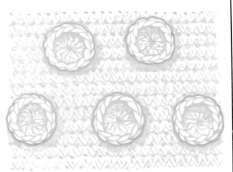

3 Then work (one half treble in the
space between the next two half
treble) six times. Continue spacing
flowers in this way to the last four stitches
and end with a half treble worked as
before. On the next flower row, begin with
seven half treble worked between half
treble to move the position of the
flowers.

1st row 2ch, 1htr into sp between htr to end.
Turn.
Rep last row twice more.
4th row 2ch, 1htr into sp between htr 3 times, *work flower, 1htr into sp between htr 6 times, rep from * to last 4 htr, work flower, 1htr into sp between htr to end.
Turn.
5th-9th rows As 5th-9th rows on back and fronts.
10th row 2ch, 1htr into sp between htr 7 times, *work flower, 1htr into sp between htr 6 times, rep from * to end.
Turn.
11th and 12th rows As 11th and 12th rows on back and fronts.
These 12 rows form patt. Cont in patt until sleeve measures 32 [38:45:46] cm from beg. Mark last row with a contrasting thread.
Cont in patt until sleeve measures 35 [42:50:51.5] cm from beg.
Fasten off.

To make up
Do not press.
Join shoulder and sleeve seams.
Set in sleeves.
Front band
With RS facing, join yarn to left shoulder seam.
1st round Work one round of dc evenly into edge of work, working down left front, along lower edge, up right front and across back neck, so that the number of sts is divisible by 4; join with a ss to first st.
2nd round 1ch, 1dc into first dc, *miss next dc, 5tr into next dc, miss next dc, 1dc into next dc, rep from * to last 3 sts, miss next dc, 5tr into next dc, join with a ss to first ch.
Fasten off.
Sleeve band
With RS facing, join yarn to lower edge at sleeve seam.
1st round Work one round of dc evenly into edge of work so that number of sts is divisible by 4; join with a ss to first st.
2nd round Work as for front band.
Fasten off.
Make a twisted cord of the length required and thread it evenly through the sts at the waist.

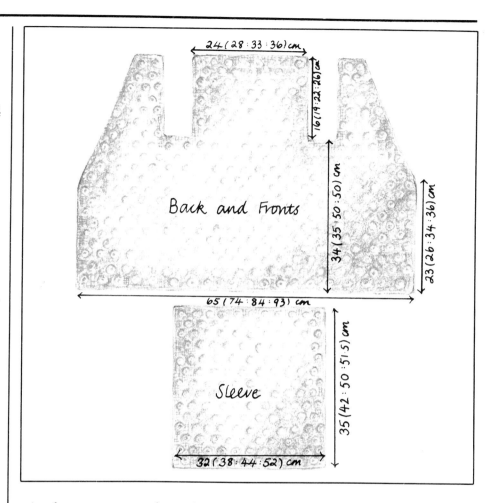

Adapting the basic floral beach robe

Use floral patterns to bring interesting textures to your crochet.

The simple flowers on the beach robes on page 69 are worked as part of the main pattern by working treble round the stem of half treble.
A simple but effective variation would be to work the treble in a colour contrasting with that of the background, changing colour either at random or in a regular pattern.

Other variations
Those with more experience might like to work the flowers in a different type of yarn. A slightly bouclé yarn could be very interesting, and a glitter yarn would make the garment into an evening wrap.
The stitches that form the flowers could be varied to form petals: for example, instead of working six treble round the stem, you could work (one half treble and two treble) twice or (one treble and two double treble) twice. You should, of course, check your tension carefully before working the pattern in this or any other variation.

Individual flowers
Instead of working an all-over pattern, you could simply work a plain half treble fabric, then sew individual crochet flowers onto it, arranging them as you like. Leaves and stems could also be added, using crochet or embroidery.

Pattern Library: Floral patterns

Daisy (1)

Use 2 colours, A and B.
Using A, wind yarn twice round index finger to form a circle, remove circle from finger.
1st round 1ch, 8dc into circle, ss to first ch. Fasten off. Pull end of yarn to close centre of circle.
2nd round *Using B make 5ch, with WS facing, ss to first dc on first round, 1ch, 1dc into each of next 4ch, 3dc into last ch, working into other edge of ch, 1dc into each of next 4ch, ss to same dc on first round, fasten off, rep from * into each dc of first round.

Tulip (3)

Make 10ch.
1dc into 2nd ch from hook, 1dc into each of next 7ch, 3dc into last ch.
Working into other edge of foundation ch work 1dc into each of next 8ch, 3dc into turning ch.
Working into *back* loop only of each dc work 1dc into each of next 8dc. Turn.
1ch, miss first dc, working into *front* loop only of each dc, work 1dc into each of next 8dc, 3dc into next dc, 1dc into each of next 8dc. Turn.
1ch, miss first dc, working into *back* loop only of each dc, work 1dc into each of next 7dc, ss into next dc. Fasten off.

Dahlia (4)

Make 5ch, join with a ss to form a circle.
1st round 1ch, 12dc into circle, ss to first ch.
2nd round Working into *back* loop only of each dc, 12ch, ss to first dc, * ss into next dc, 12ch, ss into same dc, rep from * to end.

3rd round Work as for 2nd round, but work into the *front* loop only of each dc and work 8ch only between ss. Fasten off.

Forget-me-not pattern (2)

Make a multiple of 3ch plus 5 extra.
Base row (RS) (2tr, 2ch, 1dc) into 5th ch from hook, *miss next 2ch, (2tr, 2ch, 1dc) into next ch, rep from * to last 3ch, miss 2ch, 1dc into last ch. Turn.
1st row 3ch to count as first tr, *(2tr, 2ch, 1dc) into next 2ch sp, rep from * to end, 1dc into 4th of first 4ch. Turn.
2nd row As first, but ending with 1dc into 3rd of first 3ch. Turn.
Rep 2nd row throughout for patt.

Periwinkle (5)

Make 6ch, join with a ss to form a circle.
1st round 3ch, 20tr into circle, ss to 3rd of first 3ch.
2nd round 1ch, 1dc into ss of previous round, (1ch, 1tr into next tr, 2tr into next tr, 1tr into next tr, 1ch, 1dc into next tr) 5 times, ss to first ch. Fasten off.

Rose (6)

Make 4ch, join with a ss to form a circle.
1st round 5ch, (1tr, 2ch) 7 times into circle, ss to 3rd of first 5ch.
2nd round 1ch, (1dc, 1tr, 1dtr, 1tr, 1dc) into each 2ch sp to end, ss to first ch. Turn.
3rd round With WS of work facing, (3ch, 1dc under both vertical threads at base of next dc) 8 times. Turn.
4th round 1ch, (1dc, 2tr, 1dtr, 2tr, 1dc) into each 3ch sp to end, ss to first ch. Turn.
5th round With WS of work facing, (4ch, ss under both horizontal threads between 2 petals on last round) 8 times. Turn.
6th round 1ch, (1dc, 2tr, 3dtr, 2tr, 1dc) into each 4ch sp to end, ss to first ch. Fasten off.

Wallflower pattern (7)

Make a multiple of 8ch plus 5 extra.
Base row 1tr into 4th ch from hook, *2ch, miss next 3ch, 1dc (4ch, 1dc) 3 times into next ch, 2ch, miss next 3ch, 1tr into next ch, rep from * to last ch, 1tr into last ch. Turn.
1st row (RS) 4ch, 1dtr into first tr, (2ch, 1dc, 4ch, 1dc) into next tr, 3ch, miss next 4ch loop, 1tr into next 4ch loop, 3ch, *1dc, (4ch, 1dc) 3 times into next tr, 3ch, miss next 4ch loop, 1tr into next 4ch loop, 3ch, rep from *, ending with (1dc, 4ch, 1dc, 3ch) into last tr, 1tr into top of turning ch.
Turn.
2nd row 2ch, 1dc into next 3ch loop, *3ch, 1dc into next tr, 3ch, miss next 4ch loop, 1dc into next 4ch loop, rep from *, ending with 3ch, 1dc into next tr, 3ch, 1dc into last dtr, 1dc into top of turning ch. Turn.
3rd row 2ch, miss first dc, 1dc into next dc, *1dc into each of next 3ch, 1dc into next dc, rep from *, ending with 1dc into top of turning ch. Turn.
4th row 2ch, miss first dc, 1dc into each dc to end, 1dc into top of turning ch. Turn.
5th row 3ch, miss first dc, 1tr into next dc, *2ch, miss next 3dc, 1dc, (4ch, 1dc) 3 times into next dc, 2ch, miss next 3dc, 1tr into next dc, rep from * to end, 1tr into turning ch. Turn.
Rep first–5th rows throughout.

Elongated stitches

Dazzling patterns of zigzags, triangles and bricks can be added to a double crochet fabric by working longer stitches in a contrasting yarn. Two shades of grey are used for this good-looking waistcoat.

The basic elongated-stitch waistcoat

Sizes
To fit 97-102 [102-107] cm chest
Length (from back neck) 50cm
Note: *Instructions for the larger size are in brackets [ ]; where there is only one set of figures it applies to both sizes.*

Materials
200 [250] g of a double knitting yarn in main colour A
100 [150] g in contrast colour B
4.00mm and 3.00mm crochet hooks
Pair of 3½mm knitting needles.

Note: *Strand yarn not in use loosely up side of work. Change colours by using new colour to complete last st worked in old colour.*

Tension
15sc and 22 rows to 10cm worked on 4.00mm hook. Knitted rib tension, 27 sts and 30 rows to 10cm worked on 3½mm needles

To save time, take time to check tension.

Left front (both sizes worked alike)
Using 4.00mm hook and A, make 3ch.
Base row 1dc into 3rd ch from hook. Turn.
1st row 2ch, 1dc into 2nd ch from hook, 1dc into next dc, 1dc into turning ch. Turn.
2nd row 2ch, 1dc into 2nd ch from hook, (1dc into each of next 2dc, 2dc into last dc). Turn.
3rd row 2ch, 1dc into 2nd ch from hook, 1dc into each dc to last dc, 2dc into last dc. Turn.
Rep last row 3 times more. 13dc.
Change to B.
7th row 2ch, 1dc into 2nd ch from hook, (1dc into each of next 2dc, 1dc into next st one row below, 1dc into next st 2

rows below, 1dc into next st 3 rows below, 1dc into next st 4 rows below, 1dc into next st 5 rows below, 1dc into next st 4 rows below, 1dc into next st 3 rows below, 1dc into next st 2 rows below, 1dc into next st one row below, 1dc into next st of previous row, 2dc into last st. Turn.
Rep 3rd row 5 times. 25dc.
Change to A.
13th row 2ch, 1dc into 2nd ch from hook, 1dc into each of next 3dc, *1dc into next st one row below, 1dc into next st 2 rows below, 1dc into next st 3 rows below, 1dc into next st 4 rows below, 1dc into next st 5 rows below, 1dc into next st 4 rows below, 1dc into next st 3 rows below, 1dc into next st 2 rows below, 1dc into next st one row below, 1dc into next st of previous row, rep from * once more, 1dc into next dc, 2dc into last st. Turn.
Rep 3rd row 3 times. 33dc.
17th and 18th rows 1ch, miss first dc, 1dc into each st to end. Turn.
Change to B.
19th row 1ch, miss first dc, 1dc into next dc, *1dc into next st one row below, 1dc into next st 2 rows below, 1dc into next st 3 rows below, 1dc into next st 4 rows below, 1dc into next st 5 rows below,

1dc into next st 4 rows below, 1dc into next st 3 rows below, 1dc into next st 2 rows below, 1dc into next st one row below, 1dc into next st of previous row, rep from * twice more, 1dc into turning ch. Turn.
20th-24th rows As 17th row.
Change to A.
25th row 1ch, miss first dc, 1dc into next st 5 rows below, *1dc into next st 4 rows below, 1dc into next st 3 rows below, 1dc into next st 2 rows below, 1dc into next st 1 row below, 1dc into next st of previous row, 1dc into next st one row below, 1dc into next st 2 rows below, 1dc into next st 3 rows below, 1dc into next st 4 rows below, 1dc into next st 5 rows below, rep from * twice more, 1dc into turning ch.
Turn.
26th-30th rows As 17th row.
Keeping colour sequence correct, work 19th-30th rows twice more, then work 19th to 25th rows once more.
Shape front
Keeping patt correct, beg front shaping:
62nd row 1ch, miss first dc, 1dc into each st to end. Turn.
63rd row 1ch, miss first dc, 1dc into each dc to end, dec 1 st at inner edge by omitting 1dc into turning ch. Turn.

SPECIAL TECHNIQUE
Working a pointed lower edge

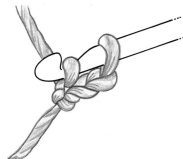

1 The pointed lower edges on the fronts of the basic waistcoat are worked by increasing from a small number of chain, while at the same time keeping the elongated stitch pattern correct. Begin with three chain and work one double crochet into the third chain from the hook. Turn.

2 On the next row begin with two chain and increase by working one double crochet into the second chain from the hook. Work one double crochet into the next double crochet and finish the row with one crochet into the turning chain. Turn.

3 The third row begins as before with two chain. Work one double crochet into the second chain from the hook, one double crochet into each of the next two double crochet and two double crochet into the last double crochet. Turn. Continue increasing in this way for the required width.

64th-66th rows As 62nd row.

67th row As 63rd row.

68th row As 62nd row.

Shape armhole

Cont to dec 1 st at inner edge on every 4th row, *at the same time* beg armhole shaping:

69th row Ss into each of first 3dc, 1dc into each st to end. Turn.

70th row 1ch, miss first dc, 1dc into each of next 25dc. Turn.

71st row As 63rd row

72nd row 1ch, miss first dc, 1dc into each of next 22dc, turn.

73rd row As 62nd row.

74th row 1ch, miss first dc, 1dc into each of next 21dc, turn.

75th row As 63rd row.

76th row 1ch, miss first dc, 1dc into each of next 19dc, turn.

77th row As 62nd row.

78th row 1ch, miss first dc, 1dc into each of next 18dc, turn.

79th row As 63rd row.

Keeping armhole edge straight, cont in patt, dec 1 st at inner edge on every foll 4th row, until 10dc rem and work measures 24cm from beg of armhole.

Next row Ss into each of first 3dc, 1dc into each st to end. Turn.

Next row 1ch, miss first dc, 1dc into each of next 5dc. Turn.

Next row Ss into each of first 3dc, 1dc into each st to end. Turn.

Fasten off.

Right front (both sizes worked alike)

Work as for left front, reversing shaping.

Front border

Mark positions of 4 buttonholes on left front.

1st row With RS facing and using 3.00mm hook, join A to lower side edge of right front, and work 1dc into each row end or st to top of shoulder, make 40ch for back neck border, cont down left front and lower edge, working 1dc into each row end and st as before. Turn.

2nd row 1ch, miss first dc, *1dc into each dc to dc at point, 3dc into next dc, 1dc into each dc to corner, 2dc into next dc, (1dc into each dc to buttonhole marker, 3ch, miss next 3dc) 4 times, 1dc into each dc to beg of front shaping, 2dc

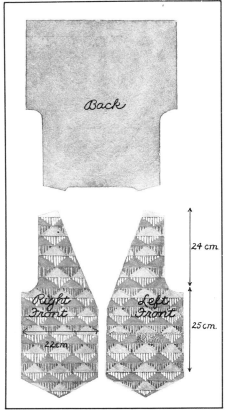

into next dc, 1dc into each dc to 40ch at back neck *, 1dc into each of next 40ch, rep from * to *, omitting buttonholes and reversing order of working.

3rd row 1ch, miss first dc, 1dc into each dc to end, inc at points and corners as on last row and omitting 1dc into turning ch. Turn.

4th row As 3rd row, but do not turn.

5th row 1ch, miss first dc, *working from left to right,* 1dc into each dc to end (see page 18). Fasten off.

Buttons (make 4 alike)

Using 3.00mm hook and A, leave an end of 50cm and make 3ch, 9tr into 3rd ch from hook, ss to top of 3ch, 1dc into each tr.

Break yarn and thread into yarn needle. Wind 50cm length of yarn into tight little ball and insert into button. Thread the yarn in the needle through the button and draw up tightly to form a round button.

Sew buttons to right front to match buttonholes.

Back

Using knitting needles and A, cast on 122 [134] sts.

Work in K1, P1 rib until work measures same as side fronts to armholes including band at lower edge.

Shape armholes

Keeping patt correct, cast off 7 [13] sts at beg of next 2 rows.

Dec 1 st at both ends of every foll row until 80 sts rem.

Cont without further shaping until work measures 25cm from beg of armhole shaping.

Shape shoulders

Cast off 3 sts at beg of next 4 rows.

Next row Cast off 3 sts, patt 44 sts, turn, cast off 24 sts, patt to end.

Cont on rem sts, cast off 3 sts at beg of every row until no more sts remain.

Fasten off.

Work other shoulder to match.

To make up

Press crochet only.

Seam shoulders and back neck.

Join side seams.

Armhole borders (both alike)

1st round Using 3.00mm hook and A, beg at underarm seam and work in dc around armhole edge. Join with a ss to first st. Turn.

2nd round 1ch, miss first dc, 1dc into each dc to end, join with a ss to first ch. Turn.

3rd and 4th rounds. As 2nd round, but do not turn at end of 4th round.

5th round Work one round of dc from left to right as for front border.

Fasten off.

Adapting the elongated-stitch waistcoat

Use our patterns to create beautiful zigzag fabrics

Colour variations

It is possible to vary the basic waistcoat quite considerably by using different colour combinations.

We have used a soft combination of greys for this waistcoat, but bright, contrast colours would also be attractive. Try red and yellow or black and white.

Substituting patterns

Using another elongated stitch pattern to work the fronts of the basic waistcoat is more difficult, and you should make certain that the pattern can be fitted into the basic shaping. For this reason, it is best to use a variation that has exactly the same number of stitches and rows in the repeat as the basic pattern.

Finally, make sure to check very carefully to see where the points fall on the sample – for example, whether they fall in between or on top of each other – and make sure that you understand the pattern before you begin to crochet.

Pattern Library: Elongated stitch patterns

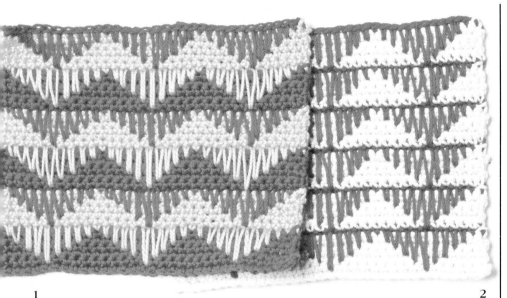

1

2

Slanted diamonds (3)

Use 2 colours, A and B.

Using A, make a multiple of 8ch plus 4.

Base row 1dc into 2nd ch from hook, 1dc into each ch to end. Turn.

1st row 1ch, miss first dc, 1dc into each dc to end. Turn.

2nd-7th rows Work in dc.

8th row (RS) Using B, 1ch, miss first dc, 1dc into next dc, *1dc into next dc 7 rows below, 1dc into next dc 6 rows below, 1dc into next dc 5 rows below, 1dc into next dc 4 rows below, 1dc into next dc 3 rows below, 1dc into next dc 2 rows below, 1dc into next dc 1 row below, 1dc into next dc of previous row, rep from * to turning ch, 1dc into turning ch. Turn.

9th-15th rows Using B, work in dc.

16th row As 8th row, using A.

Rep first-16th rows throughout.

3

Zigzag (1)

This pattern could be used to make the waistcoat on page 74.

Use 2 colours, A and B.

Using A, make a multiple of 10ch plus 4 extra.

Base row 1dc into 2nd ch from hook, 1dc into each ch to end. Turn.

1st row 1ch, miss first dc, 1dc into each dc to end. Turn.

2nd-5th rows Work in dc.

6th row (RS) Using B, 1ch, miss first dc, 1dc into next dc, *1dc into next dc one row below, 1dc into next dc 2 rows below, 1dc into next dc 3 rows below, 1dc into next dc 4 rows below, 1dc into next dc 5 rows below, 1dc into next dc 4 rows below, 1dc into next dc 3 rows below, 1dc into next dc 2 rows below, 1dc into next dc one row below, 1dc into next dc of previous row, rep from * to turning ch, 1dc into turning ch. Turn.

7th-11th rows Using B, work in dc.

12th row As 6th row, using A.

Rep first-12th rows throughout.

Triangles (2)

This pattern could be used to make the waistcoat on page 74.

Work as given for Zigzag, but work base row, first-5th and 7th-11th rows in A, and 6th and 12th rows in B.

4

6

Three-colour points (7)

Use 3 colours, A, B and C.
Using A, make a multiple of 6ch plus 4
extra.
Base row 1dc into 2nd ch from hook,
1dc into each ch to end. Turn.
1st row 1ch, miss first dc, 1dc into each
dc to end. Turn.
2nd and 3rd rows Work in dc.
4th row (RS) Using B, 1ch, miss first dc,
1dc into next dc, *1dc into next dc one
row below, 1dc into next dc 2 rows
below, 1dc into next dc 3 rows below,
1dc into next dc 2 rows below, 1dc into
next dc one row below, 1dc into next dc
of previous row, rep from * to end, 1dc
into the turning ch. Turn.
5th-7th rows Using B, work in dc.
8th row Using C, work as 4th row.
9th-11th rows Using C, work in dc.
12th row Using A, work as 4th row.
Rep first-12th rows throughout, ending
with a 4th, 8th or 12th row.

Arrows (4)

Use 2 colours, A and B.
Using A, make a multiple of 8ch plus 4
extra.
Base row 1dc into 2nd ch from hook,
1dc into each ch to end. Turn.
1st row 1ch, miss first dc, 1dc into each
dc to end. Turn.
2nd-7th rows Work in dc.
8th row (RS) Using B, 1ch, miss first dc,
1dc into next dc, *1dc into next dc 7
rows below, 1dc into next dc 6 rows
below, 1dc into next dc 5 rows below,
1dc into next dc 4 rows below, 1dc into
next dc 3 rows below, 1dc into next dc 2
rows below, 1dc into next dc one row
below, 1dc into next dc of previous row,

rep from * to turning ch, 1dc into ch.
9th-15th rows Using B, work in dc.
16th row Using A, 1ch, miss first dc, 1dc
into next dc, *1dc into next dc, 1dc into
next dc one row below, 1dc into next dc
2 rows below, 1dc into next dc 3 rows
below, 1dc into next dc 4 rows below,
1dc into next dc 5 rows below, 1dc into
next dc 6 rows below, 1dc into next dc 7
rows below, rep from * to turning ch,
1dc into turning ch. Turn.
Rep first-16th rows throughout.

Parti-colour arrows (6)

Work as given for Arrows, but work
base row, first-8th and 9th-15th rows in
A, and 8th and 16th rows in B.

Bricks (5)

Use 2 colours, A and B.
Using A, make a multiple of 8ch plus 4
extra.
Base row Using A, 1dc into 2nd ch from
hook, 1dc into each ch to end. Turn.
1st row Using B, 1ch, miss first dc, 1dc
into each dc to end.
2nd and 3rd rows Work in dc.
4th row (RS) Using A, 1ch, miss first dc,
1dc into next dc 4 rows below, *1dc into
each of next 7dc of previous row, 1dc

into next dc 4 rows below, rep from * to
turning ch, 1dc into turning ch. Turn.
5th-7th rows Using B, work in dc.
8th row Using A, 1ch, miss first dc, 1dc
into each of next 4dc, *1dc into next dc
4 rows below, 1dc into each of next 7dc
of previous row, rep from * to last 7 sts,
1dc into next dc 4 rows below, 1dc into
each of next 5 sts of previous row. Turn.
Rep first-8th rows throughout, ending
with a 4th or 8th row.

7

5

Patchwork

Beautiful fabrics can be formed by sewing together crochet motifs. Although geometric motifs such as squares and hexagons can be used, diamonds are especially suitable for patchwork; sew them together to make a colourful harlequin-style sweater.

The basic patchwork sweater

Size
To fit 86-96 cm bust
Length 58cm
Sleeve seam 50cm

Materials
300g of a four-ply yarn in main colour A
100g in contrast colour B
150g in C
100g in D
100g in E
3.00mm crochet hook
Pair of 3mm knitting needles
3mm circular knitting needle 40cm long

Tension
22 sts and 17 rows to 10cm worked over
motif pattern on 3.00mm crochet hook

To save time, take time to check
tension.

Note: *Sweater is made up of
diamond-shaped and triangular
motifs with a ribbed crochet yoke and
knitted welt and cuffs. Motifs are
worked separately and sewn together.*

Diamond motif
Make 2 motifs in A, 2 in B and 4 each in
C, D and E.
* * Using 3.00mm hook, make 3ch.
1st row (WS) 1dc into 2nd ch from
hook, 1dc into next ch. 2 sts. Turn.
2nd row 3ch, 1tr into first (edge) st, 2tr
into next st. Turn. 4 sts.

3rd row 1ch, 1dc into first (edge) st, 1dc
into each st, 2dc into top of turning
ch. Turn. 6 sts.
4th row 3ch, 1tr into first (edge) st, 1tr
into each st to last st, 2tr into last st.
Turn. 8 sts.
Rep 3rd and 4th rows, inc one st at each
end of row until there are 40 sts in all.
Next row 1ch, 1dc into each st to end,
1dc into turning ch. Turn.* *
Next row (dec) 3ch to count as first tr,
miss first st, keeping last loop of each st
on hook, work 1tr into each of next 2
sts, yrh and through all loops on hook –
called dec 1 – 1tr into each st to last 3 sts,
dec 1, 1tr into top of turning ch. Turn.
38 sts.
Next row (dec) 1ch, miss first 2 sts, 1dc
into each st to last 2 sts, miss one st, 1dc
into last st. Turn. 36 sts.
Rep last 2 rows until 4 sts rem.
Next row 3ch, miss first st, dec 1, turn. 2
sts.
Next row 1ch, 1dc into each st. Fasten
off.

Triangular motif
Make 5 motifs in A, 4 in B, 9 in C and 6
each in D and E.
Work as given for diamond motif from
* * to * *. Fasten off.

Split diamond motifs for underarm (Make 2)
Using C, work as given for diamond

motif from * * to * *. Cont dec as given
for diamond motif until 30 sts rem, thus
ending with a RS row.
Divide for armhole
Next row 1ch, miss first 2 sts, 1dc into
each of next 17 sts, turn.
Next row 3ch, miss first st, 1tr into each
st to last 3 sts, dec 1, 1tr into last st. Turn.
Cont dec one st on every row at outer
edge until one st rem. Fasten off.
Return to missed tr and complete to
match first half.
Work one more motif in D.

Half triangle (right)
Using A, make 21ch.
Base row (WS) 1dc into 2nd ch from
hook, 1dc into each st to end. 20 sts.
1st row (dec) 3ch, miss one st, 1tr into
each st to last 3 sts, dec 1, 1tr into
turning ch. Turn. 19 sts.
2nd row (dec) 1ch, miss first 2 sts, 1dc
into each st to end. Turn. 18 sts. Rep first
and 2nd rows until one st rem. Fasten
off.
Using B, make another half triangle in
the same way.

Half triangle (left)
Using A, make 21ch.
Work base row as given for half triangle
(right).
1st row (dec) 3ch, miss first st, dec 1, 1tr
into each st to end. 19 sts.
2nd row (dec) 1ch, 1dc into each st to

SPECIAL TECHNIQUE
working a diamond

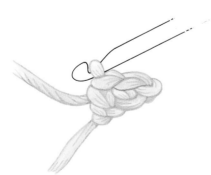

1 *Begin the diamond with three chain.
Work one double crochet into the
second chain from the hook and one
double crochet into the last chain to form
two stitches.*

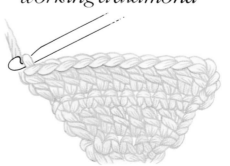

2 *On the next and every following row,
increase one stitch at each end of the
alternating treble and double crochet
rows until the diamond is the required
width.*

3 *Work one row without shaping.
Decrease one stitch at each end of the
next and every following row until two
stitches remain. Work one row and fasten
off.*

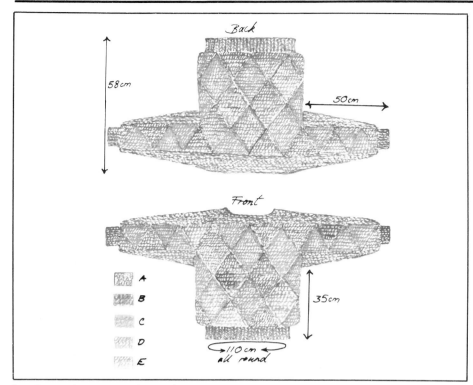

Back

58cm

50cm

Front

A
B
C
D
E

35cm

110 cm
all round

last 2 sts, miss one st, 1dc into last st. 18 sts.
Complete as given for half triangle (right), reversing shaping.
Using B, make another half triangle in same way.

To make up

Sleeves
Join 5 triangular motifs and 1 half triangle to form front and back of each sleeve as shown in the measurement diagram.

Underarm sections
Left front and right back Using A and with RS of work facing, start at apex of triangle at underarm and work 100dc along lower edge of sleeve.
Work into back loop only of each st.
1st row 1ch, 1dc into each st to end. Turn.

Shape sleeve seam
2nd row 1ch, 1dc into each of next 90 sts, turn.
3rd and every alt row Ss over first 10 sts, 1dc into each st to end. Turn.
4th row 1ch, 1dc into each of next 70 sts, turn.
6th row 1ch, 1dc into each of next 50 sts, turn.

8th row 1ch, 1dc into each of next 30 sts, turn.
10th row 1ch, 1dc into each of next 10 sts, turn. Fasten off.

Right front and left back
Using A and with RS of work facing, start at base of half triangle and work 100dc along lower edge of sleeve.
Work into back loop only of each st throughout.
1st row 1ch, 1dc into each st to end. Turn.

Shape sleeve seam
2nd and every alt row Ss over first 10 sts, 1dc into each st to end.
3rd row 1ch, 1dc into each of next 80 sts, turn.
5th row 1ch, 1dc into each of next 60 sts, turn.
Cont shaping in this way on every alt row and complete as given for left front and right back sections.

Back
Join motifs as shown in diagram, attaching corresponding sleeve sections. Join straight edge of each underarm section to opening in split diamond motifs.

Back yoke
Using A and with RS of work facing, start at right cuff * *, work 320dc evenly along top to left cuff. Work into back loop only of each st throughout.
Next row 1ch, 1dc into each st to end. Work 5 more rows in same way.

Shape top
Next 2 rows Ss over 12 sts, 1dc into each st to last 12 sts, turn.* *
Next 7 rows Ss over 16 sts, 1dc into each st to last 16 sts, turn. Fasten off.
Mark rem 48 sts at centre for back neck with contrasting thread.

Front
Join motifs as in diagram, then join underarm sections as for back.

Front yoke
Using A and with RS of work facing, beg at left cuff and work as given for back yoke from * * to * *.
Next 2 rows Ss over 16 sts, 1dc into each st to last 16 sts, turn.

Shape front neck
Next row (WS) Ss over 16 sts, 1dc into each of next 98 sts, turn.
Cont working on these sts for right side of neck shaping.
Next row Ss over 6 sts, 1dc into each of next 76 sts, turn.
Next row Ss over 16 sts, 1dc into each of next 54 sts, turn.
Next row Ss over 6 sts, 1dc into each of next 32 sts, turn.
Next row Ss over 16 sts, 1dc into each of next 16 sts. Fasten off.
With WS of work facing, miss centre 12 sts, rejoin yarn to next st, 1dc into each st to last 16 sts, turn.
Complete as given for right side of neck, reversing shaping.

Neck border
Join shoulder and top arm seam. Using A and with RS of work facing, work 1 row dc round neck opening. Fasten off.

Cuffs
Using A and with RS of work facing and using 3mm knitting needles, K up 50 sts along lower edge of each sleeve and work 5cm in K1, P1 rib. Cast off loosely in rib.

Welt
Join sleeve seams. With RS facing, using A and 3mm circular needle, K up 204 sts along lower edge and work 6cm in K1, P1 rib. Cast off loosely in rib.

Adapting the basic patchwork sweater

Work a variation of the basic sweater or design your own colourful patchwork crochet fabric with the diamond motifs.

Crochet lends itself particularly well to patchwork, since many favourite afghan motifs – such as the traditional granny square – can be joined together to make colourful fabrics. On these two pages and on pages 121-122 you'll find other motifs that can be used to make beautiful patchwork crochet.

Diamonds

The diamond is a shape that is especially well suited to patchwork. Some alternatives to the plain diamonds in the basic sweater are given in the Pattern Library. A random design needs very little planning, but if you want to construct a regular patchwork, you should draw a plan of how you want the diamonds to fit together. Note that striped shapes will form strikingly different patterns, depending on how they are joined. Any of these samples can be used for the basic sweater.

1

Pattern Library: Patchwork patterns

Narrow striped pattern (1)

Use two main colours, A and B, plus one extra colour, C, for centre row. Work 2 rows each in A and B. Using A, make 3ch.

1st row 1dc into 2nd ch from hook, 1dc into next ch. Turn. 2 sts.

2nd row Using A, 3ch, 1tr into first (edge) st, 2tr into next st, changing to B while working last st. Turn. 4 sts.

3rd row Using B, 1ch, 1dc into first (edge) st, 1dc into each st, 2dc into top of turning ch. Turn. 6 sts.

4th row Using B, 3ch, 1tr into first st, 1tr into each of next 2 sts, 2tr into last st, changing to A while working last st. Turn. 8 sts.

Cont to work stripes as set, working from diamond motif pattern on page 80 until there are 40 sts, changing to C at end of row.

Next row Using C, 1ch, 1dc into each st to end, changing to B at end of row. Beg with B cont working in stripe patt working from diamond motif on page 80.

Triple-colour diamond (2)

Use 3 colours, coded as A, B and C. Work diamond motif pattern as shown on page 80, working 14 rows in A, 13 rows in B and 14 more rows in C.

Half-triangle diamond (3)

Use three colours, coded as A, B and C, with C in a sharply-contrasting colour. Using A, work diamond motif pattern as shown on page 80 until there are 40 sts in all, changing to C at end of last row.

Next row Using C, 1ch, 1dc into each st to end. Turn, changing to B at end of this row.

Using B, complete diamond motif as shown on page 80.

2

3

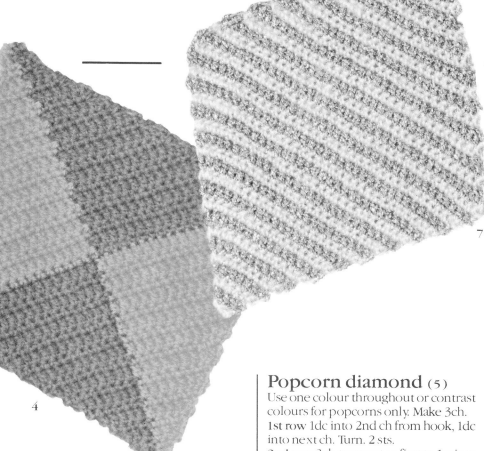

4

7

5

6

Mohair and gold diamond (7)

Use mohair (A) and glitter yarn (B) throughout. Using A, make 3ch.
1st row Using A, 1dc into 2nd ch from hook, 1dc into next ch, changing to B while working last dc. Turn. 2 sts.
2nd row Using B, 3ch, 1tr into first (edge) st, 2tr into next st, changing to A while working last st. Turn. 4 sts. Cont in patt as set working every tr row in B, working from diamond motif pattern shown on page 80.

Popcorn diamond (5)

Use one colour throughout or contrast colours for popcorns only. Make 3ch.
1st row 1dc into 2nd ch from hook, 1dc into next ch. Turn. 2 sts.
2nd row 3ch to count as first tr, 1tr into first (edge) st, 2tr into last st. Turn. 4 sts.
3rd row 1ch, 1dc into first (edge) st, 1dc into each st, 2dc into last st. Turn. 6 sts.
4th row 3ch, 1tr into first (edge) st, 1tr into next st, 1 popcorn into each of next 2 sts, 1tr into next st, 2tr into turning ch. Turn.
5th row 1ch, 1dc into first (edge) st, 1dc into each st and into top of each popcorn, to last st, 2dc into last st. Turn. 10 sts.
Cont working diamond motif (page 80), working 2 popcorns on alt rows until 6 sts rem.

Centre stripes (6)

Use main colour A for triangle at each end of diamond, with contrast colours B and C for stripes at centre. Work diamond motif pattern in A until there are 22 sts in all. 10 rows have been worked. Change to B. Cont in patt working (1 row B, 1 row C) 9 times. Work one row in B. Change to A. Complete diamond as given on page 80.

Harlequin diamond (4)

Use 2 colours, coded as A and B. Use separate balls of yarn for each colour and twist colours at centre to make a neat join, changing colours while working last st in each colour and making sure that colours are always changed on WS.
Using A, make 3ch.
1st row Using A, 1dc into 2nd ch from hook, using B, 1dc into next ch. Turn. 2 sts.
2nd row Using B, 3ch, 1tr into first (edge) st, using A, 2tr into next st. Turn. 4 sts.
Cont in diamond pattern (page 80) as set until there are 40 sts in all. Break off A and B.
Next row (reverse colours) Using B (over A), 1ch to count as first dc, 1dc into each of next 19 sts, changing to A while working last dc, using A, 1dc into each st to end. Turn.
Cont working in A and B as set and complete diamond motif as given on page 80.

Rice and bullion stitches

Although rice and bullion stitches need some practice, they are fascinating to work and form rich, dense fabrics. You can also use them for contrasting details, as on this baseball jacket.

The basic baseball jacket

Sizes
To fit 65 [70:75:80] cm chest
Length 41 [46:46:50] cm
Sleeve seam 30 [34:38:42] cm
Note: *Instructions for larger sizes are in square brackets [ ]; where there is only one set of figures it applies to all sizes.*

Materials
300 [300:350:350] g of a double knitting yarn in main colour A
100 [100:150:150] g in colour B
4.50mm crochet hook
Pair of 3¼mm knitting needles
Open-ended zip, 36 [41:41:46] cm long

Tension
17 sts and 12 rows to 10cm in patt worked on 4.50mm hook

To save time, take time to check tension.

Pocket linings (make 2)
Using A, make 22 [24:24:26] ch.
Base row 1tr into 4th ch from hook, 1tr into each ch to end. Turn.
20 [22:22:24] sts.
1st row (WS) 1ch to count as first dc, miss first st, 1dc into each tr to end, ending with 1dc into top of first 3ch. Turn.
2nd row 3ch, miss first st, 1tr into each dc to end, ending with 1tr into first ch. Turn.
First and 2nd rows form patt.
Patt 5 [5:7:7] more rows, ending with a first row. Fasten off.

Left front
**Using A, make 33 [35:37:39] ch.
Work base row and patt rows as given for pocket linings. 31 [33:35:37] sts.
Patt 5 [5:7:7] more rows, ending with a first row. * *
Divide for pockets
Next row Patt next 11 [11:13:13] sts, with RS facing patt across 20

[22:22:24] sts of pocket lining, turn. 31 [33:35:37] sts. Patt 8 [8:10:10] more rows, ending with a 2nd row. Fasten off.
With RS facing, rejoin A to next dc at base of pocket opening.
Shape pocket
Dec one st at pocket edge on next and every foll row until 11 [13:11:13] sts rem, ending with a 2nd row.
Next row Patt to end, miss first 11 [13:11:13] sts of pocket linings, 1dc into next st of pocket lining, patt to end. Turn. 31 [33:35:37] sts.
Cont in patt until front measures 32 [37:37:40] cm from beg, ending with a first row.
Shape neck
Next row Patt to within last 7 [8:8:9] sts, work next 2 sts tog, turn. 25 [26:28:29] sts.
Dec one st at neck edge on next 5 rows. 20 [21:23:24] sts. Fasten off.

Right front
Work as for left front from * * to * *
Divide for pockets
Next row Patt 18 [20:20:22] sts, work next 2 sts tog, turn.
19 [21:21:23] sts.
Shape pocket
Dec one st on pocket edge on next and every foll row until 11 [13:11:13] sts rem. Fasten off.
Next row Rejoin A to first st of pocket lining, patt to end, with RS facing work 1tr into next st at base of pocket opening, patt to end. Turn. 31 [33:35:37] sts.
Patt 8 [8:10:10] more rows.
Next row Patt 20 [22:22:24] sts, patt across first side of pocket. Turn. 31 [33:35:37] sts. Turn.
Cont in patt until work measures 32 [37:37:40] cm from beg, ending with a first row.
Shape neck
Next row Ss across first 6 [7:7:8] sts, work next 2 sts tog, patt to end. Turn. 25 [26:28:29] sts.

Complete as given for left front.

Back
Using 4.50mm hook and A, make 63 [67:71:75] ch.
Work base row and patt rows as given for pocket linings. 61 [65:69:71] sts.
Patt 1 [3:3:5] more rows, ending with a first row.
Beg rice-st jacquard
1st row (RS) Using A patt next 19 [21:23:25] sts, using B yrh 8 times, insert hook into next st, yrh and draw through all 9 loops on hook, 1ch – rice st formed –, rice st into each of next 22 sts, using A patt to end.
Turn.
2nd and every alt row Patt to end, working 1dc in B into each rice st of previous row.
3rd row Using A patt next 19 [21:23:25] sts, (using B rice st into each of next 3 sts, using A patt next 17 sts) twice, using A patt to end. Turn.
5th and 7th rows As 3rd row.
9th row Using A patt next 19 [21:23:25] sts, (using B rice st into each of next 8 sts, using A patt next 7 sts) twice, using A patt to end. Turn.
11th row Using A patt next 24 [26:28:30] sts, (using B rice st into each of next 3 sts, using A patt next 7 sts) twice, using A patt to end. Turn.
13th, 15th, 17th and 19th rows As 11th row.
21st row Using A patt next 24 [26:28:30] sts, using B rice st into each of next 3 sts, using A patt next 7 sts, using B rice st into each of next 8 sts, using A patt to end. Turn.
23rd row Using A patt next 24 [26:28:30] sts, (using B rice st into each

of next 3 sts, using A patt next 12 sts) twice, using A patt to end. Turn.
25th row Using A patt next 24 [26:28:30] sts, (using B rice st into each of next 3 sts, using A patt next 10 sts) twice, using A patt to end. Turn.
27th row Using A patt next 24 [26:28:30] sts, (using B rice st into each of next 3 sts, using A patt next 8 sts) twice, using A patt to end. Turn.
29th row Using A patt next 24 [26:28:30] sts, (using B rice st into each of next 3 sts, using A patt next 6 sts) twice, using A patt to end. Turn.
31st row Using A patt next 24 [26:28:30] sts, (using B rice st into each of next 3 sts, using A patt next 4 sts) twice, using A patt to end. Turn.
33rd row Using A patt next 24 [26:28:30] sts, using B rice st into each of next 8 sts, using A patt to end. Turn.
34th row As 2nd row.
Cont in A only, working in patt until work measures same as fronts to shoulders, ending with a first row. Fasten off.

Sleeves (alike)
Using A, make 46 [50:54:58] ch. Work base row and patt rows as for pocket linings. 44 [48:52:56] sts. Cont in patt until sleeve measures 18 [22:26:29] cm from beg, ending with a first row.
Next row Using B, 3ch, miss first st, rice st into each st to turning ch, 1tr into turning ch. Turn.
Next row Using B, 1ch to count as first dc, miss first st, 1dc into each st to end, ending with 1dc into top of turning ch. Turn.
Next 2 rows Patt 2 rows in A.
Rep last 4 rows once more.
Patt 2 more rows in A. Fasten off.

To make up
Front welts (alike)
With RS facing and using knitting needles and B, K up 41 [43:45:47] sts from lower edge.
1st rib row (WS) K1, (P1, K1) to end.
2nd row P1, (K1, P1) to end.
Rep rib rows for 9cm, ending with a first row. Cast off loosely in rib.
Back welt
With RS facing, using knitting needles and B, K up 81 [85:89:91] sts from lower edge.
Rep rib rows as for front welts for 9cm, ending with a first row.
Cast off loosely in rib.
Cuffs (alike)
With RS facing and using knitting needles and B, K up 44 [48:52:56] sts from lower edge.
Dec row P3 [5:2:4], P2 tog, (P2 [2:3:3], P2 tog) to last 3 [5:3:5] sts, P to end. 34 [38:42:46] sts. Work 9cm of K1, P1 rib. Cast off loosely in rib.
Pocket borders (alike)
With RS facing and using crochet hook, join B to first row end on pocket edge.
Next row 3ch, work a row of rice st into edge, working one st into dc row ends and 2 sts into tr row ends and ending with 1tr. Turn.
Next row 1ch to count as first dc, miss first st, 1dc into each rice st to end, 1dc into top of 3ch.
Fasten off. Join shoulder seams.
Mark depth of armholes 14 [15:17:18] cm from shoulders on back and fronts. Set in sleeves between markers, matching centre of sleeve with shoulder seam.
Join side and sleeve seams. Turn welt and cuffs to WS and slipstitch into position. Sew pocket linings to WS of fronts and ends of pocket borders to RS fronts.

Left front edging
With RS facing and using 4.50mm hook, join A to first row end on neck edge.
Next row Work in dc along front edge, working one dc into each dc row end and 2dc into each tr row end, to beg of welt, using B work in dc through double thickness of welt to lower edge. Turn.

stitch-by-stitch seaming

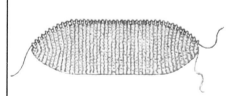

1 The collar on the basic jacket is attached to the neck edge by a particularly neat method of seaming. Knit the collar, shaping the short rows as instructed in the pattern. Do not cast off, but break the yarn and leave the stitches on a spare needle or length of yarn.

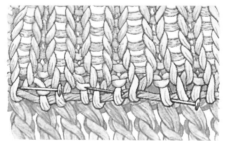

2 Stretching the collar to fit if necessary, pin the wrong side of the last row of the collar to the right side of the neck edge. Align the short ends of the collar with the last row of the front edgings, overlapping the collar with the neck by about 5mm.

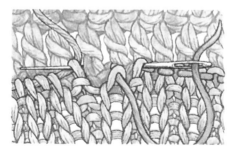

3 Using yarn to match the collar, backstitch the collar to the neck edge. Insert the needle through the loops of the last row and remove the needle or yarn from the loops as you sew. Fold the collar to the wrong side; slip stitch it into place round the neck.

Work 2 more rows of dc in B.
Fasten off.
Right front edging
With RS facing and using 4.50mm hook, join B to lower edge of welt.
Next row Work in dc to top of welt, working through double thickness, using A work in dc along front edge as for left front edging. Turn.
Work 2 more rows of dc in B.
Fasten off.

Collar
Using knitting needles and B, cast on 81 [87:87:93] sts.
Shape collar
Beg with a 2nd row, work 2 rib rows as for front welt throughout and *at the same time:*
1st row Rib to last st, turn.
2nd row Sl 1, rib to last st, turn.
3rd and 4th rows Sl 1, rib to last 2 sts, turn.
5th and 6th rows Sl 1, rib to last 4 sts, turn.
7th and 8th rows Sl 1, rib to last 6 sts, turn.
9th and 10th rows Sl 1, rib to last 9 sts, turn.
11th and 12th rows Sl 1, rib to last 12 sts, turn.
13th row Sl 1, rib to end.
14th row Rib to end across all sts.

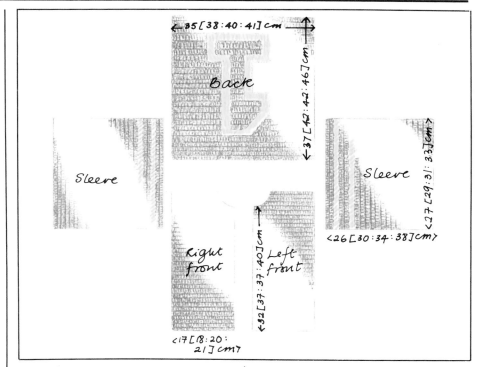

15th-25th rows As 12th, 11th, 10th, 9th, 8th, 7th, 6th, 5th, 4th, 3rd and 2nd rows.
Work 2nd row, 13th and 14th rows once more. Break yarn and leave sts on a spare length of yarn.
Place WS of last row of collar on to RS of neck and sew into position, working neat backstitch through open loops of last row. See Special Technique opposite.
Double collar to WS to slipstitch into position.
Sew in the zip fastener.

Adapting the basic baseball jacket

Vary the jacket look by using softer, pastel shades or working a different number or letter.

The basic baseball jacket has contrasting rice-stitch bands and a number on the back.

It would be possible to work more rice stitch bands on the sleeves or to work a different number or letter.

Charting a number
Draw the outline of the back of the jacket on graph paper so that one square equals one stitch. Draw a line between the centre stitch on the lower and top edges to indicate the centre back.
Draw each stitch of the outline of the number on the graph, at the same time centring the number on the centre back line. Remember that, since the number will be worked in alternate rows of rice stitch (on treble pattern rows) and double crochet, the chart will be taller than the crocheted number.

Pattern Library: Rice and bullion patterns   1

Simple rice stitch (1)
Make a multiple of 2ch plus 5 extra.
Base row Yrh 8 times, insert hook into 5th ch from hook, yrh and draw through all loops on hook – rice st formed –, *1ch, miss next ch, rice st into next ch, rep from * to end. Turn.
Patt row 3ch, miss first st, *rice st into next 1ch sp, 1ch, rep from * to turning ch, rice st into top of turning ch. Turn.
Rep patt row throughout.

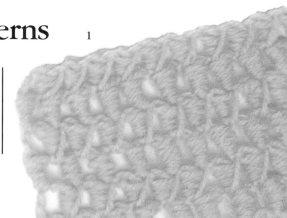

Picket fence (5)

3

Make any number of ch plus 3 extra.
Base row Yrh 5 times, insert hook into 4th ch from hook, yrh and draw through a loop, yrh and draw through all 7 loops on the hook – bullion st formed –, *bullion st into next st, rep from * to end. Turn.
1st row (WS) 1ch to count as first dc, miss first st, 1dc into each st to end. Turn.
2nd row 3ch, miss first st, bullion st into each st to end. Turn.
Rep first and 2nd rows throughout.

Pebble pattern (3)

2

Make a multiple of 10ch plus 2 extra.
Base row 1dc into 2nd ch from hook, 1dc into each ch to end. Turn.
1st row (RS) 3ch, miss first st, 1tr into each of next 2 sts, *yrh 10 times, insert hook into next st, yrh and draw through a loop, yrh and draw through all 12 loops on hook – bullion st formed –, bullion st into each of next 4 sts, 1tr into each of next 5 sts, rep from * to last 8 sts, bullion st into each of next 5 sts, 1tr into last 3 sts. Turn.
2nd row 1ch to count as first dc, miss first st, 1dc into each st to end. Turn.
3rd row 3ch, miss first st, bullion st into each of next 2 sts, *1tr into each of next 5 sts, bullion st into each of next 5 sts, rep from * to last 8 sts, 1tr into each of next 5 sts, bullion st into each of next 2 sts, 1tr into last st. Turn.
4th row As 2nd row.
Rep first-4th rows throughout.

Vertical rice pattern (2)

Make a multiple of 4ch plus 5 extra.
Base row 1dc into 2nd ch from hook, 1dc into each ch to end. Turn.
1st row 1ch to count as first dc, miss first st, *1dc into each of next 2 sts, yrh 3 times, insert hook into next st, yrh and draw through all loops on hook – rice st formed –, 1ch, miss next st, rep from * to last 3 sts, 1dc into each of last 3 sts.
2nd row 1ch to count as first dc, miss first st, 1dc into each of next 2 sts, *rice st into next 1ch sp, 1ch, miss next st, 1dc into each of next 2 sts, rep from * to last st, 1dc into last st. Turn.
Rep 2nd row throughout.

Rice stitch with trebles (4)

Make an odd number of ch plus 4 extra.
Base row (RS) Yrh 5 times, insert hook into 5th ch from hook, yrh and draw through all loops on hook – rice st formed, *1ch, miss next ch, rice st into next ch, rep from * to end. Turn.
1st row 3ch, miss first st, *1tr into next

4

1ch sp, 1tr into next rice st, rep from * to turning ch, 1tr into sp formed by turning ch, miss next turning ch, 1tr into next turning ch. Turn.
2nd row 4ch, miss first 2 sts, *rice st into next st, 1ch, miss next st, rep from * to last st, rice st into last st. Turn.
Rep first and 2nd rows throughout.

5

Horizontal patterns

Horizontal patterns are highly versatile, being suitable for anything from fashionable garments, such as this casual cardigan, to the simplest baby clothes. Choose beautiful yarns and colours to display the strong crosswise lines of these useful patterns.

The basic striped cardigan

Size
To fit 86-96cm bust
Length including welt 54cm
Sleeve seam 49cm

Materials
150g of a double knitting yarn in main colour A
150g in contrast colour B
100g in contrast colour C
50g in each of contrast colours and D and E
4.50mm and 5.00mm crochet hooks
5 buttons

Tension
15dc and 14 rows to 10cm worked on 4.50mm hook

To save time, take time to check tension.

Note: *The cardigan is worked in two sections, each beginning at the cuff, which are then joined at the centre back.*

Left side
Cuff Using 4.50mm hook and A, make 21ch.
Base row 1dc into 2nd ch from hook, 1dc into each ch to end. Turn. 20 sts.

Next row 1ch, miss first st, 1dc into *back* loop only of each st to end. Turn.
Rep last row 34 times more. Change to 5.00mm hook and use loop on hook to beg to work into one edge of cuff:
Next row (RS) 3ch, miss first row end, 1tr into each row end to end. Turn. 36 sts.
Next row 1ch, miss first st, 1dc into next st, (2dc into next st, 1dc into each of next 7 sts) 4 times, 2dc into next st, 1dc into last st. Turn. 41 sts.

Pattern band A
Change to B.
1st row (RS) Work in dc, inc one st at each end of the row. 43 sts.
2nd row (RS) Work in tr.
Change to A.
3rd row Work in dc, inc one st at each end of the row. 45 sts.
4th row Work in dc. Change to B.
5th row 1ch, miss first st, * inserting hook from front to back work 1tr round stem of next st on last tr row – 1tr front below worked – 1dc into each of next 2dc, rep from * to last 2 sts, 1tr front below, 1dc into last st. Turn.
6th row Work in tr.
Rep 3rd-6th rows once more, inc one st at each end of 7th row, and working each tr front below on 9th row into

corresponding tr on 4th row. 47 sts.
Next row Change to D and work in dc working into back loops only and inc one st at each end of row. 49 sts.
Next row Change to A and work in dc.

Pattern band B
Change to C.
1st row (RS) 4ch, miss first st, * 1tr into next st, 1htr into next st, 1dc into each of next 3 sts, 1htr into next st, 1tr into next st, 1dtr into next st, rep from * to end. Turn.
Change to D.
2nd row 1ch, 1dc into first dtr, * 3ch, leaving last loop of each st on hook work 1tr into each of next 7 sts, yrh and draw through all 8 loops on hook – half whirl formed –, 3ch, 1dc into next dtr, rep from * to end, working last dc into top of turning ch. Turn.
3rd row 1ch, 1dc into first dc, * (6tr, 1dtr) into sp at top of half whirl, 1dc into next dc, rep from * to end. Turn. Change to C.
4th row As for first row.
Next row Change to A and work in dc.
Next row Change to D and work in dc.
Next row Change to E and work in dc working into front loops only. Cont in tr, working in stripe sequence as foll: 1 row in E, 2 rows in B, 3 rows in C, 2 rows in

---

SPECIAL TECHNIQUE
whirl pattern

1 Pattern band B on the basic cardigan is a two-colour whirl pattern. Using the first colour, work the first graduated stitch (see page 41) row as given in the pattern. Change to the second colour. After working the edge stitch, work seven treble together into the next seven stitches to form the first half whirl.

2 Continue in this way to the end of the row. Complete the whirl on the third row by working six treble and one double treble into the space formed at the top of each group of seven treble. Work one double crochet into each double crochet between half whirls to anchor the whirl.

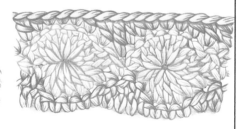

3 Return to the first colour and for the last pattern row follow the instructions given for the first pattern row. This straightens the top edge to allow you to work the next row of the basic cardigan instructions.

D, 2 rows in E, 3 rows in B, 3 rows in C.
At the same time shape sleeve thus:
Next row Work in tr.
Next 2 rows Work in tr, inc one st at
each end of row.
Working in stripe sequence as above,
rep last 3 rows 5 times in all. 69 sts.
Next row Work in tr. Do not turn.
Shape bodice
Using C, at the end of last row of stripe
sequence, work 27ch. Turn and remove
hook from loop. Using spare length of C,
work 26ch and fasten off. Return to loop
just left.
Next row (WS) 1dc into 2nd ch from
hook, 1dc into each of next 25ch, 1dc
into each of 69 sts on top of sleeve, 1dc
into each of 26ch just worked. Turn.
121 sts.
Next row Change to B and work in tr.
Next 3 rows Work in dc, working one
row each in E, D and A.
Change to C and work the 4 rows of
pattern band B, omitting all incs.
Next 4 rows Work in dc, working one
row each in A, D, E and B.
Cont with B and work the 10 rows of
pattern band A, working one more dc at
end of 5th row and omitting all incs.
Next row Change to E and work in dc.
Next row Change to C and work in tr.* *
Back bodice extension
Next row With RS facing and using C,
1ch, miss first st, 1dc into each of next
49 sts, turn. 50 sts.
Shape back neck
Next row Ss over first 3 sts, 1ch, miss
first st, 1dc into each st to end. Turn.
48 sts.
Next row 1ch, miss first st, 1dc into each
st to last 3 sts, work 2dc tog, 1dc into last
st. Turn.
Next row 3ch, work 2tr tog, 1tr into
each st to end. Turn. 46 sts.
Change to B and work 2 rows in tr.
Change to C and work 1 row in tr and 1
row in dc. Fasten off.

Right side
Work as for left side to * *. Fasten off.
Back bodice extension
Next row With RS facing and using C,
rejoin yarn to 72nd st of row, 1ch, miss
first st, 1dc into each st to end. 50 sts.
Complete to match left back neck,

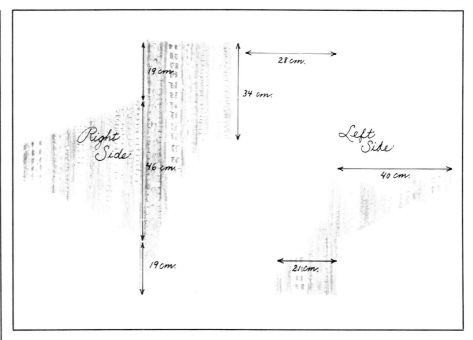

reversing all shaping.
Fasten off, but do not cut yarn.

To make up
With RS tog, join centre back seam with
crochet ss. Fasten off.
Press centre back seam lightly. Join
underarm and side seams, carefully
matching stripes at underarm.

Striped border
1st row With RS facing, join C to first st
on lower edge, 1ch, miss first st, 1dc into
each st up right front, 1dc into each row
end on back neck (at the same time
place contrast markers at beg of RH
back bodice extension, centre back
seam and beg of LH back bodice
extension), and 1dc into each st down
left front. Turn.
Next 7 rows Work in dc, working 2dc
tog at each of the markers on the back
neck and working in stripe sequence as
foll: 2 rows in B, 1 row in E, 1 row in D,
1 row in A, 1 row in B and 1 row in A.
Fasten off.

Welt
Using 4.50mm hook and A, make 21ch.
Work in double crochet rib as for cuff
until work, when slightly stretched,

measures 68cm, or your waist
measurement.
Fasten off.
Using 4.50mm hook and A, work 1 row
of dc into row ends on lower edge to
neaten edge and ease in fullness.
Sew welt to lower edge of bodice from
RS, easing in fullness. Do not press
seam.

Buttonhole band
Mark position of 5 buttonholes on
lower right front.
1st row Using 4.50mm hook and with
RS facing, join A to first st on lower
edge, 1ch, miss first st, 1dc into each st
up right front, 1dc into each dc across
back neck, working 2dc tog at markers,
and 1dc into each st down left front.
Turn.
2nd row 1ch, miss first st, * work in dc
to position of buttonhole, 2ch, miss
next 2 sts, 1dc into next st, rep from * 4
times more, 1dc into each st to end.
Turn.
3rd row Work in dc.
4th row Work in crab st as shown on
page 18.
Fasten off.
Sew buttons on to left front to
correspond with buttonholes.

Adapting the basic striped cardigan

Use the Pattern Library to make several versions of the basic, simply-shaped cardigan.

Simple substitutions

The basic cardigan is worked from cuff to cuff in horizontal bands of pattern and simple stripes to produce a vertically-striped garment.

Any of the samples in the Pattern Library could be substituted – the easiest method being to work the cardigan in any or all of the simple, striped patterns.

Enlarging the cardigan

The cardigan will fit size 86 to 96cm bust, but it can easily be made larger by working more rows on the sleeves and on the back bodice extension.

Work enough ribbed welt to fit, when slightly stretched, around your waist; sew it to the lower edge, easing any fullness to fit.

Pattern Library: Horizontal patterns

1

3

Fancy clusters (1)

Make a multiple of 9ch plus 2 extra.

Base row (RS) 1dc into 2nd ch from hook, * 1dc into each of next 3ch, (7ch, 1dc into next ch) 3 times, 1dc into each of next 3ch, rep from * to end. Turn.

1st row 7ch, * (leaving last loop of each st on hook work 4tr into next 7ch loop, yrh and draw through all 5 loops on hook – cluster formed –, 2ch) twice, cluster into next 7ch loop, 6ch, rep from * to end, omitting 6ch at end of last rep and working 2ch, 1tr tr into last dc. Turn.

2nd row 1ch, miss first tr tr, * (2dc into next 2ch loop) three times, 6dc into next 6ch loop, rep from * to end, omitting 6dc at end of last rep and working 2dc into sp formed by turning ch. Turn.

3rd row 3ch, miss first st, 1tr into each st to end. Turn.

4th row 1ch, miss first st, * 1dc into each of next 3 sts, (7ch, 1dc into next st) 3 times, 1dc into each of next 3 sts, rep from * to end. Turn.

First-4th rows form patt. Rep them throughout, ending with a 2nd row.

Note: *This pattern can be worked in one or two colours as shown.*

Narrow stripes (2)

Use 2 colours, A and B, and work alternate rows of htr and dc, changing colour after every row or every alt row.

Simple clusters (3)

Make a multiple of 2ch plus 2 extra.

Base row (RS) 1dc into 2nd ch from hook, 1dc into each ch to end. Turn.

1st row 3ch, leaving last loop of each tr on hook work 2tr into first st, yrh and draw through all 3 loops on hook – cluster worked –, * miss next st, (1tr, 1 cluster) into next st, rep from * to last 2 sts, miss next st, 1tr into last st. Turn.

2nd row 1ch, miss first st, * 1dc into top of next cluster, 1dc into next tr, rep from * to end, ending with 1dc into top of turning ch.

Rep first and 2nd rows throughout.

2

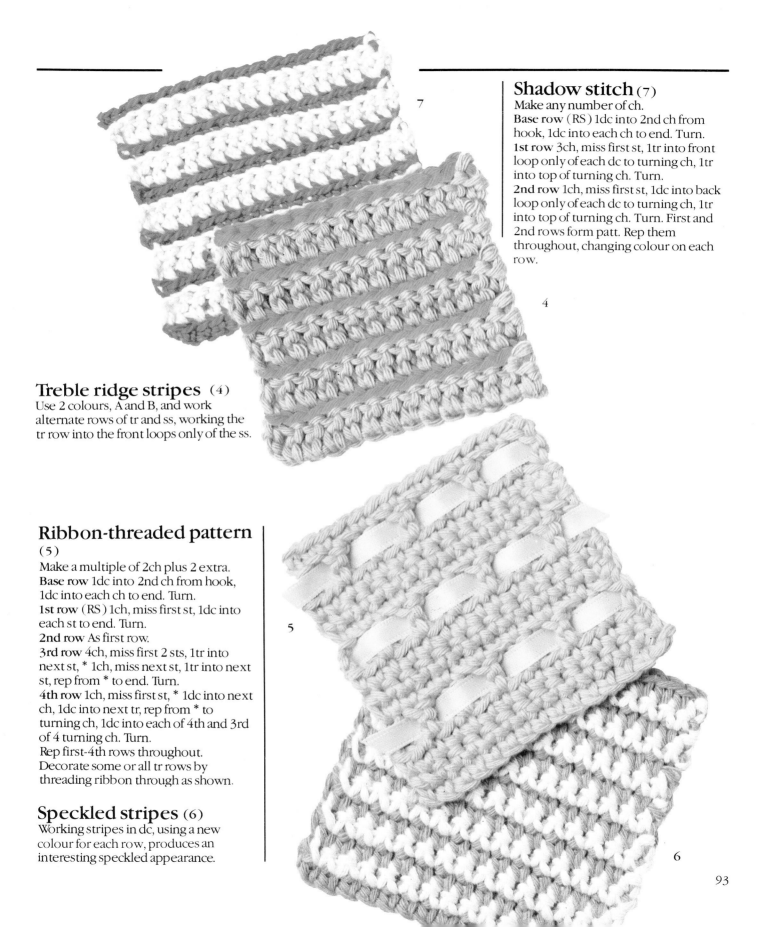

7

Shadow stitch (7)

Make any number of ch.
Base row (RS) 1dc into 2nd ch from hook, 1dc into each ch to end. Turn.
1st row 3ch, miss first st, 1tr into front loop only of each dc to turning ch, 1tr into top of turning ch. Turn.
2nd row 1ch, miss first st, 1dc into back loop only of each dc to turning ch, 1tr into top of turning ch. Turn. First and 2nd rows form patt. Rep them throughout, changing colour on each row.

4

Treble ridge stripes (4)

Use 2 colours, A and B, and work alternate rows of tr and ss, working the tr row into the front loops only of the ss.

Ribbon-threaded pattern (5)

Make a multiple of 2ch plus 2 extra.
Base row 1dc into 2nd ch from hook, 1dc into each ch to end. Turn.
1st row (RS) 1ch, miss first st, 1dc into each st to end. Turn.
2nd row As first row.
3rd row 4ch, miss first 2 sts, 1tr into next st, * 1ch, miss next st, 1tr into next st, rep from * to end. Turn.
4th row 1ch, miss first st, * 1dc into next ch, 1dc into next tr, rep from * to turning ch, 1dc into each of 4th and 3rd of 4 turning ch. Turn.
Rep first-4th rows throughout.
Decorate some or all tr rows by threading ribbon through as shown.

5

Speckled stripes (6)

Working stripes in dc, using a new colour for each row, produces an interesting speckled appearance.

6

Lacets

Lacets are V-shaped stitches, which can either be used by themselves to create a variety of openwork patterns or be combined with blocks and spaces to form lacy filet fabrics. Here they are used for a cool summer T-shirt.

The basic lacet T-shirt

Sizes

To fit 96 [101:106]cm chest
Length 64 [65:66]cm
Sleeve seam 21cm
Note: *Instructions for larger sizes are in square brackets [ ]; where there is only one set of figures it applies to all sizes.*

Materials

350 [400:450]g of a four-ply yarn
2.50mm crochet hook
Pair of 2¾mm knitting needles
3 small buttons

Tension

7 patt reps and 20 rows to 10cm worked on 2.50mm hook

To save time, take time to check tension.

Back

Using knitting needles, cast on 145 [149:157] sts. Work in K1, P1 rib until work measures 6cm from beg. Cast off loosely in rib until one loop rem. Transfer loop to 2.50mm hook.
1st row (RS) 5ch, * miss next cast-off st, 1dc into next cast-off st, 2ch, miss next cast-off st, 1tr into next cast-off st, 2ch, rep from * to end, omitting last 2ch and working 1tr into last cast-off st. 36 [37:39] patt reps.
2nd row 1ch, 1dc into first tr, * 3ch, 1dc into next tr, rep from * to end, working last dc into 3rd turning ch. Turn.
3rd row 5ch, * 1dc into next 3ch sp, 2ch, 1tr into next dc, 2ch, rep from * to end, omitting last 2ch and working 1tr into last dc. Turn.
2nd and 3rd rows form patt.
Cont in patt until work measures 42cm from beg, ending with a 2nd patt row.
Yoke
Next row 3ch, miss first st, * 2tr into next 3ch sp, 1tr into next dc, rep from * to end. Turn.
109 [112:118] sts.

Shape armholes

Next row Ss over first 9tr, 3ch, 1tr into each of next 92 [95:101]tr, turn leaving 8tr unworked. 93 [96:102] sts.* *
Cont in tr without further shaping until work measures 64 [65:66]cm from beg. Fasten off.

Front

Work as for back to * *.

Divide for front opening

Next row 3ch, miss first st, 1tr into each of next 42 [44:47] sts, turn. 43 [45:48] sts.
Cont in tr on these sts only until work measures 56 [57:58]cm from beg, ending at neck edge.
Shape neck
Next row Ss over first 8tr, 3ch, work in tr to end. Turn.
Dec 1tr at neck edge on every row until 31 [32:33]tr rem.
Cont without further shaping until work measures same as back from beg. Fasten off.
Return to beg of front opening, miss next 7 [6:6]tr and join yarn to next st.
Complete second side to match.

Sleeves (both alike)

Using knitting needles, cast on 93 [101:109] sts. Work in K1, P1 rib until work measures 4cm from beg. Cast off in rib until one loop rem. Transfer loop to 2.50mm hook. Work first-3rd rows as for back then 2nd row once more. 23 [25:27] patt reps.
Shape sleeve
Next row 4ch, 1tr into dc at base of 4ch, patt to last dc, (1tr, 1ch, 1tr) into last dc. Turn.
Next row 1ch, 1dc into first tr, 1ch, 1dc

---

finishing a front opening

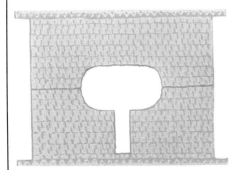

1 *The front opening usually begins just above the start of the armhole shaping. Work each side separately, reversing shaping on the second side. Press or block the front and back as instructed in the pattern. Join shoulder seams.*

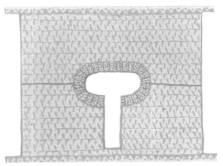

2 *With right side facing, pick up stitches evenly round the neck and work in rib as required. Cast off loosely in rib.*

3 *Pick up stitches on each side of the neck, including the row ends of the neckband. Remember to work buttonholes in the rib. Lap the buttonhole band over the button band and sew both neatly to the beginning of the front opening.*

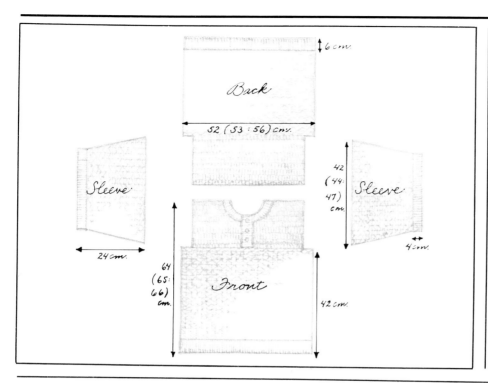

into next tr, patt to last 2 sts, 1dc into last tr, 1ch, 1dc into 3rd of 4 turning ch. Turn.

Next row 5ch, 1dc into next 1ch sp, 2ch, 1tr into next dc, patt to end, ending with 2ch, 1dc into next 1ch sp, 2ch, 1tr into last dc. Turn.

Patt 7 rows without shaping.

Rep last 10 rows twice more.

29 [31:33] patt reps. Cont in patt without further shaping until sleeve measures 24cm from beg. Fasten off.

Neckband

Join shoulder seams. With RS facing and using knitting needles, K up 110 [116:122] sts round neck edge. Work in K1, P1 rib for 10 rows. Cast of ribwise.

Button band

With RS facing and using knitting needles, K up 50 [54:58] sts down right side of neck. Work in K1, P1 rib for 10 rows. Cast off ribwise.

Pattern Library: Lacet patterns

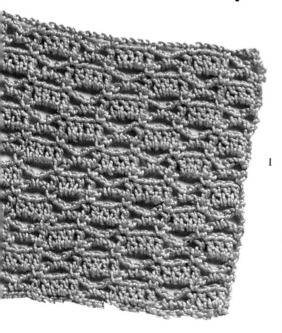

1

Crossed lacets (1)

This could be used for the T-shirt on page 94.

Make a multiple of 8ch plus 2 extra.

Base row 1dc into 2nd ch from hook, * 4ch, miss next 3ch, 1dc into next ch, rep from * to end. Turn.

1st row (RS) 3ch, miss first st, * 3tr into next 4ch sp, 1tr into next dc, 2ch, 1dc into next 4ch sp, 2ch, 1tr into next dc, rep from * to end. Turn.

2nd row 5ch, * 1dc into first of next 5tr, 4ch, 1dc into last of same 5tr, 4ch, rep from * omitting 4ch at end of last rep and working last dc onto top of turning ch. Turn.

3rd row 5ch, * 1dc into first 4ch sp, 2ch, 1tr into next dc, 3tr into next 4ch sp, 1tr into next dc, 2ch, rep from * omitting 2ch at end of last rep and working last tr into 3rd of 5 turning ch. Turn.

4th row 1ch, 1dc into first tr, * 4ch, 1dc into last of next 5tr, 4ch, 1dc into first of next 5tr, rep from * to end working last dc into 3rd turning ch. Turn.

First-4th rows form the pattern; rep them throughout.

Vertical lacets (2)

Make a multiple of 8ch plus 7.

Base row (RS) 1tr into 4th ch from hook, 1tr into each of next 3ch, * 2ch, miss next ch, 1dc into next ch, 2ch, miss next ch, 1tr into each of next 5ch, rep from * to end. Turn.

1st row 3ch, miss first tr, 1tr into each of next 4tr, * 3ch, miss next (2ch, 1dc, 2ch), 1tr into each of next 5tr, rep from * to end. Turn.

2nd row 3ch, miss first tr, 1tr into each of next 4tr, * 2ch, 1dc into next 3ch sp, 2ch, 1tr into each of next 5tr, rep from * to end, working last tr into top of turning ch. Turn.

Rep first and 2nd rows throughout.

2

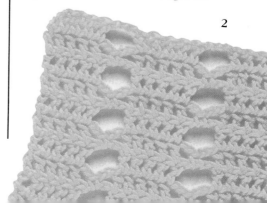

Buttonhole band

K up sts down left side of neck as for button band. Work 5 rows in K1, P1 rib ending at top of neck.

Buttonhole row Rib 6, * cast off 3 sts, rib 12 [13:14]* , rep from * to * once, cast off 3 sts, rib to end.

Next row Rib to first buttonhole, * cast on 3 sts, rib 12 [13:14], rep from * once, cast on 3 sts, rib to end. Work 13 more rows in rib. Cast off.

To make up

Join side seams. Join sleeve seams, leaving top 7 rows open. Set in sleeves, sewing 7 rows at sleeve top to sts of armhole shaping. Overlap buttonhole band over button band and sew ends to tr at base of neck opening. Sew on buttons.

Adapting the basic lacet T-shirt

Some of the lacet patterns in this section could be used for the T-shirt. Others could be used for edgings.

The patterns suitable for the T-shirt are so designated under their names. Make a sample first, using your chosen yarn and hook, then calculate the number of pattern repeats that will produce a fabric of the desired width.

Lacet edgings

These patterns can also be adapted for use as edgings on household linen. You should experiment before you begin the edging to ensure that your chosen pattern can be used, but the following method can be applied to most simple lacet patterns. Work chain the length of the edging plus about 20 extra.

Work the base row of your chosen lacet patterns into the chain.

When the edging is the required length, turn, and work the first pattern row. Fasten off, and work the first pattern row. Fasten off. If you want a deeper edging, work more pattern rows before fastening off.

Do not worry about the few chain left unworked after the base row. After fastening off, cut the beginning slip knot and undo the chains.

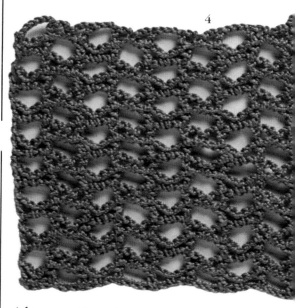

4

Cluster lacet (3)

This could be used for the T-shirt on page 94.

Make a multiple of 6ch plus 3 extra.

Base row 1tr into 4th ch from hook, * 2ch, miss next ch, 1dc into next ch, 2ch, miss next ch, 1tr into each of next 3ch, rep from *, ending last rep with 1tr into each of last 2ch. Turn.

1st row (RS) 3ch, miss first tr, 1tr into next tr, * 3ch, 1tr into first of next 3tr, leaving last loop of each st on hook work 5tr into next tr, yrh and draw through all 6 loops on hook – cluster formed –, 1tr into next tr, rep from * omitting cluster in last rep and working last tr into top of turning ch. Turn.

2nd row 3ch, miss first tr, 1tr into next tr, * 2ch, 1dc into next 3ch sp, 2ch, 1tr into next tr, 1tr into top of cluster, 1tr into next tr, rep from * ending last rep with 1tr into last tr, 1tr into top of turning ch.

Rep first and 2nd rows throughout.

3

Alternating lacets (4)

Make a multiple of 8ch plus 9.

Base row (RS) 1dc into 7th ch from hook, 2ch, miss next ch, 1tr into next ch, * 3ch, miss next 3ch, 1tr into next ch, 2ch, miss next ch, 1dc into next ch, 2ch, miss next ch, 1tr into next ch, rep from * to end. Turn.

1st row 6ch, miss first tr, * 1tr into next tr, 2ch, 1dc into next sp, 2ch, 1tr into next tr, 3ch, 1tr into next tr, rep from * to end. Turn.

2nd row 5ch, 1dc into first sp, 2ch, * 1tr into next tr, 3ch, 1tr into next tr, 2ch, 1dc into next sp, 2ch, rep from * to end ending miss first 3 turning ch, 1tr into next ch. Turn.

Rep first and 2nd rows throughout.

Openwork patterns

A variety of attractive lacy fabrics can be made from different combinations of loops, clusters and shells. Use them to make beautiful shawls, like the one shown here, and evening clothes.

The basic lace shawl

Size
Shawl measures about 180cm in diameter

Materials
600g of a four-ply yarn
5.00mm crochet hook

Tension
7 3tr clusters to 10cm in patt worked on 5.00mm hook

To save time, take time to check tension.

Note: *Never use a knot to join in a new ball of yarn; instead, splice the ends together. (See Special Technique.)*

Shawl
Using 5.00mm hook make 4ch, join into a circle with a ss.
1st round 3ch to count as first tr, work 11tr into circle, ss into 3rd of first 3ch. 12tr.

2nd round 5ch to count as first tr and 2ch sp, * 1tr into next tr, 2ch, rep from * all round, ss to 3rd of first 5ch.
3rd round 1dc into same place as ss, * 2dc into next 2ch sp, 1dc into next tr, rep from * ending with 2dc into last sp, ss into first dc. Turn.
4th round 2ch, leaving last loop of each st on hook, work 2tr into first st, yrh and draw through all loops on hook – called 2tr Cl –, * 2ch, miss 1dc, leaving last loop of each st on hook, work 3tr into next dc, yrh and draw through all loops on hook – called 3tr Cl –, rep from * to end, ending with 2ch, ss into top of first Cl. Turn.
5th round Work 4dc into each sp to end, ss into first dc.
6th round 5ch, * miss 1dc, 1tr into next dc, 2ch, rep from * to end, ss into 3rd of first 5ch.
7th round 5ch, * 3tr Cl into next tr, 2ch, 1tr into next tr, 2ch, rep from * ending with 3tr Cl into next tr, 2ch, ss into 3rd of first 5ch.

8th round 1ch to count as first dc, 1dc into first sp, * 1dc into next 3tr Cl, 2dc into next sp, rep from * to end, ss into first ch.
9th round As 4th round.
10th round * 3dc into next sp, 4dc into next sp, rep from * ending with 4dc into last sp, ss into first dc.

11th round 1dc into same place as ss, * 1ch, miss 1dc, 1dc into next dc, rep from * ending with 1ch, ss into first dc.
12th round Ss into first 1ch sp, 3ch, 1tr into same sp, * 2tr into each 1ch sp, rep from * to end of round, ss into 3rd of first 3ch.
13th round 2ch, work 2tr Cl into same place as ss, 1ch, miss 1tr, * 3tr Cl into next tr, 1ch, miss 2tr, rep from * to end, ss into first 2tr Cl.
14th round * 1dc into next sp, 5ch, rep from * ending with 2ch, 1tr into first dc at beg of round.
15th-19th rounds 1dc into loop just made, * 5ch, 1dc into next loop, rep from * ending with 2ch, 1tr into first dc.

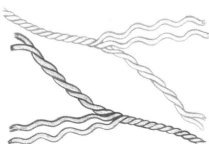

20th round 1dc into loop just made, * 3ch, 1dc into next loop, rep from * ending with 3ch, ss into first dc.

21st round 1dc into same place as ss, * 3dc into next loop, 1dc into next dc, rep from * ending with 3dc into last loop, ss into first dc. Turn.

22nd round As 4th round.

23rd round 2dc into each of first 2 sps, 3dc into each foll sp, ss into first dc.

24th round As 6th round.

25th round As 7th round.

26th round * 2dc into each of next 5 sps, 3dc into next sp, rep from * ending with 1dc into each of last 2 sps, ss into first dc. Turn.

27th round 2ch, 2tr Cl into first st, * 2ch, miss 1dc, 3tr Cl into next dc, 2ch, miss 2dc, 3tr Cl into next dc, rep from * omitting 3tr Cl at end of last rep, ss into first 2tr Cl. Turn.

28th round 3dc into each sp to end, ss into first dc.

29th round As 11th round.

30th round As 12th round.

31st round 2ch, 2tr Cl into same place as ss, * 1ch, miss 2tr, 3tr Cl into next tr, rep from * ending with 1ch, ss into top of first 2tr Cl.

32nd round As 14th round.

33rd-39th rounds As 15th round.

40th round As 20th round.

41st round As 21st round, inc 4dc evenly in round.

42nd round 2ch, 2tr Cl into same place as ss, * 2ch, miss 1dc, 3tr Cl into next dc, (2ch, miss 2dc, 3tr Cl into next dc) twice, rep from * omitting a Cl at end of last rep, ss into top of first 2tr Cl. Turn.

Adapting the basic shawl

Openwork patterns combine chain lace and groups, clusters and shells in various ways. Any of the ones shown could be used to make a pretty shawl.

Using openwork patterns

Openwork patterns can be worked in either rounds or rows, and so are suitable for making not only shawls, but also bags, scarves, summer tops and evening wraps. Worked in crochet cotton, they have a crisp look; for evening wear, choose one of the many pretty glitter yarns available.

The patterns can also be worked in strips and used as decoration – either as a lace insertion or as edging – on household items, baby clothes and adults' garments.

Pattern Library: Openwork patterns

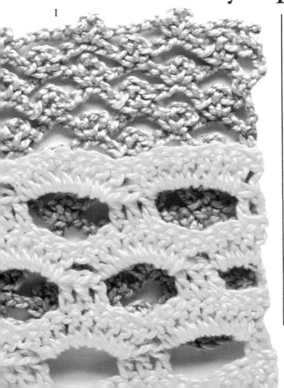

1

Picot chain lace (1)

Make a multiple of 4 plus 1 ch with 5 extra turning ch.

Base row (1dc, 3ch, 1dc) into 10th ch from hook, 5ch, miss 3ch, (1dc, 3ch, 1dc) into next ch, rep from * to last 4ch, 5ch, miss 3ch, 1dc into last ch. Turn.

Patt row 5ch, * (1dc, 3ch, 1dc) into 3rd ch of next 5ch loop, 5ch, rep from * to end, 1dc into 3rd of last 5ch loop. Turn.

Rep patt row throughout.

Diamond eyelets (2)

Make a multiple of 8 ch plus 3 extra turning ch.

Base row 1tr into 4th ch from hook, 1tr into next ch, * 5ch, miss 5ch, 1tr into each of next 3ch, rep from * , ending with 1tr into each of last 2ch. Turn.

1st row 3ch to count as first tr, * 9tr into next 5ch sp, rep from * to end, 1tr into top of turning ch. Turn.

2nd row 5ch to count as first tr and 2ch sp, * miss first 3tr of next 9tr group, 1tr into each of next 3tr at centre of group, 5ch, miss next 3tr of same group, rep from *, ending with 3tr at centre of last 9tr group, 2ch, 1tr into top of turning ch. Turn.

3rd row 3ch, 4tr into first 2ch sp, * 9tr into next 5ch sp, rep from * to end, working 4tr into last 2ch sp before turning ch, 1tr into 3rd of 5 turning ch. Turn.

4th row 3ch, miss 1tr, 1tr into next tr, 5ch, 1tr into each of 3 centre tr of next 9tr group, rep from * to end, ending with miss 3tr of last 9tr group and first 3tr of last 5tr group, 1tr into next tr, 1tr into turning ch. Turn.

Rep first-4th rows throughout.

43rd round 2dc into first sp, 3dc into each foll sp all round, ss into first dc.
44th round As 6th round, working 1ch instead of 2ch between tr.
45th round As 7th round, working 1ch instead of 2ch between tr.
46th round 3dc into each of first 3 sps, 2dc into each foll sp all round, ss into first dc. Turn.
47th round As 27th round.
48th round * 2dc into next sp, 3dc into next sp, rep from *, working 2dc into last sp.
49th round As 11th round.
50th round As 12th round.
51st round As 31st round, working 2ch instead of 1ch between each 3tr Cl.
52nd round As 14th round.

53rd-61st round As 15th round.
62nd round As 20th round.
63rd round 1dc into same place as ss, * 2dc into next sp, 1dc into next dc, 3dc into next sp, 1dc into next dc, rep from * ending with 3dc into last sp, ss into first dc.
64th round As 4th round.
65th round As 28th round.
66th round As 44th round.
67th round As 45th round.
68th round 3dc into first sp, 2dc into each foll sp, ss into first dc. Turn.
69th round As 4th round, but missing 2dc instead of 1ch between 3tr Cls.
70th round 2dc into first sp, 3ch into each foll sp all round, ss into first dc.
71st round As 11th round.

72nd round As 12th round.
73nd round As 30th round, working 2ch instead of 1ch between each 3tr Cl.
74th round As 14th round.
75th-78th round As 15th round.
79th round 1dc into loop just made, * 5ch, 1dc into next dc, rep from * to end, ending with 5ch, ss into first dc.
80th round 1dc into same place as ss, * 6ch, 1dc into next dc, rep from * to end, ending with 6ch, ss into first dc.
81st round As 79th round, working 7ch instead of 6ch for each loop. Fasten off.

Treble block and picot (3)

Make a multiple of 10 plus 7 ch with 2 extra turning ch.
Base row 1tr into 4th ch from hook, 1tr into each of next 4ch, * 3ch, miss 2ch, (1dc, 3ch, 1dc) into next ch – called picot dc –, 3ch, miss 2ch, 1tr into each of next 5ch, rep from * to end, 1tr into last ch. Turn.
1st row 3ch to count as first tr, 1tr into each of next 5tr, 5ch, 1tr into each of next 5tr, rep from * to end, 1tr into top of turning ch. Turn.
2nd row 6ch to count as first tr and 3ch sp, picot dc into centre of first 5tr block, 3ch, 5tr into next 5ch sp, 3ch, picot dc into centre of next 5tr block, 3ch, rep from * to end, 1tr into top of turning ch. Turn.
3rd row 8ch to count as first tr and 5ch sp, * miss next picot, 1tr into each of next 5tr, 5ch, rep from * to end, 1tr into 3rd of 6 turning ch. Turn.
4th row 3ch to count as first tr, 5tr into first 5ch sp, * 3ch, 1 picot dc into centre tr of next 5tr block, 3ch, 5tr into next 5ch sp, rep from * to end, 1tr into 3rd of 8 turning ch. Turn.
5th row As 2nd row.
2nd-5th rows form patt; rep them throughout.

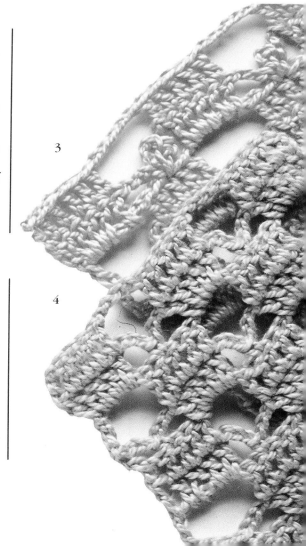

3

4

Crown lace (4)

Make a multiple of 10 plus 7 ch.
Base row 1tr into 4th ch from hook, 1tr into each of next 3ch, * 3ch, miss 2ch, 1dc into next ch, 3ch, miss 2ch, 1tr into each of next 5ch, rep from * to end. Turn.
1st row 3ch, miss first tr, 1tr into each of next 4tr, *4ch, 1tr into each of next 5tr, rep from * ending with 1tr into each of last 4tr, 1tr into top of turning ch. Turn.
2nd row 6ch, 1dc into centre tr of next 5tr group, * 3ch, 5tr into next 4ch sp, 3ch, 1dc into centre tr of next 5tr group, rep from * ending with 3ch, 1tr into top of turning ch. Turn.
3rd row 6ch, miss first dc, * 1tr into each of next 5tr, 5ch, rep from * ending with 4ch, 1tr into 3rd of turning ch. Turn.
4th row 3ch, 4tr into first ch sp, * 3ch, 1dc into centre tr of 5tr group, 3ch, 5tr into next 5ch sp, rep from * ending with 4tr into last sp, 1tr into turning ch. Turn.
Rep first-4th rows throughout.

Shells

Shells are probably the best known of crochet stitches, and their popularity is well justified. Use these lacy fabrics, formed from groups of treble, to make traditional baby clothes, such as this christening gown and shawl, as well as lightweight sweaters and lacy edgings.

The basic christening gown and shawl

Sizes
Gown to fit 43-48cm chest (0-6 months)
Length 75cm
Sleeve seam 4cm
Shawl measures 110 x 110cm

Materials
Gown 250g of a four-ply yarn
Approx 2m of 7mm-wide, double-faced satin ribbon
5 small buttons
Shawl 450g of a four-ply yarn
Approx 5.5m of 7mm-wide, double-faced satin ribbon
3.50mm crochet hook

Tension
8tr and 5 rows to 5cm worked on 3.50mm hook

To save time, take time to check tension.

Gown
Skirt and bodice
Make 184ch.
Base row 2tr into 4th ch from hook, * miss next 2ch, 1dc into next ch, miss next 2ch, 5tr into next ch, rep from * to last 6ch, miss next 2ch, 1dc into next ch, miss next 2ch, 3tr into last ch. Turn.
Beg patt
1st row (RS) 1ch, 1dc into first tr, 2ch, leaving last loop of each st on hook work 3tr into next dc, yrh and draw through all 4 loops on hook – called cluster –, * 2ch, 1dc into 3rd of next 5tr, 2ch, cluster into next dc, rep from * to turning ch, 2ch, 1dc into top of turning ch. Turn.
2nd row 3ch, 2tr into first dc, 1dc into next cluster, * 5tr into next dc, 1dc into next cluster, rep from * to last dc, 3tr into last dc. Turn.

First and 2nd rows form patt.
Cont in patt until work measures 60cm, ending with a WS row.

Bodice
Next row 3ch, 1tr into first tr, * (miss next tr, 1tr into next tr) 24 times, miss next tr, 2tr into next tr, rep from * twice more. Turn. 80 sts.
Next row 3ch, miss first tr, 1tr into each of next 29 sts, 1dc into next st, miss next 2 sts, 5tr into next st, miss next 2 sts, 1dc into next st, 1tr into each of next 6 sts, 1dc into next st, miss next 2 sts, 5tr into next st, miss next 2 sts, 1dc into next st, 1tr into each of last 30 sts. Turn.

SPECIAL TECHNIQUE
beginning the bodice

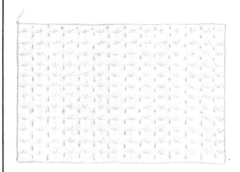

1 The skirt and bodice of the gown are worked in one piece to the armholes, the skirt edges being sewn together to form the centre back seam. Work the skirt for the length required, ending with a second pattern row.

2 Turn and work three chain and one treble into the first treble. * Miss the next treble and work one treble into the next treble. Repeat from * 24 times. Miss the next treble, then work two treble into the next treble.

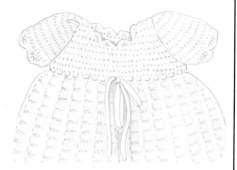

3 Continue in this way to the end of the row so that there are 80 stitches. When the garment is completed, thread narrow satin ribbon between stitches on the first row of the bodice and tie in a bow at the centre front. Use buttons in a colour matching the ribbon.

Rep last row twice more.
Divide for backs and front
Next row 3ch, miss first st, 1tr into each of next 17 sts, turn. 18 sts.
Left back
Cont on these sts only for bodice left back.

Shape armhole
Next row 3ch, miss first st, work next 2tr tog, 1tr into each st to end. Turn. 17 sts.
Next row 3ch, miss first st, 1tr into each st to last 3 sts, work next 2tr tog, 1tr into last st. Turn. 16 sts. Work 3 more rows in

tr without further shaping.
Shape neck
Next row Ss across first 7sts, 3ch, miss st at base of 3ch, 1tr into each st to end. Turn. 10 sts.
Next row 3ch, miss first st, 1tr into each st to last 3 sts, work next 2tr tog, 1tr into

last st. 9 sts. Fasten off.

Front

With RS facing, return to sts missed at beg of left back, miss next 4 sts and using hook rejoin yarn to next st.

Next row 3ch, miss first st at base of join, 1tr into each of next 7 sts, 1dc into next dc, 5tr into 3rd of next 5tr, 1dc into next dc, 1tr into each of next 6tr, 1dc into next dc, 5tr into 3rd of next 5tr, 1dc into next tr, 1tr into each of next 8 sts, turn.

Shape armholes

Next row 3ch, miss first st, work next 2tr tog, patt to last 3 sts, work next 2tr tog, 1tr into last st.

Rep last row once more.

Work 2 rows in patt without further shaping.

Shape right front neck

Next row 3ch, miss first st, 1tr into each of next 5 sts, 1tr into next dc, 1tr into next tr, miss next tr, 1tr into next tr, turn. 9 sts.

Next row 3ch, miss first st, 1tr into each st to end. Turn.

Rep last row once more. Fasten off.

Left front neck

With WS facing, return to sts missed at beg of front neck, and using hook rejoin yarn to 3rd tr of next shell.

Next row 3ch, miss first st at base of join, miss next tr, 1tr into next tr, 1tr into next dc, 1tr into each of next 6 sts. 9 sts.

Complete to match first side of neck, reversing all shaping.

Right back

With RS facing, return to sts missed at beg of front, miss next 4 sts and rejoin yarn to next st.

Next row 3ch, miss first st at base of join, 1tr into each st to end. Turn. 18 sts.

Complete to match left back, reversing all shaping.

Sleeves

Make 28ch.

Base row (RS) 1tr into 4th ch from hook, 1tr into each ch to end. Turn. 26 sts.

Next row 3ch, miss first st, * 2tr into next st, 1tr into next st, 2tr into next st, 1tr into each of next 2 sts, rep from * to end. Turn. 36 sts.

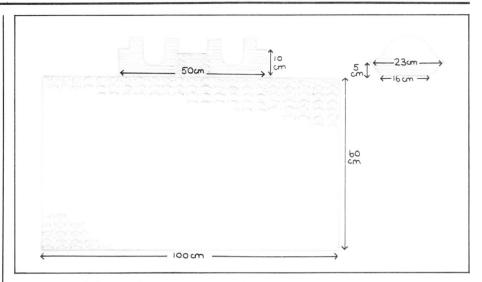

Next 2 rows 3ch, miss first st, 1tr into each st to end. Turn.

Shape top

Next row Ss across first 3 sts, 3ch, 1tr into each st to last 2 sts, turn. 32 sts.

Next row 3ch, miss first st, work next 2tr tog, 1tr into each st to last 3 sts, work next 2tr tog, 1tr into last st. Turn. 30 sts.

Rep last row until 22 sts rem.

Work 2 more rows in tr without further shaping.

Fasten off.

To make up

Do not press.

Join shoulder seams.

Join skirt seam including first row of bodice to form centre back. Join sleeve seams. Set in sleeves, easing in the fullness.

Neck and bodice edging

With RS facing and using hook, join yarn to top of centre back seam at beg of left back bodice.

Next row 1ch, 1dc into same place as join, (5tr into top of st at next row end, 1dc into top of st at next row end) 4 times, 5tr into top of st at corner of left-back bodice, 1dc into top of 4th st on neck edge, 5tr into top of st at neck row end, 1dc into shoulder seam, miss next row end, 5tr into next row end, 1dc into next row end, 5tr into centre tr of next shell, 1dc into top of next dc, 5tr between 3rd and 4th of next 6tr, 1dc

into top of next dc, 5tr into centre tr of next shell, 1dc into next row end, 5tr into next row end, miss next row end, 1dc into shoulder seam, 5tr into top of st at next row end, 1dc into 3rd st on neck edge, 5tr into top of st at corner of right back bodice, (1dc into top of st at next row end, 5tr into top of st at next row end) 4 times, 1dc into top of centre back seam. Fasten off.

Sleeve edgings (both alike)

With RS facing and using hook join yarn to first st on lower edge.

Next row 1ch, 1dc into next st, * miss next 2 sts, 5tr into next st, miss next 2 sts, 1dc into next st, rep from * to end. Fasten off.

Skirt edging

With RS facing and using hook join yarn to centre back seam.

Next row 3ch, 2tr into same place as join, * miss next 2 sts, 1dc into next st, miss next 2 sts, 5tr into next st, rep from * to last 6 sts, miss next 2 sts, 1dc into next st, miss next 2 sts, 2tr into last st, ss to top of first 3ch. Fasten off.

Thread ribbon through first row of bodice, adjust gathers to fit and tie ribbon in a bow at centre front. Sew buttons on to bottom of centre tr of 5 shells on right back edge of bodice. Use holes formed when working corresponding shells on left back edge of bodice as buttonholes.

Shawl

Centre square
Make 160ch. Work base row as for Gown skirt. Cont in patt as for skirt until work measures approx 88cm from beg and 94 rows in all have been worked. Do not turn at end of last row, but cont working into row ends.

Edging
1st round 3ch, * * 1tr into first row end, * (2tr into next row end, 1tr into next row end) twice, 3tr into next row end, 1tr into next row end, rep from * to last 3 row ends, 2tr into next row end, 1tr into next row end, 2tr into last row end, 3tr into st at corner, 1tr into each of next 156 sts, 3tr into st at corner* *, rep from * * to * * once more, ending last rep with 2tr into base of 3ch, ss to top of 3ch. 636 sts.
2nd and 3rd rounds 3ch, miss first st, (1tr into each st to centre tr of 3 corner tr, 3tr into corner tr) 4 times, 1tr into

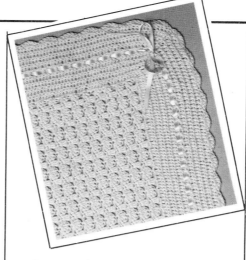

each st to end, ss to top of first 3ch. 652 sts.
4th round 4ch, miss first 2 sts, * (1tr into next st, 1ch, miss next st) to within 3 sts of next corner st, 1tr into each of next 3 sts, 3tr into corner st, 1tr into each of next 3 sts, rep from * 3 times more, ss to top of first 3ch.
5th round 3ch, miss first st, * (1tr into

next 1ch sp, 1tr into next tr) to within 3 sts of next corner st, 3tr into corner st, 1tr into each of next 3 sts, rep from * 3 times more, ss to top of first 3ch.
6th-9th rounds As 2nd and 3rd rounds. 700 sts. Fasten off.
10th round With RS facing, rejoin yarn to a corner st, 3ch, 4tr into same place as join, * (miss next 2 sts, 1dc into next st, miss next 2 sts, 5tr into next st) to within 6 sts of next corner st, miss next 2 sts, 1dc into next st, miss next 3 sts, 5tr into next corner st, rep from * 3 times more, omitting 5tr at end of last rep, ss to top of first 3ch.
Fasten off.

To make up
Do not press.
Cut ribbon into four equal lengths.
Thread a length of ribbon through the holes on the 4th round of the edging on each side of the shawl.
Tie the ends of ribbon in a neat bow at each corner.

Adapting the basic shell pattern

Shell patterns are ideal for delicate, traditional baby clothes such as christening gowns.

Christening robes are traditionally made in white or cream, but there is no reason why you should not introduce pastel-coloured yarn as a contrast.
For example, the treble rows on the robe and shawl could be striped. Similarly, a colour could be introduced when working the shell edging. If you do decide to use another colour, buy ribbon and buttons to match it.

Designing with shells
Unless you are experienced, increasing and decreasing can be difficult when working shell patterns, so avoid shaping wherever possible. Instead, make simple garments from squares and rectangles; some possibilities include summer tops, scarves, T-shaped pullovers and cardigans.

Pattern Library: Shell patterns

Little shells (1)
Make an odd multiple of 3ch plus 1 extra.
Base row (RS) 1tr into 4th ch from hook, * miss next 2ch, (1tr, 3ch, 1tr) into next ch, rep from * to last 3ch, miss next 2ch, 1tr into last ch. Turn.
1st row 3ch, 1tr into first tr, * (1tr, 3ch, 1tr) into next 3ch sp, (3tr, 1ch, 3tr) into next 3ch sp, rep from * to last 3ch sp, (1tr, 3ch, 1tr) into last 3ch sp, 1tr into top of turning ch. Turn.

2nd row 3ch, 1tr into first tr, (1tr, 3ch, 1tr) into each ch sp to end, 1tr into top of turning ch. Turn.
Rep first and 2nd rows throughout.

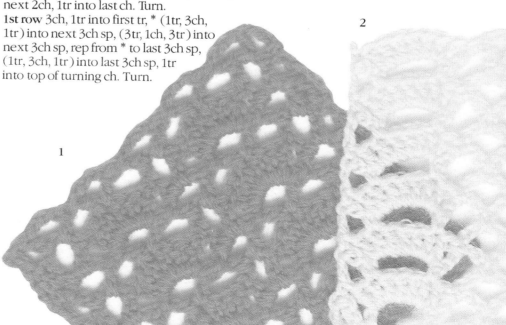

Vertical shells (2)

Make a multiple of 12ch plus 2 extra.
Base row 1dc into 8th ch from hook,
* 5ch, miss next 3ch, 1dc into next ch,
rep from * to last 2ch, 2ch, miss next ch,
1tr into next ch. Turn.
1st row (RS) 1ch, 1dc into first tr, * 7tr
into next 5ch sp, 1dc into next 5ch sp,
5ch, 1dc into next 5ch sp, rep from * to
last 5ch sp, 7tr into last 5ch sp, 1dc into
3rd turning ch. Turn.
2nd row 5ch, * miss next tr, 1dc into
next tr, 5ch, miss next 3tr, 1dc into next
tr, 5ch, 1dc into next 5ch sp, 5ch, rep
from * to last shell, miss next tr, 1dc into
next tr, 5ch, miss next 3tr, 1dc into next
tr, 2ch, 1tr into last dc. Turn.
Rep first and 2nd rows throughout.

Shells with picot (3)

Make a multiple of 8ch plus 3 extra.
Base row (RS) 1tr into 4th ch from
hook, * 1tr into next ch, 3ch, miss next
ch, 1dc into next ch, 3ch, ss into first of
3ch just worked – picot formed –, 3ch,
miss next ch, 1tr into each of next 4ch,
rep from * ending last rep with 3tr.
Turn.
1st row 1ch, 1dc into first tr, * 1dc into
each of next 2tr, 5ch, 1dc into each of
next 3tr, rep from * ending last rep with
1dc into top of turning ch. Turn.
2nd row 1ch, 1dc into first dc, * 3ch, 5tr
into next 5ch loop, 3ch, miss next 2dc,
1dc into next dc, picot, 3ch, rep from *
to last 5ch loop, 5tr into last 5ch loop,
3ch, 1dc into last dc. Turn.
3rd row 5ch, * 1dc into each of next 5tr,
5ch, rep from * ending last rep with
2ch, 1tr into last dc. Turn.
4th row 3ch, 2tr into first tr, * 3ch, miss
next 2dc, 1dc into next dc, picot, 3ch,
5tr into next 5ch loop, rep from *
ending last rep with 3tr into 3rd turning
ch. Turn.
Rep first-4th rows throughout.

Openwork shells (4)

Make a multiple of 6ch plus 4 extra.
Base row 1dc into 2nd ch from hook,
* 3ch, miss next 2dc, 1dc into next ch,
rep from * to last 2ch, 1ch, 1dc into last
ch.
Turn.

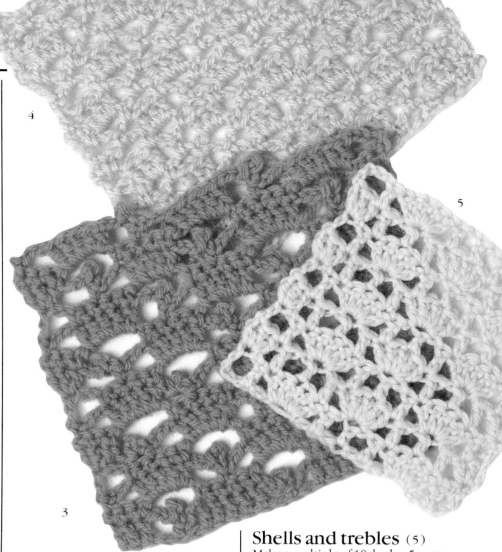

4

5

3

1st row (RS) 1ch, 1dc into first 1ch sp,
* 2ch, 3tr into next 3ch sp, 2ch, 1dc into
next 2ch sp, rep from * to turning ch,
2ch, 1tr into top of turning ch. Turn.
2nd row 4ch, * 1dc into next 2ch sp,
3ch, rep from * to last 2ch sp, 1dc into
last 2ch sp, 1ch, 1tr into top of turning
ch. Turn.
3rd row 2ch, 1tr into first dc, * 2ch, 1dc
into next 3ch sp, 2ch, 3tr into next 3ch
sp, rep from * to turning ch, 1ch, 1tr into
sp formed by turning ch. Turn.
4th row 1ch, 1dc into first 1ch sp, * 3ch,
1dc into next 2ch sp, rep from * to
turning ch, 1ch, 1dc into top of turning
ch. Turn.
Rep first-4th rows throughout.

Shells and trebles (5)

Make a multiple of 10ch plus 5 extra.
Base row 1tr into 7th ch from hook,
* miss next 2ch, 5tr into next ch, miss
next 2ch, 1tr into next ch, (1ch, miss
next ch, 1tr into next ch) twice, rep
from * omitting 1ch and 1tr from end of
last rep. Turn.
1st row 3ch, 2tr into first tr, * 1tr into
first tr of shell, 1ch, 1tr into 3rd tr of
shell, 1ch, 1tr into 5th tr of shell, miss
next tr, 5tr into next tr, rep from *
ending last rep with 3tr into top of
turning ch. Turn.
2nd row 4ch, miss first 2tr, 1tr into next
tr, * miss next tr, 5tr into next tr, 1tr into
first tr of shell, 1ch, 1tr into 3rd tr of
shell, 1ch, 1tr into 5th tr of shell, rep
from * ending last rep with miss next tr,
1tr into next tr, 1ch, 1tr into top of
turning ch. Turn.
Rep first and 2nd rows throughout. The
patt is reversible.

Filet motifs

Filet crochet is derived from two basic stitches – treble and chain stitch. Motifs are created against a trellis of chain stitch and spaced treble by building up blocks of treble. Fine cotton is well-suited to this work and has been used for the summer top shown here.

The basic filet sun top

Sizes

To fit 86-91 [91-96] cm bust
Length 35cm excluding straps
Note: *Instructions for larger size are in square brackets [ ]; where there is one set of figures it applies to both sizes.*

Materials

150g of No. 20 crochet cotton
1.25mm crochet hook
5 buttons

Tension

20 spaces and 20 rows to 10cm worked on 1.25mm hook

To save time, take time to check tension.

Top (both sizes)

Make 207 ch.

1st row 1tr into 4th ch from hook, 1tr into each of next 2ch, (2ch, miss 2ch, 1tr into next ch) twice, (2 sps made), 1tr into each of next 3ch (block made), now work 60 sps, 1 block, 2 sps, 1 block. Turn.

2nd row 3ch, miss first tr, 1tr into each of next 3tr (block made over block at beg of row), (2ch, 1tr into next tr) twice, (2 sps made over 2 sps), 1tr into each of next 3tr (block made over block) now work 47 sps, (2tr into next sp, 1tr into next tr) twice, (2 blocks made over 2 sps) now work 11 sps, 1 block, 2 sps, 1tr into each of next 2tr, 1tr into next ch (block made over block at end of row). Turn.

3rd row 1ss into each of first 4tr (1 block dec) 3ch, (2tr into next sp, 1tr into next tr) twice, 2ch, miss 2tr, 1tr into next tr (sp made over block), now work 10sps, 1 block, 2sps, 1 block, 23sps, 2 blocks, 22 sps, 2 blocks. Turn.

4th row 5ch, 1tr into 4th ch from hook, 1tr into next ch, 1tr into next tr, (block inc at beg of row) 2sps, 1 block, 20sps, 1 block, 2sps, 1 block, 22sps, 1 block, 2sps, 1 block, 10sps, 1 block, 1sp, 2ch, miss 2tr, insert hook into next ch and draw yarn through, yrh and draw through one loop on hook (a foundation ch made), complete as a tr, *yrh, insert hook into foundation ch and draw yarn through, yrh and draw through one loop on hook (another foundation ch made), complete as a tr, rep from *twice more (a block inc at end of row), 3ch. Turn.

1st size only

5th-88th rows Work from chart, noting that 88th row is marked by arrow. Turn chart and work from 88th row marked by arrow back to first row. Fasten off.

2nd size only

5th-94th rows Work from chart, noting that 94th row is marked by an asterisk. Turn chart and work from 94th row marked by * back to first row. Fasten off.

Buttonhole band (both sizes)

1st row Join yarn to 3rd tr made on last row, 1dc into same place as join, (2dc into next sp, 1dc into next tr) twice, 1dc into each of next 3tr, (2dc into next sp, 1dc into next tr) 60 times, 1dc into each of next 3tr (2dc into next sp, 1dc into next tr) twice, 1ch. Turn.

2nd row 1dc into each of first 58dc, (5ch, miss 5dc, 1dc into each of next 28dc) 4 times, 5ch, miss 5dc, 1dc into each of next 4dc, 1ch. Turn.

3rd row (1dc into each dc, 5dc into next 5ch sp) 5 times, 1dc into each dc, 5ch. Turn.

4th row Miss first 3dc, 1tr into next dc, (2ch, miss 2dc, 1tr into next dc) 65 times.
Fasten off.

Button band (both sizes)

1st row Join yarn to 3rd tr made on first row, 1dc into same place as join, (2dc

---

SPECIAL TECHNIQUE
making a crochet cord

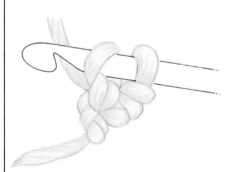

1 Start with 2 chain. Hold them between finger and thumb of left hand and work 1 double crochet into 2nd chain from hook. Turn the work so that foundation chain is at top. Insert hook into back loop and work 1 double crochet into foundation loop of 2nd chain made at beginning.

2 Turn chain so that bottom is now at top next to hook and insert hook into the 2 loops at side of chain.

3 Take yarn round hook and through 2 loops on hook. Yarn round hook and through remaining 2 loops to make a twisted stitch. By turning stitches in this way you achieve a twisted cord.

into next sp, 1dc into base of next tr)
twice, 1dc into base of each of next 3tr,
(2dc into next sp, 1dc into base of next
tr) 60 times, 1dc into base of each of
next 3tr, (2dc into next sp, 1dc into base
of next tr) twice, 1ch. Turn.
2nd row 1dc into each dc, 1ch. Turn.
3rd row 1dc into each dc, 5ch. Turn.
4th row As 4th row of buttonhole band.

Shoulder straps (make 2)
Make 9ch.
1st row 2 blocks. Turn.
2nd row 5ch, inc 1 block, 2sps, inc 1

block. Turn.
3rd row 3ch, 1 block, 2sps, 1 block .
Turn.
4th row Dec 1 block, 3ch, 2 blocks. Turn.
Rep 2nd to 4th rows until work
measures 37cm from beg, or length
required.
Fasten off.

To make up
Sew shoulder straps in place on front
and back of bodice.
Sew on buttons to correspond with
buttonholes.

Cord (make 2)
Beg with 2ch; holding this between
finger and thumb of left hand, work 1dc
into 2nd ch from hook, turn, inserting
hook into back of loop, work 1dc into
foundation loop of 2nd ch made, *turn,
insert hook into 2 loops at side, yrh and
draw through 2 loops on hook, yrh and
draw through rem 2 loops, rep from *
until work measures 120cm, or length
required. Fasten off. Slot cords through
at waistline and top.
Damp and pin out to measurements.
Leave to dry.

Adapting the filet sun top

Substitute another filet pattern
by working from one of the
following charts, placing the
motifs on to a plain filet net
background.

Filet crochet, traditionally worked in
fine cottons, is really a simple form of
lace, originally inspired by filet guipure
lace. It had its heyday at the end of the

19th century, when filet crochet could
be seen decorating almost any piece of
household linen, baby clothes and
underwear.
The motifs are worked onto a basic net
background with spaces filled in with
blocks of crochet to create the different
motifs. The motifs can either be small
and scattered all over the fabric or quite
large and used either individually or in
groups to create denser patterns over
the basic net.

The basic patterns
The basic net is made by working individual treble with either one or two
chain between, depending on the size
of mesh required. The blocks are
formed by working one or two treble
into these spaces. The size of the net
must be determined before creating a
filet design; if you are working from a
printed pattern, this will be specified at
the beginning of the instructions.

Using a filet chart
Since many filet designs are fairly intricate, the pattern is set out in the form of
a chart, since row-by-row instructions
for the motifs would be far too complicated and lengthy. Each blank square on
the chart represents a space (not a
stitch), and each block is indicated by a
symbol – for example – a •, as here, or an
X – so that you can see how many
blocks to work in one row to form the
pattern.
Right side rows are usually worked by
reading the chart from right to left, and
wrong side rows from left to right.
When making a filet chart for your own
design, remember that although spaces
and blocks are represented by squares
on the graph paper, these do not represent the actual size of the space or
block. It is therefore important to make
a tension square in the yarn and pattern
of your choice so that you can judge the
size of the completed motif, and adjust
it if necessary.

Row
2 4

1 3 5 Row   □ 1 Space ▨ 1 Block   ▲ ✳

Pattern Library: Filet patterns

Cupid's bow (1)

Worked over a basic net of 1tr and 1ch with 1tr worked into each 1ch sp to form blocks.

1st motif row 4ch, 1tr into next tr, (1ch, 1tr into next tr) 29 times, 1tr into 1ch sp, 1tr into next tr, (1ch, 1tr into next tr) to end of row, working last tr into 3rd of 4 turning ch. Foll chart, work rem 32 rows of motif.

Heart

Worked over a basic net of 1tr and 1ch with 1tr worked into each 1ch sp to form blocks.

1st motif row 4ch, 1tr into next tr, (1ch, 1tr into next tr) 4 times, 1tr into next 1ch sp, 1tr into next tr, (1ch, 1tr into next tr) to end of row working last tr into 3rd of 4 turning ch.

Foll chart work rem 9 rows of motif.

1

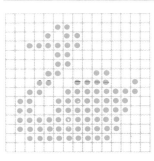

2

Swans (2)

Worked over a basic net of 1tr and 1ch with 1tr worked into each 1ch sp to form blocks.

1st motif row 4ch, 1tr into next tr, (1ch, 1tr into next tr) 4 times, (1tr into 1ch sp, 1tr into next tr) 17 times, (1ch, 1tr into next tr) to end of row working last tr into 3rd of 4 turning ch.

Foll chart, work rem 28 rows of motif.

Small swan

Worked over a basic net of 1tr and 1ch with 1tr worked into each 1ch sp to form blocks.

1st motif row 4ch, 1tr into next tr, (1ch, 1tr into next tr) 3 times, 1tr into 1ch sp, 1tr into next tr) 9 times, (1ch, 1tr into next tr) to end of row, working last tr into 3rd of 4 turning ch.

Foll chart work rem 12 rows of motif.

Large butterfly (3)

Worked over a basic net of 1tr and 2ch with 2tr worked into each 2ch sp to form blocks.

1st motif row 5ch, 1tr into next tr, (2ch, 1tr into next tr) 14 times, (2tr into next 2ch sp, 1tr into next tr) 4 times, (2ch, 1tr into next tr) to end of row, working last tr into 3rd of first 5 turning ch.

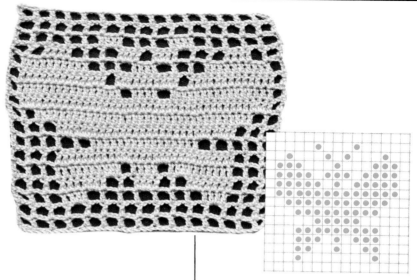

3

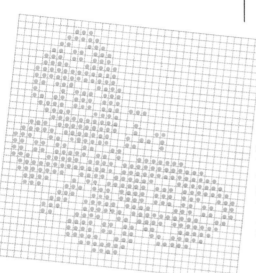

Small butterfly

Worked over a basic net of 1tr and 2ch with 2tr worked into each 2ch sp to form blocks.

1st motif row 5ch to count as first tr and 2ch sp, 1tr into next tr, (2ch, 1tr into next tr) 3 times, 2tr into next 2ch sp, 1tr

into next tr, (2ch, 1tr into next tr) 7 times, 2tr into 2ch sp, 1tr into next tr, (2ch, 1tr into next tr) 3 times working last tr into 3rd of first 5 turning ch. Following chart work rem 12 rows of chart.

Birds (4)

Worked over a basic net of 1tr and 1ch with 1tr worked into each 1ch sp to form blocks.

1st motif row 4ch, 1tr into next tr, 1ch, 1tr into next tr, 1tr into 1ch sp, 1tr into next tr, (1ch, 1tr into next tr) to end of row, working last tr into 3rd of 4 turning ch.

Foll chart, work rem 38 rows of motif.

Flying bird

Worked over a basic net of 1tr and 1ch with 1tr worked into each 1ch sp to form blocks.

1st motif row 4ch, 1tr into next tr, (1ch, 1tr into next tr) 13 times, 1tr into next 1ch sp, 1tr into next tr, (1ch, 1tr into next tr) 14 times working last tr into 3rd of 4 turning ch.

Foll chart work rem 10 rows of motif.

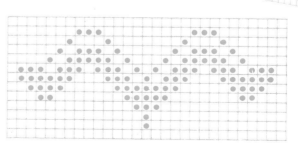

4

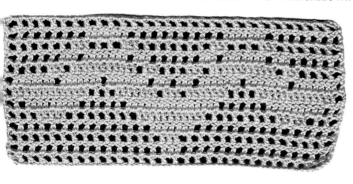

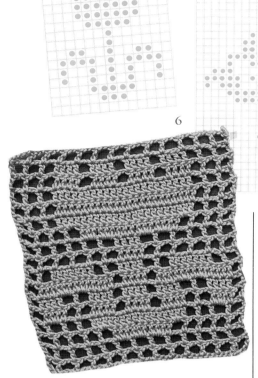

6

Tulip (6)

Worked over a basic net of 1tr and 2ch with 2tr worked into each 2ch sp to form blocks.

1st motif row 5ch, 1tr into next tr, (2ch, 1tr into next tr) 11 times, (2tr into 2ch sp, 1tr into next tr) 4 times, (2ch, 1tr into next tr) 3 times, (2tr into 2ch sp, 1tr into next tr) twice, (2ch, 1tr into next tr) to end of row working last tr into 3rd of 5 turning ch.
Foll chart work rem 29 rows of motif.

Small tulip

Worked over a basic net of 1tr and 2ch with 2tr worked into each 2ch sp to form blocks.

1st motif row 5ch, 1tr into next tr, (2ch, 1tr into next tr) 4 times, (2tr into next 2ch sp, 1tr into next tr) 3 times, (2ch, 1tr into next tr) to end of row, working last tr into 3rd of 5 turning ch.
Foll chart work rem 13 rows of motif.

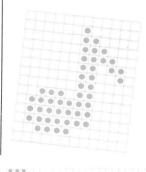

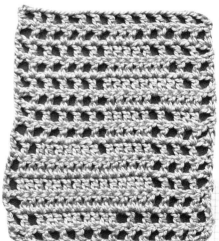

5

Treble clef and musical notes (5)

Worked over a basic net of 1tr and 1ch with 1tr worked into each 1ch sp to form blocks.

1st motif row 4ch, 1tr into next tr, (1ch, 1tr into next tr) 37 times, (1tr into 1ch sp, 1tr into next tr) 7 times, (1ch, 1tr into next tr) to end of row, working last tr into 3rd of 4 turning ch.
Foll chart, work rem 35 rows of motif.

Musical note

Worked over a basic net of 1tr and 1ch with 1tr worked into each 1ch sp to form blocks.

1st motif row 4ch, 1tr into next tr, (1ch, 1tr into next tr) 5 times, (1tr into 1ch sp, 1tr into next tr) 4 times, (1ch, 1tr into tr) to end of row, working last tr into 3rd of 4 turning ch.
Foll chart work rem 11 rows of motif.

Irish crochet

Elaborate Irish crochet fabrics, formed from a rich combination of flowers, leaves, shamrocks and picot mesh, all worked in fine cotton, are among the most beautiful of crochet laces. Use the technique to make this charming blouse for a little girl and a pretty waistcoat.

The basic Irish crochet patterns

Child's blouse

Sizes

To fit 58 [61:64] cm chest
Length 35 [38:41] cm
Sleeve seam 9cm
Note: *Instructions for larger sizes are given in square brackets [ ]; where there is only one set of figures it applies to all sizes.*

Materials

100 [100:150] g of a No. 5 crochet cotton
2.50mm crochet hook
1 small button

Tension

8 loops and 17 rows to 10cm over mesh patt worked on 2.50mm hook

To save time, take time to check tension.

Back

Make 79 [82:85] ch.
Base row 1dc into 7th ch from hook, *4ch, miss next 2ch, 1dc into next ch, rep from * to end. Turn.
25 [26:27] 4ch loops.
Patt row 6ch, *1dc into next 4ch loop, 4ch, rep from * to last loop, 1dc into last loop. Turn.
Rep patt row until work measures 21 [23:25] cm from beg.

Shape armholes

Next row Ss across first 4ch loop and to centre of next loop, 1dc into centre of same loop, work 22 [23:24] loops. Turn.
Rep last row once more, working 20 [21:22] loops. Turn. **

Next row Ss across first 4ch loop and to centre of next loop, 1dc into centre of same loop, work 19 [20:21] loops. Turn.
Cont without further shaping until work measures 33 [36:39] cm from beg.

Shape shoulders

Next row Ss across first 2 4ch loops and to centre of next loop, 1dc into same loop, work 14 [15:16] loops. Turn.
Rep last row once more, working 10 [11:12] loops. Turn.
Next row Ss across first 4ch loop and to centre of next loop, 1dc into centre of same loop, work 8 [9:10] loops. Turn.
Next row Ss to centre of first 4ch loop, 1dc into same loop, work 7 [8:9] loops.
Fasten off.

Front

Work as given for back to **.

Divide for neck

Next row Ss across first 4ch loop and to centre of next loop, 1dc into centre of same loop, work 9 [10:10] loops, turn.
Cont on these loops only without further shaping until work measures 31 [32:35] cm from beg, ending at neck edge.

Shape neck

Next row Ss across next 2 4ch loops, 1dc into next dc, 6ch, 1dc into first 4ch loop, patt to end. Turn. 7 [8:8] loops.
Patt one row without shaping.
Next row Ss to centre of first 4ch loop, 1dc into same loop, patt to end.
Turn. 6 [7:7] loops.
Patt one row without shaping.
Rep last shaping row once more.
5 [6:6] loops.

Shape shoulder

Next row Ss across first 2 4ch loops and to centre of next loop, 1dc into same loop, patt to end. Turn. 2 [3:3] loops.
Next row 6ch, 1dc into first loop, 4ch, 1dc into next loop.
Fasten off.
Rejoin yarn to next 4ch loop at beg of neck division and work 2nd side of neck to correspond with first, reversing all shaping.

SPECIAL TECHNIQUE
working raised motifs

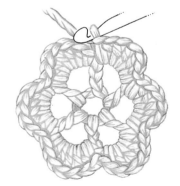

1 *The outer petals of the flowers on the blouse and waistcoat on page 113 are worked behind the previous rounds to give a three-dimensional appearance. Work the first two rounds as instructed in the pattern to form a small flower.*

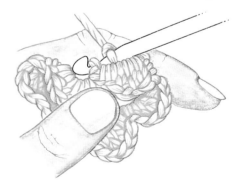

2 *Holding the work as shown and inserting the hook from back to front, work one double crochet round the stem of the next treble on the first round. Work five chain. Continue in this way, ending with a slip stitch to the first double crochet. On the next round work in the chain loops to form the petals.*

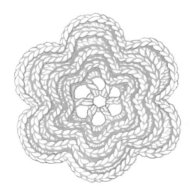

3 *To form a many-layered motif like the rose on the waistcoat, repeat step 2, working the double crochet round the corresponding double crochet on the last-but-one round. The petals are made larger by working more chain and then more graduated stitches (see page 41) on the following round.*

Sleeves (both alike)

Make 52 [55:58] ch.

Base row As for back. 16 [17:18] loops.
Cont in patt as for back until work
measures 9cm from beg.

Shape top

Next row Ss across first 4ch loop and to
centre of next loop, 1dc into same loop,
patt across 13 [14:15] loops. Turn.

Next row Ss to centre of first 4ch loop,
1dc into same loop, patt across 12
[13:14] loops. Turn.

Patt 2 rows without shaping.

Next row Ss to centre of first 4ch loop,
1dc into same loop, patt across 11
[12:13] loops. Turn.

Next row Ss to centre of first 4ch loop,
1dc into same loop, patt across 10
[11:12] loops. Turn.

Rep last 4 rows, work one loop less on
each dec row until 8 [9:10] loops rem.
Rep last 2 rows only until 4 [5:6] loops
rem.

Fasten off.

To make up

Join shoulder seams. Set in sleeves. Join
side and sleeve seams, using an invisible
seam.

Lower edging

Using hook and with RS facing, join yarn
to a side seam, 1ch, *2dc into first loop,
3ch, ss to first of 3ch – picot formed –,
3dc into next loop, picot, rep from * all
round lower edge, ending with ss to
first ch. Fasten off.

Neck edging

Using hook and with RS facing, join yarn
to a shoulder seam and work as for
lower edging.

Sleeve edgings

Using hook and with RS facing, join yarn
to sleeve seam and work as for lower
edging.

Rosebud

Using hook, make 6ch, join with a ss to
form a circle.

1st round 6ch, (1tr, 3ch) 5 times into
circle, ss into 3rd of 6 ch.

2nd round (1dc, 1htr, 3tr, 1htr, 1dc) into
each 3ch loop.

3rd round Working behind last round,
1dc round first tr on first round, *5ch,
1dc round next tr on first round, rep
from * ending with ss into first dc.

4th round (1dc, 1htr, 5tr, 1htr, 1dc) into

each 5ch loop, ss to first dc.

Fasten off. Work 3 more rosebuds in the
same way.

Leaf

Make 16ch.

Base row 1dc into 3rd ch from hook, 1dc
into each ch to last ch, 3dc into last ch,
1dc into each ch along opposite side of
foundation ch, 1dc into turning ch.

On foll rows work into *back* loop only
of each st:

1st row 1dc into each of next 11dc. Turn.

2nd row 1ch, miss first st, 1dc into each
of next 10dc (1dc, 1ch, 1dc) into centre
dc, 1dc into each dc to within 4dc of tip
of leaf, turn.

3rd row 1ch, miss first dc, 1dc into each
dc to 1ch at base of leaf, (1dc, 1ch, 1dc)
into 1ch sp, 1dc into each dc to within
3dc of previous row.

4th and 5th rows As 3rd.

6th row As 3rd, working 3dc into 1ch sp
at base of leaf. Fasten off.

Work 5 more leaves in the same way.

To make up

Sew motifs around neck as shown.
Sew on button.
Work 6ch. Fasten off. Sew to neck
opposite button.

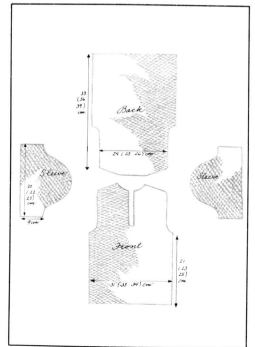

Traditional Irish waistcoat

Note: *Before beginning, see
Know-How, page 154. Because of the
method of working, it is not possible
to give exact yarn quantity, size and
tension.*

Materials

No. 5 crochet cotton as required
(waistcoat shown was made from
200g)
2.50mm crochet hook
Paper dressmaking pattern for simple
waistcoat
Medium-weight interfacing as required

Rose

Make 8ch, join with a ss to form a circle.

1st round 6ch, (1tr, 3ch) 7 times into
circle, ss to 3rd of 6ch.

2nd round (1dc, 1htr, 3tr, 1htr, 1dc) into
each 3ch loop.

3rd round Working behind last round,
1dc round first tr on first round, (5ch, 1dc
round next tr) 7 times, 5ch, ss to first dc.

4th round (1dc, 1htr, 5tr, 1htr, 1dc) into
each 5ch loop.

5th round Working behind last round,
1dc round first dc of 3rd round, (7ch,
1dc round next dc) 7 times, 7ch, ss to
first dc.

6th round (1dc, 1htr, 7tr, 1htr, 1dc) into
each 7ch loop.

7th round Working behind last round,
1dc round first dc of 5th round, (9ch,
1dc round next dc) 7 times, 9ch, ss to
first dc.

8th round (1dc, 1htr, 9tr, 1htr, 1dc) into
each 9ch loop, ss to first dc.

Fasten off. Make one more rose in the
same way.

Rosebud

Work as for child's blouse. Make 21.

Leaf

Work as for child's blouse. Make 22.

To make up

Cut out back and fronts of waistcoat
from interfacing, omitting seam
allowances round neck, armholes and
front and lower edges. Join side seams.
Tack motifs into position on to
interfacing as shown.

Using hook, join yarn to first motif and work picot mesh as foll:
Base row *2ch, 1 picot (3ch, ss into first of 3ch), 3ch, 1 picot, 2ch, ss into next motif or same motif, rep from * to end. Turn.
Patt row 2ch or ss along a motif as necessary, *1 picot, 3ch, rep from * to end.
Cont filling in between motifs, working straight rows of picot mesh across back. When all motifs are joined and interfacing covered with picot mesh, remove all tacking.
Join shoulder seams.
Edging
Working over a cord of 3 strands of yarn; *(3dc, 1 picot) into each ch loop all round neck, front and lower edges and round armholes.

Adapting the basic Irish crochet patterns

Use the rich motifs and meshes of Irish crochet to work either modern or traditional lace.

Adapting the blouse
The child's blouse is adapted simply by substituting motifs from among those given here for those given in the basic pattern. You could sew smaller motifs around the neckline as shown on page 113, or arrange larger motifs over the bodice. Use matching sewing thread to sew the motifs invisibly to the mesh. If you do not want to substitute motifs, vary the blouse by working the motifs in the pattern in contrast colours.

Adapting the waistcoat
The basic waistcoat could be worked using any of the motifs or meshes given here, though a picot mesh is traditional. The waistcoat shown has motifs round the front and edges only, but using motifs all over the waistcoat would create a beautifully ornate fabric.

Pattern Library: Irish crochet patterns

Fancy clover (1)
Make 7ch, join with a ss to form a circle.
1st round 1ch, 15dc into circle, ss to first dc.
2nd round *4ch, miss next dc, (1tr, 2ch, 1tr) into next dc, 4ch, miss next dc, ss into each of next 2dc, rep from *, ending with ss into last dc.
3rd round *(3dc, 4ch, 3dc) into next 4ch loop, (2dc, 4ch, 2dc) into next 2ch loop, (3dc, 4ch, 3dc) into next 4ch loop, ss between 2ss of 2nd round, rep from * to end.
Stem Make 16ch, 1dc into 2nd ch from hook, 1dc into each ch to end, ss to base of clover. Fasten off.

Bluebell (2)
Make 10ch. From now on, work over a cord.
Base row 1dc into 2nd ch from hook, 1dc into each of next 7ch, 5dc into last ch, 1dc into each of next 8ch along opposite side of foundation, 3dc over cord only, 1dc into each of next 7dc, 3dc over cord only. Turn.
From now on work into back loop only of each st.
1st row 1ch, miss first dc, 1dc into each of next 10dc, 3dc into end dc, 1dc into each of next 8dc, 3dc over cord only. Turn.
2nd row 1ch, miss first dc, 1dc into each of next 13dc, work 20dc over cord for stem. Fasten off.

Honeycomb mesh (3)
Make a multiple of 4ch plus 10.
Base row 1tr into 10th ch from hook, *4ch, miss next 3ch, 1tr into next ch, rep from * to end. Turn.
Patt row 8ch, 1tr into first 4ch loop, *4ch, 1tr into next 4ch loop, rep from * to end. Turn.
Rep patt row for length required.

Triple leaf (4)
Make 15ch. From now on work each st over a cord.
1st row 1dc into 2nd ch from hook, 1dc into each of next 12ch, 5dc into last ch, 1dc into each ch along opposite side of foundation ch, work 3dc over cord only, working into back loop of each st, work 1dc into each of next 11dc. Turn.
From now on work into back loop only of each st.
2nd row 1ch, miss first dc, 1dc into each of next 11dc, 3dc into centre of 3dc of previous row, 1dc into each of next 12dc. Turn.
3rd row 1ch, miss first st, 1dc into each of next 12dc, 3dc into centre dc of 3dc of previous row, 1dc into each of next 10dc. Turn.
4th row 1ch, miss first st, 1dc into each of next 10dc, 3dc into centre dc of 3dc of previous row, 1dc into each of next 11dc. Turn.
5th row 1ch, miss first st, 1dc into each of next 11dc, 3dc into centre dc of 3dc of previous row, 1dc into each of next 9dc. Turn.
6th row 1ch, miss first st, 1dc into each of next 9dc, 3dc into centre dc of 3dc of previous row, 1dc into each of next 9dc. Fasten off.
Make 2 more leaves in the same way and sew tog as shown.

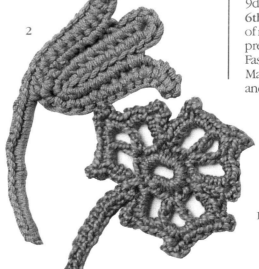

2

1

Picot flower (5)

Make 8ch, join with a ss to form a circle.
1st round 1ch, 20dc into circle, ss to first ch.
2nd round 1dc into same place as ss, *10ch, miss 3dc, 1dc into next dc, rep from *, ending with ss into first dc.
3rd round (1ch, 1htr, 2tr, 1 picot – 3ch, ss into first of 3ch –, 3dtr, 1 picot, 3dtr, 1 picot, 2tr, 1htr, 1dc) into each 10ch loop, ss to first ch.
Fasten off.

Wheel (6)

Make 6ch, join with a ss to form a circle.
1st round 1ch, 12dc into circle, ss to first dc.
2nd round 4ch, (1tr, 1ch) into each dc, ss to 3rd of 4ch.
3rd round 1ch, 3dc into each 1ch sp, ss to first dc.
4th round *4ch, ss to first ch to form a picot, 1dc into each of next 3dc, rep from * to end, ss to base of first picot.
Fasten off.

Flour-leaf clover (7)

Stem Working over a triple cord, work 24dc.
Flower centre Work 21dc over cord, join with a ss to first of these 21dc. Pull the cord to form a circle.
Petal Leave the cord and work into the dc of the circle thus:
1st row (1ch, 1dc into next st) 4 times. Turn.
2nd row 1ch, 1dc into first dc, (1ch, 1dc under next 1ch of 1st row) 4 times, 1ch, 1dc into same place as last dc. Turn.
3rd row (1ch, 1dc under 1ch) 6 times, 1ch, 1dc into same place as last dc. Turn.
Work 2 more rows without shaping, then one more row, missing one st at each end. Fasten off. Work 3 more petals in the same way, missing 1dc of ring between 2 petals.
From now on work over cord:
Edging Work a row of dc all round outer edges of petals, working (1dc into same place at last st at beg of petal, 1dc into missed dc on circle, 1dc into same place as first st of next petal) between 2 petals. At end of last petal cont working dc into sts of stem. Fasten off.

Ornate medallions

Whether worked in knitting yarn or crochet cotton, these unusual crochet squares can be used to make beautifully textured fabrics. You can use the medallions to make an entire fabric, as in this beautiful bedspread, or you can combine them with simpler squares for variety.

The basic crochet bedspread

Sizes
Single bed size measures 180 x 240cm
Double bed size measures 215 x 240cm

Materials
Single bed size: 1900g of a four-ply yarn
Double bed size: 2100g
3.00mm crochet hook

Tension
One motif measures approx 34cm square

To save time, take time to check tension.

Square
Make 8ch. Join with a ss to form a circle.
1st round 3ch, 1tr into circle, * (3ch, 2tr into circle), rep from * 6 times more, 3ch. Join with a ss to top of first 3ch. 8 2tr groups.

2nd round Ss to centre of next 3ch loop, 1dc into same place as ss, * (4ch, 1dc) into next 3ch loop, rep from * 6 times more, 4ch. Join with a ss to first dc.
3rd round Into each 4ch loop work (1dc, 1htr, 5tr, 1htr, 1dc).
4th round * 6ch, inserting hook from back of work, work 1dc round next dc of 2nd round, rep from * to end.
5th round Into each 6ch loop work (1dc, 1htr, 7tr, 1htr, 1dc).
6th round As 4th, working 8ch instead of 6ch.
7th round As 5th, working 9tr instead of 7tr.
8th round As 4th, working 10ch instead of 6ch.
9th round 9ch, 1tr tr into st at base of 9ch, * (1ch, 1tr into 10ch loop) 3 times into same loop, (1ch, 1tr into 10ch loop) 3 times into next loop, 1ch, (1tr tr, 3ch,

1tr tr) into dc between next 2 loops, rep from * to end omitting (1tr tr, 3ch, 1tr tr) at end of last rep. Join with a ss to 6th of first 9ch.
10th round Ss into first 3ch loop, 3ch, (1tr, 3ch, 2tr) into same loop, * 1tr into tr tr, (1tr into next 1ch sp, 1tr into next tr) 6 times, 1tr into next 1ch sp, 1tr into next tr tr, (2tr, 3ch, 2tr) into 3ch sp, rep from * to end omitting (2tr, 3ch, 2tr) at end of last rep. Join with a ss to top of first 3ch.
11th round 3ch, * 1tr into next tr, (2tr, 3ch, 2tr) into next 3ch sp, 1tr into each of next 18tr, rep from * to end omitting 1tr at end of last rep. Join with a ss to top of first 3ch.
12th round 3ch, * 1tr into each of next 3tr, (2tr, 3ch, 2tr) into next 3ch sp, 1tr into each of next 20tr, rep from * to end omitting 1tr at end of last rep. Join with

---

SPECIAL TECHNIQUE

making a popcorn

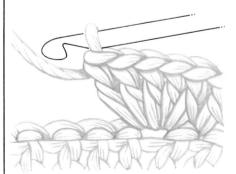

1 With right side of work facing, crochet in pattern to the point where popcorn stitch is to be made. Work five treble into the next stitch.

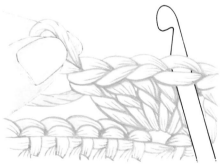

2 Withdraw the hook from the working loop and insert it from front to back through the top of the first of the five treble just made, while holding the working loop with the left hand.

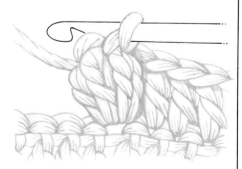

3 Keeping the hook in place, re-insert it into working loop and draw this loop through the first treble of the five treble group to make the popcorn stitch. Make sure that the stitches are drawn together neatly to achieve a good shape.

a ss to top of first 3ch.

13th round 4ch, * miss 1tr, 1tr into next tr, 1ch, miss next tr, 1tr into next tr, 1ch, miss next tr, (2tr, 3ch, 2tr) into next 3ch sp, (1ch, miss next tr, 1tr into next tr) 11 times, 1ch, rep from * to end omitting 1tr and 1ch at end of last rep. Join with a ss to 3rd of first 4ch.

14th round Ss into next 1ch sp, 4ch, * (1tr into next sp, 1ch) twice, (2tr, 3ch, 2tr) into next 3ch sp, (1ch, 1tr into next sp) 12 times, 1ch, rep from * to end omitting 1tr and 1ch at end of last rep. Join with a ss to 3rd of first 4ch.

15th round 3ch, * (1tr into next sp, 1tr into next tr) 3 times, 1tr into next tr, (2tr, 3ch, 2tr) into next 3ch sp, 1tr into each of next 2tr, (1tr into next sp, 1tr into next tr) 12 times, rep from * to end omitting 1tr at end of last rep. Join with a ss to top of first 3ch.

16th round 3ch, * work 5tr into next tr, withdraw hook from working loop, insert hook through top of first of these 5tr then back into working loop and draw working loop through first of 5tr – called 1 popcorn – 1pc –, 1tr into each of next 3tr, 1pc into next tr, 1tr into each of next 4tr, (2tr, 3ch, 2tr) into 3ch sp, 1tr into each of next 4tr, (1pc into next tr, 1tr into each of next 3tr) 6 times, rep from * to end omitting 1tr at end of last rep. Join with a ss to top of first 3ch.

17th round 3ch, * (1tr into top of next pc, 1tr into each of next 3tr) twice, 1tr into each of next 3tr, (2tr, 3ch, 2tr) into next 3ch sp, 1tr into each of next 6tr, (1tr into top of next pc, 1tr into each of next 3tr) 6 times, rep from * to end omitting 1tr at end of last rep. Join with a ss to top of first 3ch.

18th round 4ch, * (miss 1tr, 1tr into next tr, 1ch) 6 times, (2tr, 3ch, 2tr) into 3ch sp, (1ch, miss 1tr, 1tr into next tr) 16 times, 1ch, rep from * to end omitting 1tr and 1ch at end of last rep. Join with a ss to 3rd of first 4ch.

19th round Ss into next sp, 4ch, * (1tr into next sp, 1ch) 6 times, (2tr, 3ch, 2tr) into next 3ch sp, 1ch, (1tr into next sp, 1ch) 17 times, rep from * to end omitting 1tr and 1ch at end of last rep. Join with a ss to 3rd of first 4ch.

20th round 3ch, * (1tr into next sp, 1tr into next tr) 7 times, 1tr into next tr,

(2tr, 3ch, 2tr) into next 3ch sp, 1tr into next tr, (1tr into next tr, 1tr into next sp) 17 times, rep from * to end. Join with a ss to top of first 3ch.

21st round Ss to next tr, 3ch, * 1tr into each of next 2tr, (1pc into next tr, 1tr into each of next 3tr) 3 times, 1tr into each of next 2tr, (2tr, 3ch, 2tr) into next 3ch sp, 1tr into each of next 5tr, (1pc

into next tr, 1tr into each of next 3tr) 8 times, 1pc into next tr, 1tr into next tr, rep from * to end omitting 1tr at end of last rep. Join with a ss to top of first 3ch.

22nd round 3ch, * 1tr into each of next 18 sts, (2tr, 3ch, 2tr) into next 3ch sp, 1tr into each of next 41 sts, rep from * to end omitting 1tr at end of last rep. Join with a ss to top of first 3ch.

23rd round Ss to next tr, 4ch, * (miss next tr, 1tr into next tr, 1ch) 9 times, (2tr, 3ch, 2tr) into next 3ch sp, 1ch, (miss next tr, 1tr into next tr, 1ch) 22 times, rep from * to end omitting 1tr and 1ch at end of last rep. Join with a ss to 3rd of first 4ch.

Fasten off.

Make 35 squares in all for single bed size and 42 squares in all for double bed size.

To make up
Block and press each square lightly on WS to correct size.

Sew squares into strips of five by seven for single bed size and six by seven for double bed size.

Fringe
Make a fringe along two sides and one end of bedspread: for each clump of fringe cut four lengths of yarn 20cm long; knot these four strands into each 1ch sp along edge. Trim evenly as necessary.

Adapting the basic bedspread

Choose any of the medallions featured in the next two pages to make a beautiful bedspread.

Substituting motifs
Substituting one crochet square for another is quite simple: all you need do, if they differ in size, is to make fewer or more squares, depending on the size required for the completed fabric. To calculate the number of squares you will need, make a sample square using the hook and yarn of your choice, measure the size of the finished square and calculate the number needed for

the bedspread from this measurement. In some cases the final round of a motif can be repeated, with additional stitches worked on each side of the motif until it is the desired size. If you choose one of these squares as an alternative to the bedspread medallion featured on page 119, you can use this method to make your motif exactly the same size, and so make the same number of squares as are used for the original bedspread.

The squares should be blocked and pressed (if appropriate) before they are sewn together, so that they are all of equal size and fit together smoothly.

Pattern Library: Ornate medallions

Diamond cluster motif (1)

Make 6ch. Join with a ss to form a circle.
1st round 3ch to count as first tr, 2tr into circle, (2ch, 3tr into circle) 3 times, 2ch. Join with a ss to top of first 3ch. Four blocks of 3tr.
2nd round 3ch, * leaving last loop of each st on hook, work 5dtr into next tr, yrh and draw through all loops on hook – called 5dtr cluster –, 1tr into next tr, (2tr, 2ch, 2tr) into next 2ch sp, 1tr into next tr, rep from * to end omitting 1tr at end of last rep. Join with a ss to top of first 3ch.
3rd round 3ch, * 1tr into top of cluster, 1tr into next tr, 5dtr cluster into next tr, 1tr into next tr, (2tr, 2ch, 2tr) into next 2ch sp, 1tr into next tr, 5dtr cluster into next tr, 1tr into next tr, rep from * to end omitting 1tr at end of last rep. Join with a ss to top of first 3ch.
4th round 3ch, * 5dtr cluster into next tr, 1tr into next tr, 1tr into top of next cluster, 1tr into next tr, 5dtr cluster into next tr, 1tr into next tr, (2tr, 2ch, 2tr) into 2ch sp, 1tr into next tr, 5dtr cluster into next tr, 1tr into next tr, 1tr into top of next cluster, 1tr into next tr, rep from * to end omitting 1tr at end of last rep. Join with a ss to top of first 3ch.
5th round 3ch, * 1tr into top of next cluster, 1tr into next tr, 5dtr cluster into next tr, 1tr into each of next 5 sts, (2tr, 2ch, 2tr) into next 2ch sp, 1tr into each of next 5 sts, 5dtr cluster into next tr, 1tr into next tr, rep from * to end omitting 1tr at end of last rep. Join with a ss to top of first 3ch.
6th round 3ch, * 5dtr cluster into next tr, 1tr into each of next 9 sts, (2tr, 2ch, 2tr) into next 2ch sp, 1tr into each of next 9 sts, rep from * to end omitting 1tr at end of last rep. Join with a ss to top of first 3ch.
7th round 3ch, * 1tr into each of next 12 sts, (2tr, 2ch, 2tr) into next 2ch sp, 1tr into each of next 11 sts, rep from * to end omitting 1tr at end of last rep. Join with a ss to top of first 3ch.
Fasten off.

Shells and popcorns (2)

Make 6ch. Join with a ss to form a circle.
1st round 3ch to count as first tr, 1tr into circle, (3ch, 3tr into circle) 3 times, 3ch, 1tr into circle. Join with a ss to top of first 3ch. Four 3tr blocks.
2nd round 3ch, * work 5tr into next st, withdraw hook from working loop and insert through top of first of 5tr, insert hook back into working loop and draw through first of 5tr – called 1pc –, 5tr into 3ch sp, 1pc into next tr, 1tr into next tr, rep from * to end omitting 1tr at end of last rep. Join with a ss to top of first 3ch.
3rd round 5ch, * miss first pc, 1pc into next tr, 1tr into next tr, 3tr into next tr, 1tr into next tr, 1pc into next tr, 2ch, miss 1pc, 1tr into next tr, 2ch, rep from * to end omitting 1tr and 2ch at end of last rep. Join with a ss to 3rd of first 5ch.
4th round Ss into next 2ch sp, 5ch, * miss 1pc, 1pc into next tr, 1tr into next tr, 3tr into next tr, 1tr into next tr, 1pc into next tr, 2ch, miss next pc, 1tr into 2ch sp, 2ch, 1tr into next 2ch sp, 2ch, rep from * to end omitting 1tr and 2ch at end of last rep. Join with a ss to 3rd of first 5ch.
5th round Ss into next sp, 5ch, * miss 1pc, 1pc into next tr, 1tr into next tr, 3tr into next tr, 1tr into next tr, 1pc into next tr, 2ch, (1tr into next 2ch sp, 2ch) 3 times, rep from * to end omitting 1tr and 2ch at end of last rep. Join with a ss to 3rd of first 5ch.
6th round Work as 5th, but working section in brackets 4 times instead of 3.
7th round As 5th, but working section in brackets 5 times instead of 3.
Cont working in this way until motif is required size. Fasten off.

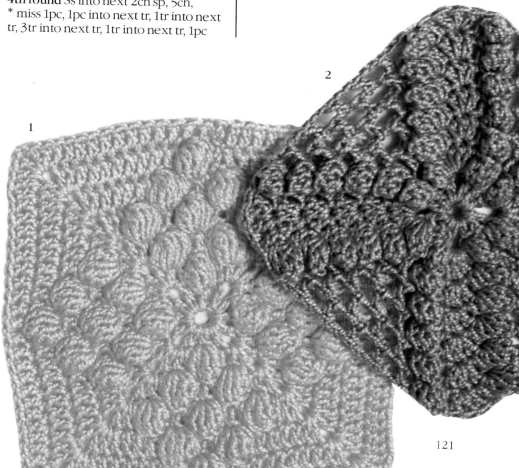

1

2

Openwork popcorn motif (3)

Make 8ch. Join with a ss to form a circle.
1st round 3ch, leaving last loop of each st on hook work 3dtr into circle, yrh and draw through all loops on hook – called 3dtr cluster –, (3ch, leaving last loop of each st on hook work 4dtr into circle, yrh and draw through all loops on hook – called 4dtr cluster –, 5ch, 4dtr cluster into circle) 3 times, 3ch, 4dtr cluster into circle, 5ch. Join with a ss to top of first cluster. 8 clusters.
2nd round Ss to 2nd of 3ch, 1dc into same place, * 9dtr into next 5ch sp, 1dc into 3ch sp, rep from * to end omitting 1dc at end of last rep. Join with a ss to first dc.
3rd round 3ch, into st at base of 3ch work (5tr into next st, withdraw hook from working loop and insert into first of 5tr, then back into working loop and draw loop through first of 5tr – called 1pc –), * 2ch, miss 2dtr, 1tr into next dtr, 2ch, miss 1dtr, (2tr, 3ch, 2tr) into next dtr, 2ch, miss 1dtr, 1tr into next dtr, 2ch, 1pc into next dc, rep from * to end omitting 1pc at end of last rep. Join with a ss to top of first pc.
4th round 3ch, * (2tr into 2ch sp, 1tr into next tr) twice, 1tr into next tr, (2tr, 3ch, 2tr) into next 3ch sp, 1tr into next tr, (1tr into next tr, 2tr into 2ch sp) twice, 1tr into top of next pc, rep from * to end omitting 1tr at end of last rep. Join with a ss to top of first 3ch.
5th round 6ch, 1tr into st at base of 6ch, * miss 2tr, 1tr into each of next 3tr, 1pc into next tr, 1tr into each of next 3tr, (2tr, 3ch, 2tr) into 3ch sp, 1tr into each of next 3tr, 1pc into next tr, 1tr into each of next 3tr, miss 2tr, (1tr, 3ch, 1tr) into next tr, rep from * to end omitting (1tr, 3ch, 1tr) at end of last rep. Join with a ss to 3rd of first 6ch.
6th round Ss to 2nd of first 3ch, 4ch, * miss next tr, 1tr into next tr, (1ch, miss next st, 1tr into next st) 4 times, (2tr, 3ch, 2tr) into 3ch sp, 1tr into next tr, (1ch, miss next st, 1tr into next st) 4 times, 1ch, 1tr into 2nd of 3ch, 1ch, rep from * to end omitting 1tr and 1ch at end of last rep. Join with a ss to 3rd of first 4ch. Fasten off.

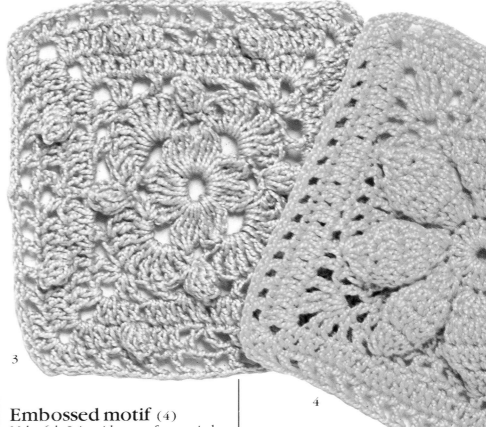

3

4

Embossed motif (4)

Make 6ch. Join with a ss to form a circle.
1st round 3ch to count as first tr, work 15tr into circle. Join with a ss to top of first 3ch. 16tr.
2nd round 4ch, (5tr into next tr, 1ch, 1tr into next tr, 1ch) 7 times, 5tr into next tr, 1ch. Join with a ss to 3rd of first 4ch.
3rd round 4ch, 1tr into same place as ss, 1ch, (2tr into each of next 5tr, 1ch, 1tr into next tr, 1ch, 1tr into same place as last tr, 1ch) 7 times, 2tr into each of next 5tr, 1ch. Join with a ss to 3rd of first 4ch.
4th round 3ch, 1tr into same place as ss, 1ch, 2tr into next tr, 1ch, (work 2tr tog 5 times over next 10tr, 1ch 2tr into next tr, 1ch, 2tr into next tr, 1ch) 7 times, work 2tr tog 5 times over next 10tr, 1ch. Ss to top of first 3ch.
5th round 4ch, (1tr into next tr, 1ch) 3 times, * work next 5tr tog, 1ch, (1tr into next tr, 1ch) 4 times, rep from * all round ending with tr worked tog over next 5tr, 1ch. Ss to 3rd of first 4ch.
6th round 4ch, * 1tr into next tr, 1ch, (2dtr, 3ch, 2dtr) into next 1ch sp, (1ch, 1tr into next tr) twice, 1ch, 1htr into top of next cluster, (1ch, 1dc into next tr) 4 times, 1ch, 1htr into top of next cluster, 1ch, 1tr into next tr, 1ch, rep from * to end omitting 1tr and 1ch at end of last

rep. Join with a ss to 3rd of first 4ch.
7th round 3ch, * 1tr into 1ch sp, 1tr into next tr, 1tr into 1ch sp. 1tr into each of next 2dtr, (2tr, 2ch, 2tr) into 3ch sp, 1tr into each of next 2dtr, (1tr into 1ch sp, 1tr into next tr) twice, 1tr into next 1ch sp, 1tr into next htr, (1tr into next 1ch sp, 1tr into next dc) 4 times, 1tr into next sp, 1tr into next htr, 1tr into next sp, 1tr into next tr, rep from * to end omitting 1tr at end of last rep. Join with a ss to top of first 3ch.
8th round 4ch, miss next tr, 1tr into next tr, (1ch, miss next tr, 1tr into next tr) twice, * 1ch, miss next tr, (2tr, 2ch, 2tr) into 2ch sp, (1ch, miss next tr, 1tr into next tr) 14 times, rep from * to end working (1ch, miss next tr, 1tr into next tr) 10 times, 1ch at end of last rep. Join with a ss to 3rd of first 4ch. Fasten off.

Chapter 2
Crochet Plus

Crochet plus embroidery

Firm crochet fabrics, especially those worked in double crochet, are ideal backgrounds for embroidery. With a little practice, you will find it remarkably easy to beautify anything from a favourite sweater to a baby's layette like the one shown here.

The basic embroidered set

Size
Coat to fit 0-6 months (45cm chest)
Length 25cm
Sleeve seam 14cm
Rug 76cm long by 63cm wide

Materials
Coat and hat 150g of a double knitting yarn in main colour A
50g in contrast colour B
Rug 250g in main colour A
100g in contrast colour B
4.50mm crochet hook
Small amounts of embroidery thread in green and two shades of pink

Tension
18dc and 19 rows to 10cm worked on 4.50mm hook
To save time, take time to check tension.

Coat back
Using A, make 43ch.
Base row (RS) 1dc into 2nd ch from hook, 1dc into each dc to end. Turn. 42dc.
Pattern row 1ch, miss first dc, 1dc into each dc to end. Turn.
Cont in patt on these 42dc until work measures 24cm. Fasten off.
Edging
With RS facing, miss the turning ch, and join B to first dc at beg of last row worked, 1ch, 1dc into each dc to end of row, *1ch to form corner miss first row end of side edge, 1dc into each row end to next corner, 1ch to form corner*, 1dc into each ch on lower edge, rep from * to * once more, 1dc into turning ch at beg of last row working in A.
Fasten off.

Fronts (alike)
Using A, make 22ch.
Base row (RS) 1dc into 2nd ch from hook, 1dc into each ch to end. Turn. 21dc.
Cont in patt as given for back on these 21dc until work measures 24cm from beg. Fasten off.
Edging
Work as for back.

Sleeves (alike)
Using A, make 33ch.
Base row (RS) 1dc into 2nd ch from hook, 1dc into each ch to end. Turn. 32dc.
Cont in patt as given for back on these 32dc until work measures 13cm from

---

SPECIAL TECHNIQUE
crochet seaming

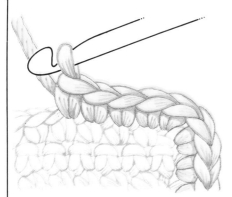

1 First edge the garment pieces with one row of double crochet, working one stitch into each row end at the side edges and into each stitch at the upper and lower edges. Turn corners either by working one chain at each corner, as on the baby's outfit shown here, or by working three double crochet into each of the corner stitches.

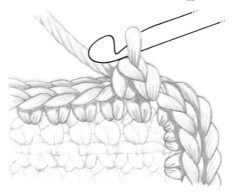

2 To join the pieces, place the edged pieces together with wrong sides facing. Using the same yarn as that used for the edging, join the yarn to the end of the seam. Work one chain and miss the first stitch on the edging. Insert the hook through both edgings under all four loops. Work one double crochet.

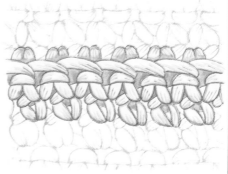

3 Continue in this way, joining the edgings by working one double crochet into each pair of stitches on the edging. Seaming a garment in this way produces a raised decorative seam, which looks particularly attractive when worked in a colour contrasting with the main fabric.

beg. Fasten off.

Edging
Work as for back.

To make up
Using 4.50mm hook and B, crochet pieces tog with WS facing and working through both loops of edging of each piece as foll:

Left shoulder
With back behind left front, join B to 1ch at top corner, 1ch, miss first dc, 1dc into each of next 12dc.
Fasten off.

Right shoulder
With back behind right front, join B to 13th st from top corner, 1ch, miss first dc, 1dc into each of next 11dc, 1dc into 1ch at corner. Fasten off.

Left armhole
With sleeve behind front and back, join

B to left side at 16th row end from outer edge of shoulder seam and to 1ch at top corner of sleeve, 1ch, miss first dc, 1dc into each of next 15dc, 1dc into 1ch at top corner of front, 1dc into 1ch at top corner of back, 1dc into each of next 15dc, 1dc into next dc on back and 1ch at top corner of sleeve. Fasten off.

Right armhole
With sleeve behind front and back, join B to back at 16th row end from outer edge of shoulder seam and to 1ch at top corner of sleeve, 1ch, miss first dc, 1dc into each of next 15dc, 1dc into 1ch at top corner of back, 1dc into 1ch at top corner of front, 1dc into each of next 15dc, 1dc into next dc on front and 1ch at top corner of sleeve. Fasten off.

Left side and sleeve seams
With back behind front, join B to 1ch at lower edge of left front and back, 1ch,

miss first dc, 1dc into each dc to sleeve, 1dc into each dc on sleeve, ending with 1dc into 1ch at lower corners. Fasten off.

Right side and sleeve seams
With back behind front, join B to 1ch at lower edge of right sleeve, 1ch, 1dc into each dc to front, 1dc into each dc of front and back, ending with 1dc into 1ch at lower corners. Fasten off.

Ties (make 2)
Using B, work a length of ch 18cm long. Fasten off.
Sew one end of each tie to front edge 9cm from top corner.
Fold back revers as shown and catch stitch corners neatly in place.

Hat

Sides (make 2)
Using A, make 27ch.
Base row (RS) 1dc into 2nd ch from

hook, 1dc into each ch to end. 26dc.
Cont in patt as given for Coat on these
26dc until work measures 14cm from
beg. Fasten off.

Edging
Work as given for Coat back.

To make up

With WS tog and working through both
loops of the edge of each piece, join B to
1ch at top right-hand corners. 1ch, 1dc
into each dc to corner, 2dc into 1ch at
corner.
1dc into each dc at row ends of sides to
corner, 1dc into 1ch at corner. Fasten off.

Ties (make 2)
Using B, work a length of ch 25cm long.
Fasten off.
Fold corners of hat on to RS as shown
and sew corners neatly in place.
Sew ties to hat.

Rug

To make a square
Using A, make 22ch.
Base row (RS) 1dc into 2nd ch from
hook, 1dc into each ch to end. Turn.
21dc. Fasten off.
Work patt row as for Coat back on these
21dc 21 times.
Make a total of 30 squares in the same
way.

Edging
Work as for Coat back.

To make up

Note: *Squares are arranged so that rug
is 6 squares long by 5 squares wide.
Place alternate squares tog
horizontally and vertically, and using*

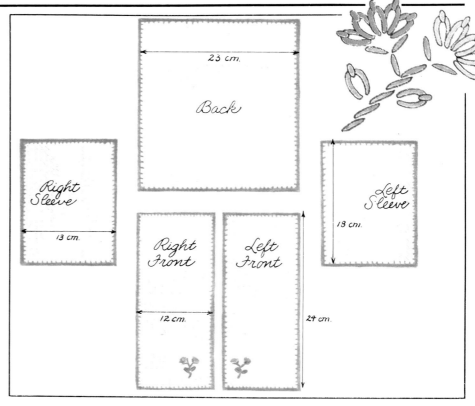

B oversew tog neatly at the edges.

Edging
With RS facing, join B to 1ch at any
corner, 1ch, 1dc into each dc to next
corner of first square, 1dc into 1ch at
corner, * 1dc into 1ch at corner of next
square, 1dc into each dc to 1ch at next
corner of same square, rep from * round
edge of rug, working 2dc into 1ch at
corners of blanket and ending with 1dc
into first corner of blanket, join with a ss
to first ch. Fasten off.

Embroidery
The motif above has been embroidered
on to the coat and rug, with a slightly
smaller version on the hat.
Position the motif at the centre of
alternate squares on the rug, reversing
the light and dark flowers on alternate
rows. Reverse the motif completely for
the left-hand corner of the coat and hat.
Using wool or matte embroidery
thread, work the stem in stem stitch, the
upper stem and sepals in straight stitch
and the leaves and petals in lazy-daisy.

Adapting the baby's embroidered set

**Any simple crochet fabric can be
enhanced by adding embroidery.**

Embroidery on double crochet
Most of the simpler embroidery
stitches can be worked on a firm double
crochet fabric in much the same way as
when embroidering a woven fabric.
Easy designs can be worked freehand
on the fabric, but more complicated
motifs are best planned first on paper.

Draw the motif on graph paper so that
each square on the paper represents
one double crochet. Use different symbols or colours to represent stitches.
There is no need to confine yourself to a
plain double crochet fabric as a background for embroidery. Introduce bobbles or holes into the fabric and then
outline them with embroidery stitches.
Or work a simple embroidery motif and
then outline it with surface crochet.

Other variations
Embroidery on other crochet fabrics is
less easy, since longer crochet stitches
do not provide such a firm base. However, such fabrics can still be decorated
for an 'embroidered' look.
Surface slip stitch produces much the
same effect as embroidered chain stitch,
and embroidered braid or velvet ribbon
can be woven through a treble or treble
mesh fabric for an interesting effect.

Pattern Library: Embroidered patterns

Sampler (1)
Work alternate rows of treble and double crochet. Embroider rows of stitches – here herringbone, threaded stitch and French knots – using contrasting yarns.

Poppies (2)
Thread narrow braid through double crochet and embroider 'wheat-ears' on either side using lazy-daisy stitch. Work poppies in cross stitch and back stitch, with centres in French knots.

Rainbow (3)
Use the colours of the rainbow to work chain stitch or surface slip stitch arcs on to a double crochet fabric.

Bobble flowers (4)
Work treble bobbles in a double crochet fabric. Work stems and leaves in lazy-daisy stitch.

127

Crochet plus quilting

Firm crochet fabrics lend themselves particularly well to quilting with wadding. The resulting thick fabric is ideal for winter jackets and coats, such as this bodywarmer, bomber jacket and coat.

The basic quilted jackets and coat

Sizes
To fit 56-60[60-64]cm chest
Length: Bodywarmer 37[40]cm
Bomber jacket 38[41]cm
Coat 42[46]cm
Sleeve seam: Bomber jacket 27[29]cm
Coat 25[27]cm
Note: *Instructions for the larger size are given in square brackets [ ]; where there is only one set of figures it applies to both sizes.*

Materials
Bodywarmer 100g of a four-ply yarn in main colour A and in each of 2 contrast colours, B and C
Bomber jacket 400g in main colour A 100g in contrast colour B
Coat 500[550]g
3.50mm crochet hook
Pair of 3¼mm knitting needles
For each garment 50cm of 94cm-wide, 56g (2oz) synthetic wadding
Bomber jacket only 40cm open-ended zip
Coat only 6 buttons

Tension
21htr and 16 rows to 10cm worked on 3.50mm hook

To save time, take time to check tension.

Bodywarmer
Body section
* Using A, make 124 [134] ch.
Base row 1htr into 3rd ch from hook, 1htr into each ch to end. Turn. 123[133] sts.
Pattern row 2ch to count as first htr, miss first st, 1htr into each st to end. Turn.
Rep patt row 5[6] times more, placing contrasting marker at 62nd[67th] st of first and last row.
Fasten off. * Rep from * to * once more. Cut a strip of wadding measuring 5mm less *all round* than the crochet strips. Place wadding between two strips of crochet so that top, lower edges and coloured markers match.
Using matching yarn, oversew all edges of crochet tog, matching corresponding sts (see page 164) and so enclosing the wadding.
Make two padded strips in B and one in C in the same way.

Back yoke
* Using A, make 56[60] ch.

Work base row as for body section. 55[59] sts.
Work in patt as for body section, placing contrasting marker at 28th[29th] st of first and last row.*
Rep from * to * once more.
Sew in wadding as for body section.
Make one padded strip each in B and C in the same way.

Front yokes (alike)
* Using A, make 26[28]ch.
Work base row as for body section. 25[27] sts.
Work in patt as for body section, omitting marker.*
Rep from * to * once more.
Sew in wadding as for body section.
Make one more padded strip in A and two in B in the same way.
Shape neck
* Using C, make 16[18]ch.
Work base row as for body section. 15[17] sts.
Work in patt as for body section, omitting marker.*
Rep from * to * once more.
Sew in wadding as for body section.
Make one more padded strip in C in the same way.

SPECIAL TECHNIQUE
working half-treble bobbles

1 *Simple half-treble bobbles are worked on alternate strips of the basic coat. With the right side facing, work to the position of the first bobble. Work five half treble into the next stitch, turn and work one half treble into each of the five half treble.*

2 *Insert the hook into the fifth stitch of the five half treble just worked. Wind the yarn round the hook and then draw through all loops on the hook to form a bobble.*

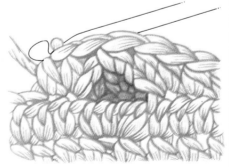

3 *The following row is a wrong side row. Work to the position of the bobble. Work one half treble into the top of the bobble.*

To make up
Matching corresponding sts (see Know How page 162), oversew tog four padded strips of body section, making sure that the top of one strip is sewn to the lower edge of the next and so on. Sew tog strips of back and front yokes in the same way.
Join shoulder seams, matching corresponding sts.

Armhole borders (alike)
With RS facing, using knitting needles and C *double,* K up 90[96] sts across armhole edge.
Work in K1, P1 rib for 2.5cm. Cast off in rib.

Neckband
With RS facing, using knitting needles and C *double,* K up 14 sts across right front neck edge, one st in corner, 11 sts up right front neck, one st in corner, 27[31] sts across back neck, one st in corner, 11 sts down left front neck, one st in corner, 14 sts across left front neck. 81[85] sts.
Next row (WS) Beg with P1, work in K1, P1 rib to end.
Next row Work in K1, P1 rib, ending with K1.
Next row Rib 12, P2 tog, K1, P2 tog, rib 7, P2 tog, K1, P2 tog, rib 23[27], P2 tog, K1, P2 tog, rib 7, P2 tog, K1, P2 tog, rib 12. 73[77] sts.
Rib 2 rows.
Next row Rib 11, K2 tog, P1, K2 tog, rib 5, K2 tog, P1, K2 tog, rib 21[25], K2 tog, P1, K2 tog, rib 5, K2 tog, P1, K2 tog, rib 11. 65[69] sts.
Rib 1 row.
Cast off in rib.

Welt
With RS facing, using knitting needles and A, K up 123[133] sts across lower edge of body section.
Work in K1, P1 rib for 5cm. Cast off in rib.

Front bands (alike)
Join top edge of body section to lower edges of yokes, matching corresponding sts and markers. Sew row ends of armhole borders to missed sts on top of body section.
With RS facing, using crochet hook and A, work 3 rows of dc across front edge. Fasten off.
Using C, work 3 rows of dc across neckband. Fasten off.

Bomber jacket
Body section
Work three padded strips in A and one in B as for Bodywarmer body section.

Back and front yokes
Work all strips in A as for Bodywarmer yokes.

Sleeves (both alike)
* Using 3.50mm hook and A, make 64[68]ch.
Work base row as for Bodywarmer body section. 63[67] sts.
Work in patt as for Bodywarmer body section, placing coloured marker at 32nd[34th] st of first and last rows.*
Sew in wadding as for Bodywarmer body section.
Make three more padded strips in A and one in B.

To make up
Matching corresponding sts, oversew tog four padded strips of body section as on page 162, making sure that top of one strip is sewn to the lower edge of the next and so on.
Oversew tog strips of back and front yokes in the same way.
Oversew tog strips of sleeves, as on page 162, in the same way.
Cuffs (alike)
With RS facing, using knitting needles and A, K up 63[67] sts across lower edges of sleeve.
Work in K1, P1 rib for 5cm. Cast off in

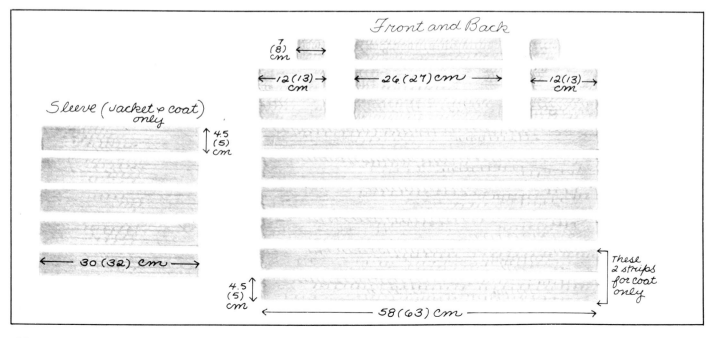

Sleeve (Jacket & coat) only

7 (8) cm

←12(13)→ cm

Front and Back

←26 (27) cm→

←12(13)→ cm

↑ 4.5 (5) ↓ cm

These 2 strips for coat only

← 30 (32) cm →

4.5 (5) cm

← 58(63) cm →

rib.
Join sleeve seams, leaving 5[6] row ends at top of sleeve unseamed.
Fold cuff to WS. Using matching yarn and herringbone st, sew cast-off edge to edge of padded strips to form double cuff.

Neckband
With RS facing, using knitting needles and A, K up 81[85] sts as for Bodywarmer neckband.
Work in K1, P1 rib for 5cm. Cast off in rib.
Make double neckband as for cuffs.

Welt
With RS facing, using knitting needles and A, K up 123[133] sts across lower edge of body section.
Work in K1, P1 rib for 12cm. Cast off in rib.
Make double welt as for cuffs.

Front bands (alike)
Sew top edge of body section to lower edge of yokes.
With RS facing, using crochet hook and A, work 3 rows of dc evenly across front edge, working into both thicknesses of welt and neckband. Sew zip neatly to front bands.

Coat

Body section
Work as for Bodywarmer body section from * to * 9 times.
Bobble strips Work as for plain strips, but work bobbles on 4th[5th] row as foll:
Bobble row 2ch to count as first htr, miss first htr, 1htr into each of next 5htr, * 5htr into next htr, turn, 1htr into each of 5htr just worked, turn, insert hook into first of last 5htr, yrh and draw though all loops on hook – bobble formed –, 1htr into each of next 9[10] htr, rep from * to last 7[6] sts, bobble, 1htr into each of last 6[5] sts. Turn.
Make 2 more bobble strips.
Make 3 plain padded strips and 3 padded strips with a bobble strip on RS.

Back yoke
Work as for Bodywarmer back yoke from * to * 5 times.

Bobble strips Work as for plain strips, but work bobbles on 4th [5th] row as foll:
Bobble row 2ch to count as first htr, miss first st, 1htr into next htr, * bobble, 1htr into each of next 9htr, rep from * to last 3 [2] sts, bobble, 1htr into each of last 2 [1] sts. Turn. Make 2 plain strips and one padded strip with bobble strip on RS.

Right front yoke
Work as for Bodywarmer front yokes from * to * 3 times.
Bobble strip Work as for plain strip, but work bobbles on 4th[5th] row as foll:
Bobble row 2ch to count as first htr, miss first st, 1htr into each of next 5htr, bobble, 1htr into each of next 9[10] htr, bobble, 1htr into each of next 8[9] sts. Turn.
Make one plain padded strip and one padded strip with a bobble strip on the RS.

Left front yoke
Work as for Bodywarmer front yoke from * to * 3 times.
Bobble strip Work as for plain strip, but work bobbles on 4th[5th] row as foll:
Bobble row 2ch to count as first htr, miss first st, 1htr into each of next 7[8] sts, bobble, 1htr into each of next 9[10] sts, bobble, 1htr into each of next 6[5] sts. Turn.
Make one plain padded strip and one padded strip with bobble strip on RS.
Shape neck
Work as for Bodywarmer.

Sleeves (alike)
Work as for Bomber jacket sleeves from * to * 16 times.

Bobble strip Work as for plain strips, but work bobbles on 4th[5th] row as foll:
Bobble row 2ch to count as first htr, miss first st, 1htr into each of next 5[4] htr, * bobble, 1htr into each of next 9[10]htr, rep from * 4 times more, bobble, 1htr into each of next 6[6] htr. Turn.
Make 3 more bobble strips.
Make 6 plain padded strips and 4 padded strips with bobble strip on RS.

To make up
Work as given for Bomber jacket, noting that there are 2 extra strips in the length and alternating plain and bobble strips.
Join sleeve seams, leaving 5[6] row ends open at top. Set in sleeves.
Front edgings (alike)
Make 7ch.
Base row 1dc into 2nd ch from hook, 1dc into each ch to end. Turn. 6 dc.
Pattern row 1ch, miss first dc, 1dc into each dc to end. Turn.
Rep patt row until work fits along front edge. Fasten off.
Sew edging in place.
Lower edging
Work 3 rows of dc into lower edge. Fasten off.
Cuff
Work 3 rows of dc into lower edge of sleeve. Fasten off.
Neck edging
Work one row of dc round neck edge, marking 4 corner dc with a contrast thread. Work 5 more rows of dc, dec 1dc at corners on next and foll 2 alt rows. Fasten off.
Sew buttons to left side, sewing top button on neckband, bottom button 8cm from lower edge and rem 4 buttons evenly spaced in between. Make button loops (see page 164) to correspond on right front.

Adapting the basic quilted jackets and coat

Use these techniques and designs to create warm and stylish garments for the whole family.

The children's garments on page 128 can be varied quite simply by introducing more colours into the design – for example, the bodywarmer would look very striking worked in bold primary-coloured stripes.

The more experienced crocheter might introduce simple bobble, cluster or jac-quard patterns into the stripes.

When making your own designs, keep basic shapes very simple. Avoid shaping armholes and sleeves and use square or slash necklines. Remember, too, that padded crochet is bulky, so allow more ease around the torso and the armholes.

Pattern Library: Padded patterns

Crochet quilting (1)
Quilting can be worked successfully with surface slipstitch. Place thin wadding between two pieces of crochet – thicker wadding would make it more difficult for the hook to pass through all three layers. Tack along the quilting lines. Work surface slipstitch (see page 155) through all three layers to quilt the fabric.

Note: *It is possible to use surface slipstitch to work more abstract designs.*

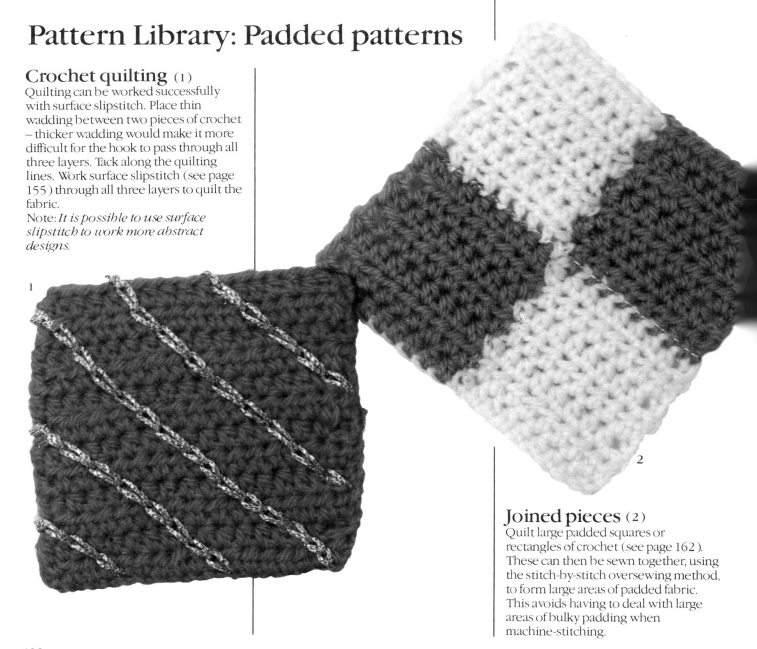

Joined pieces (2)
Quilt large padded squares or rectangles of crochet (see page 162). These can then be sewn together, using the stitch-by-stitch oversewing method, to form large areas of padded fabric. This avoids having to deal with large areas of bulky padding when machine-stitching.

3

4

Filled pockets (3)

Make the required number of ch.
Base row (RS) 1dc into 2nd ch from
hook, 1dc into each st to end. Turn.
* **1st row** (WS) 2ch to count as first htr,
skip first st, inserting hook under front
loop only of each st work in htr to end.
Turn.
2nd-3rd rows Work in htr, inserting
hook under both loops of each st as
usual. Fasten off.
With WS facing, turn work
upside-down, return to missed loops of
last dc row and rejoin yarn to first
unworked loop.
Next row 2ch to count as first htr, miss
first st, 1htr into each unworked loop to
end. Turn.
Next 2 rows Work in htr, inserting hook
under both loops of each st as usual.
Cut a piece of wadding slightly smaller
all round than the three rows of crochet
and insert it between the two pieces of
crochet. Fold the first 3 rows up to the
last row worked.
Next row Work a row of dc, inserting
the hook under both loops of the two
edges. Turn.*
Rep from * to * for length required.
Finish the edges by working a row of dc
through both thicknesses of crochet.
Note: *Increase the width of the pockets
by working in treble or by working
more rows, but always end each
pocket on a wrong-side row.*

Double-crochet padding (4)

Work small squares in double crochet
and pad as on page 162. Sew them
together to form a really warm and
highly textured fabric.

Backstitch quilting (5)

Quilting by hand, though more
time-consuming, produces as good
results as machine quilting. Tack the
lining, wadding and crochet together as
for machine quilting (see page 163).
Then, with right side facing, backstitch
along the tacked lines.

5

Crochet plus appliqué

Spirals – also known as continuous rounds – are the ideal method of working small appliqué motifs which can be sewn to most fabrics. This technique is a very simple way of adding individuality to clothes, as this charming little top illustrates.

The basic appliquéd top

Sizes
To fit 56 [61:66:71] cm chest
Length 37 [40:41:44] cm
Sleeve seam 23 [27:31:35] cm

Note: *Instructions for larger sizes are in brackets[ ]; where there is only one set of figures it applies to all sizes.*

Materials
200 [200:250:250] g of a four-ply yarn
Oddments of four-ply yarn in lemon, orange, green and white for fruit and leaves
3.00mm crochet hook

Tension
20tr and 10 rows to 10cm worked on 3.00mm hook

To save time, take time to check tension.

Note: *The top is worked in one piece, beginning at the lower edge of the back.*

Main piece
Back
Make 62 [67:72:77] ch.
Base row (RS) 1dc into 2nd ch from hook, 1dc into each ch to end. Turn. 61 [66:71:76] sts.
1st-6th rows 1ch to count as first dc, miss first st, 1dc into each st to end. Turn.
7th row 3ch, miss first st, 1tr into each st to end. Turn.
Rep last row until back measures 24 [26:27:29] cm from beg, ending with a WS row.
Shape sleeve
Using a separate length of yarn, make 45 [53:61:69] ch. Fasten off and return to main piece.
Next row Make 47 [55:63:71] ch, 1tr into 4th ch from hook, 1tr into each of next 43 [51:59:67] ch, 1tr into each of next 61 [66:71:76] sts across back, 1tr into first of separate length of ch, 1tr into each ch to end. Turn. 151 [172:193:214] sts.
Cont in tr on these sts without further shaping until sleeve measures 13 [14:14:15] cm from beg, ending with a WS row.

Shape neck
Using a separate length of yarn, make 39 [40:45:48] ch. Fasten off and return to main piece.
Next row 3ch, miss first st, 1tr into each of next 55 [65:73:82] sts, 1tr into first of separate length of ch, 1tr into each ch to end, miss next 39 [40:45:48] sts on main piece, 1tr into each st to end. Turn. 151 [172:193:214] sts.

SPECIAL TECHNIQUE
"doughboy" pockets

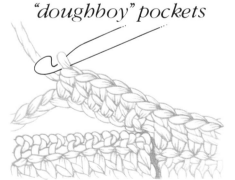

1 *After shaping the armholes at the front, work in treble for the length given in the pattern, ending with a wrong side row. Fasten off and turn. Miss stitches as instructed at the beginning of the next row and join yarn to the next stitch. Pattern the centre stitches as instructed. End with a wrong side row and fasten off.*

2 *Make a length of chain and fasten off. With right side facing, return to the stitches missed in step 1 and rejoin the yarn to the beginning of the row. Pattern across the missed stitches, place the length of chain behind the pocket and work one into each chain. Pattern across the stitches missed at the other edge.*

3 *Continue in treble on these stitches for the stated length, ending with a wrong side row. On the next row join the top of the pocket to the main fabric by working into both the pocket and pocket lining stitches. When the garment is completed, sew the top edge of the pocket lining to the wrong side of the front.*

Front and sleeve

Cont in tr on these sts without further shaping until sleeve measures 26 [28:28:30] cm from beg, ending with a WS row.

Fasten off and turn.

Shape front

With RS facing, miss first 45 [53:61:69] sts, using hook, rejoin yarn to next st.

Next row 3ch, miss first st at base of 3ch, 1tr into each of next 60 [65:70:75] sts, turn. 61 [66:71:76] sts.

Cont in tr on these sts without further shaping until front measures 8 [9:10:11] cm from armhole, ending with a WS row. Fasten off and turn.

Pocket

With Rs facing, miss first 13 [14:15:16] sts, using 3.00mm hook, rejoin yarn to next st.

Next row 3ch, miss first st at base of 3ch, 1tr into each of next 34 [37:40:43] sts. Turn. 35 [38:41:44] sts.

Cont in tr on these sts without further shaping until pocket measures 13 [14:14:15] cm from beg, ending with a WS row. Fasten off.

Pocket lining

Using a separate length of yarn, make 35 [38:41:44] ch. Fasten off and return to main piece. With RS facing, return to sts missed at beg of pocket and rejoin yarn to beg of row.

Next row 3ch, miss first st at base of 3ch, 1tr into each of next 12 [13:14:15] sts, place separate length of ch behind pocket, 1tr into first of separate length of ch, 1tr into each ch to end, miss pocket, 1tr into each of last 13 [14:15:16] sts on main piece. Turn. 61 [66:71:76] sts.

Cont in tr on these sts without further shaping until pocket lining measures 13 [14:14:15] cm from beg, ending with a WS row.

Join pocket

Next row 1ch to count as first dc, miss first st, 1dc into each of next 12 [13:14:15] sts, bring last row of pocket up in front of last row of pocket lining, 1dc into first st on pocket and next st on pocket lining, 1dc into each of next 34 [37:40:43] sts on pocket and pocket lining, 1dc into each of last 13 [14:15:16] sts on pocket lining, working through 2

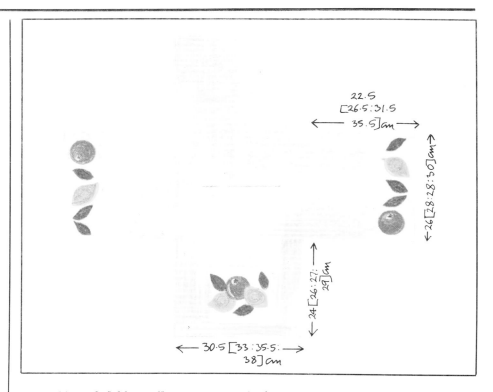

sts tog. Turn. 61 [66:71:76] sts. Cont in dc on these sts for 6 more rows. Fasten off.

To make up

Press very lightly on WS over a dry cloth with a warm iron.

Pocket edges (both alike)

With RS facing work a row of dc into side edge of pocket, working 2dc into each tr row end.

Work 4 more rows of dc. Fasten off. Sew dc row ends neatly to RS of front. Sew top of pocket lining to WS of front. Join sleeve and side seams, leaving 6 [7:7:8] cm open at bottom of each side seam to form slits.

Neck edging

With RS facing work one round of dc into neck edge, working 1dc into each st and joining last to first st with a ss. Fasten off.

Cuff edgings (both alike)

With RS facing work one round of dc into cuff edge, working 2dc into each tr row end and joining last to first st with a ss. Fasten off.

Lower edging

With RS facing join yarn to top of RH

slit.

Next row 1ch, 2dc into each row end to corner, 3dc into corner, 1dc into each st on last row of front, 3dc into corner, 2dc into each row end to top of LH slit, 2dc into each row end to corner, 3dc into corner, 1dc into each st on base row of back, 3dc into corner, 2dc into each row end to top of RH slit, ss to first ch. Fasten off.

Oranges (make 3)

Using orange, make 4ch, ss to first ch to form a circle.

1st round 8dc into circle.

2nd round 2dc into each of next 8dc. 16dc.

3rd round (2dc into next dc, 1dc into next dc) 8 times. 24dc.

4th round (2dc into next dc, 1dc into each of next 2dc) 8 times. 32dc.

5th round (2dc into next dc, 1dc into each of next 3dc) 8 times. 40dc.

Cont to inc 8dc on each round in this way until orange measures 5.5cm in diameter, ss to next dc. Fasten off. Make 2 more oranges in the same way, working a 'highlight' of 18dc in lemon yellow on the 5th round of one orange.

Lemons (make 4)
Using lemon yellow, work as for Oranges until work measures 4.5cm in diameter.
Next round * 1dc into next st, 1tr into next st, 2dtr into next st, 1tr into next st*, 1dc into each st to opposite side of circle, rep from * to * once more, 1dc into each st to end. Fasten off.
Make 3 more lemons in the same way, working a 'highlight' of 10dc in white on the 5th round of one lemon.

Leaves (make 9)
Using green, make 8ch.
1st round 1dc into 2nd ch from hook, 1dc into each of next 5ch, 3dc into last ch, 1dc into rem loop of each of next 6ch.
2nd round 3ch, miss next ch, * 1dc into next dc, 1htr into next dc, 1tr into each of next 3dc, 1htr into next dc, 1dc into next dc*, 1dc into next dc, rep from * to * once more, ss to first ch.
Fasten off.

Make 8 more leaves in the same way.

To make up
Using green, embroider one cross stitch on each orange to represent the stalk. Press each spiral on the WS over a dry cloth.
Sew 3 leaves, 2 lemons (including lemon with a white highlight) and the highlighted orange to the front pocket. Sew one orange, one lemon and 3 leaves to the lower edge of each sleeve.

Adapting the basic appliquéd top

Any of the spiral fruits and vegetables in the Pattern Library could be sewn on to the basic top. Use nature's colours for authenticity, choosing different shades to suggest, for example, the bloom on fruit or natural highlights and shadows. When sewing on the spirals, use matching yarn – split if necessary – and slip-stitches, worked just under the edge. Spiral shapes can be worked quite freely in double crochet, with other stitches, introduced to alter the shape; for example the lemons on the basic top are formed by working treble and double treble at opposite points on the spiral. You may need to experiment to obtain a convincing shape. Having a picture or the object itself in front of you while you work is a great help, especially when matching colours.

Pattern Library: Spiral patterns

Apple
Use red or green as the main colour, introducing yellow, white or pink as desired.
Work as for Orange on page 136 until work measures approx 5cm in diameter.
Next 2 rounds 1dc into each dc to opposite side of circle, ss into next st, 1dc into each dc to end.
Next round 1dc into each dc to opposite side of circle, ss into next ss. Fasten off.

Stalk Either embroider the stalk in stem stitch or join brown yarn to indentation on apple, work 4ch, ss into each ch, ss into join on apple. Fasten off.
Calyx Using brown, work a cross stitch on the opposite indentation to the stalk.
Leaf Work as given for Leaf on this page, using one or two shades of green as required.

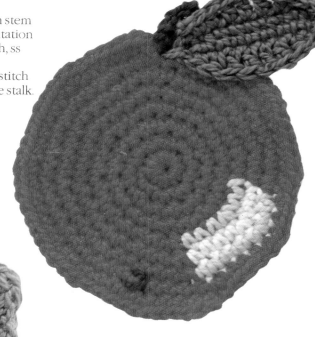

Lime
Use green as the main colour, introducing yellow and white as required. Work as for Lemon as given above.

Mushroom

Use natural for stalk and cap and brown for first row of cap.

Stalk Make 7ch.

1st round 1dc into 2nd ch from hook, 1dc into each of next 4ch, 3dc into last ch, 1dc into each of next 5 single loops on opposite side of ch, 3dc into turning ch.

Next round 1dc into each dc to end, working 3dc at each point. Fasten off.

Cap Join yarn 1cm from top of stalk.

Next row 3ch, miss st at base of join, 1tr into each dc to opposite side of stalk, ss into side of last tr worked, ss into next dc on stalk. Turn.

Next row 1dc into each st to end, ss into side of last tr, ss into next dc on stalk. Turn.

Next row Miss first ss, ss into first st, 2dc into each st to last 2 sts, ss into next st. Turn.

Rep last row twice more. Fasten off.

Pear

Use green or yellow as the main colour, introducing yellow, white or red as required. Work as for Orange on page 136 until work measures approx 4cm in diameter.

Next round 10ch, 1dc into 2nd ch from hook, 1dc into each of next 8ch, 1dc into each dc on circle, 1dc into each of next 9 single loops on opposite side of ch, 3dc into last st.

Next round 1dc into each dc to 3dc worked on last round, 1dc into next dc, 3dc into next dc, 1dc into each of next 2dc, work in htr to within 4 sts of circle, work in tr to end.

Rep last round once more, working htr and tr into other edge of top. Fasten off.

Stalk and calyx Work as for Apple, working stalk into top of pear and calyx into opposite edge.

Leaf Work as for leaf of Orange, on page 137.

Tomato

Use red as main colour, highlighting work with pink and white.

Work as for Orange on page 136 until work measures approx 4cm in diameter. Fasten off.

Stalk Using green, make 5ch.

1st row Ss into 2nd ch from hook, 3dc into next ch, ss into each of last 2ch. Fasten off.

Rejoin yarn to centre of 3dc worked on last row, make 3ch, 1dc into 2nd ch from hook, 1dc into last ch, ss into join. Fasten off.

Cherries

Use red as main colour, introducing pink and white as highlights.

Work as for Orange on page 136 until work measures approx 2.5cm in diameter. Fasten off.

Leaf Work as for Apple.

Stalk Join green to edge of Cherry, make a ch the required length, ss into each ch, ss into edge of Cherry at join. Fasten off.

Chapter 3
Edgings and Trimmings

Picot and shell edgings

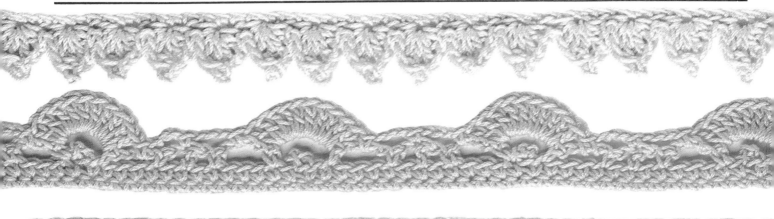

Pointed shell edging (1)

Worked on a base row of double crochet over a multiple of 3 stitches either directly on to the main fabric or as a separate edging.

Picot row (RS) 1ch, miss first dc, miss one st, (1dc, 1htr, 1tr, 1dtr, 2ch, ss into top of dtr, 1tr, 1htr, 1dc) into next dc – called shell –, *miss 2dc, 1 shell into next dc, rep from * to end, working 1dc into edge.

Lace shell edging (2)

Worked on a base row of double crochet with a number of stitches divisible by 13 plus 5, either directly on to your fabric or as a separate edging.

1st row (RS) 1ch, miss first dc, 1dc into each of next 9dc, 3ch, ss into first of these 3ch – called picot –, *1dc into each of next 13dc, 1 picot, rep from * ending last rep with 9dc, working last dc into turning ch. Turn.

2nd row 2ch, miss first st, miss next st, 1tr into next st, 1ch, miss one st, 1dc into next st, *4ch, miss 3 sts, 1dc into next dc before picot, 5ch, 1dc into dc after picot, 4ch, miss 3 sts, 1dc into next dc, 1ch, miss one st, 1tr into next st, 1ch, miss one st, 1dc into next dc, rep from * to end, 1dc into turning ch. Turn.

3rd row *3ch, 1dc into next tr, 3ch, 1dc into next 4ch sp, 10tr into next 5ch sp, 1dc into next 4ch sp, rep from * to end, 3ch, 1dc into next tr, 2ch, 1dc into turning ch.

Looped picot edging (3)

Worked on a base row of double crochet with any number of stitches, either directly on to main fabric or as a separate edging.

Picot row (RS) Ss into first st, *4ch, ss into first of these ch – called picot –, ss into next st, rep from * to end.

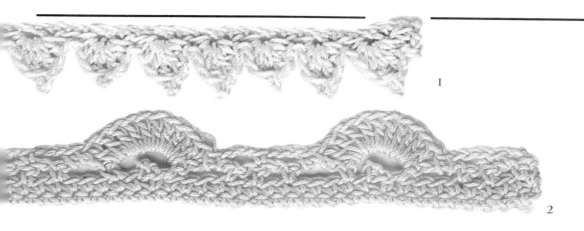

1

2

3

Irish picot edging (4)

Work at least one or more base rows of double crochet with a multiple of 3 sts, either directly on to your fabric or as a separate edging.

Picot row (RS) 1ch, miss first dc, 1dc into each of next 2dc, *4ch, remove hook and insert into first of ch just worked, pick up 4th ch and draw through first ch, 1dc into each of next 3dc, rep from * to end.

Frilled edging (5)

Work on a base row of double crochet with a multiple of 4 plus 3 stitches, either directly on to the main fabric or as a separate edging.

1st row 5ch, miss 2 sts, 1dc into next st, *5ch, miss one st, 1dc into next st, rep from * to end, working last dc into turning ch. Turn.

2nd row (RS) 3ch, 2tr into first 5ch loop, 3ch, 3tr into same loop, *2ch, ss into next 5ch loop, 2ch, (3tr, 3ch, 3tr) into next loop, rep from * to end.

3rd row 1ch, miss first dc, 1dc into each tr and ss and 5dc into each 3ch sp to end.

Buttonhole edging (6)

Worked on a base row of double crochet with a multiple of 4 plus 1 sts, either directly on to the main fabric or as a separate edging.

1st row (RS) 1ch, miss first dc, 1dc into each dc to end, 1dc into turning ch. Break off yarn and return to beg of row.

2nd row (RS) As first. Break off yarn and return to beg of row.

3rd row (RS) 1ch, miss first dc, * 6ch, miss 3dc, 1dc into next dc, rep from * to end, working last dc into last st. Turn.

4th row 1ch, miss first st, *1ss into top loop of each of next 6ch, 1ss into next dc, rep from * to end.

Panels

Large flower panel (1)

Make 28ch.

Base row 1tr into 6th ch from hook, (1ch, miss next ch, 1tr into next ch) 11 times. Turn.

1st row (RS) 4ch, miss first tr, 1tr into next tr, (1ch, 1tr into next tr) 3 times, 4ch, miss next tr, 1dtr into next tr, 4ch, miss next tr, 1tr into next tr, (1ch, 1tr into next tr) 3 times, 1ch, 1tr into last sp. Turn.

2nd row 4ch, miss first tr, 1tr into next tr, (1ch, 1tr into next tr) twice, 4ch, 1dc into next 4ch sp, 1dc into next dtr, 1dc into next 4ch sp, 4ch, miss next tr, 1tr into next tr, (1ch, 1tr into next tr) twice, 1ch, 1tr into last sp. Turn.

3rd row 4ch, miss first tr, 1tr into next tr, 1ch, 1tr into next tr, 5ch, 1tr into next 4ch sp, 1tr into each of next 3dc, 1tr into next 4ch sp, 5ch, miss next tr, (1tr into next tr, 1ch) twice, 1tr into last sp. Turn.

4th row 4ch, miss first tr, (1tr into next tr, 1ch) twice, 1tr into next 5ch sp, 5ch, miss next tr, 1dc into each of next 3tr, 5ch, 1tr into next 5ch sp, (1ch, 1tr into next tr) twice, 1ch, 1tr into last sp. Turn.

5th row 4ch, miss first tr, (1tr into next tr, 1ch) 3 times, 1tr into next 5ch sp, 3ch, 1dtr into centre dc of next 3dc, 3ch, 1tr into next 5ch sp, 1ch, (1tr into next tr, 1ch) 3 times, 1tr into last sp. Turn.

6th row 4ch, miss first tr, (1tr into next tr, 1ch) 4 times, 1tr into next 3ch sp, 1ch, 1tr into next dtr, 1ch, 1tr into next 3ch sp, 1ch, (1tr into next tr, 1ch) 4 times, 1tr into last sp. Turn.

7th row 4ch, miss first tr, (1tr into next tr, 1ch) 11 times, 1tr into last. Turn.

8th row As 7th row.

Rep first-8th rows for length required.

1

Ribbon coronet panel (2)

Make 35ch.

Base row Miss first 3ch, (1tr into next ch, 3ch, miss next 2ch, 1dc into next ch, 3ch, miss next 2ch, 1tr into next ch, 5ch, miss next 5ch) twice, 1tr into next ch, 3ch, miss next 2ch, 1dc into next ch, 3ch, miss next 2ch, 1tr into each of last 2ch. Turn.

1st row (RS) 3ch, miss first tr, 1tr into next tr, (5ch, 7tr into next 5ch sp) twice, 5ch, 1tr into next tr, 1tr into top of 3ch. Turn.

2nd row 3ch, miss first tr, 1tr into next tr, (3ch, 1dc into next 5ch sp, 3ch, 1dc into first tr of group, 5ch, 1tr into last tr of group) twice, 3ch, 1dc into next 5ch loop, 3ch, 1tr into next tr, 1tr into top of 3ch. Turn.

Rep first and 2nd rows for length required. Thread ribbon as shown.

2

Crown lacet panel (3)

Make 35ch.

Base row 1tr into 4th ch from hook, (3ch, miss next 2ch, 1dc into next ch, 3ch, miss next 2ch, 1tr into next ch) 5 times, 1tr into last ch. Turn. 5 lacets formed.

1st row (RS) 3ch, miss first tr, 1tr into next tr, (5ch, 1tr into next tr) 5 times, 1tr into top of last 3ch. Turn. 5 bars formed.

2nd row 3ch, miss first tr, 1tr into next tr, (3ch, 1dc into next 5ch sp, 3ch, 1tr into next tr) twice, 5tr into next 5ch sp, 1tr into next tr, (3ch, 1dc into next 5ch sp, 3ch, 1tr into next tr) twice, 1tr into top of 3ch. Turn. 2 lacets, 1 block, 2 lacets formed.

3rd row 3ch, miss first tr, 1tr into next tr, (5ch, 1tr into next tr) twice, (1tr into next tr) 6 times, (5ch, 1tr into next tr) twice, 1tr into top of 3ch. Turn. 2 bars, 1 block, 2 bars formed.

4th row 3ch, miss first tr, 1tr into next tr, 3ch, 1dc into next 5ch sp, 3ch, 1tr into next tr, 5tr into next 5ch sp, 1tr into next tr, 3ch, 1dc into centre tr of group, 3ch, 1tr into last tr of group, 5tr into next 5ch sp, 1tr into next tr, 3ch, 1dc into next 5ch sp, 3ch, 1tr into next tr, 1tr into top of 3ch. Turn. 1 lacet, 1 block, 1 lacet, 1 block, 1 lacet formed.

Keeping 2tr at each side edge as before, work rem patt rows as foll:

5th row 1 bar, 1 block, 1 bar, 1 block, 1 bar.

6th row 2 lacets, 1 block, 2 lacets.

7th row 2 bars, 1 block, 2 bars.

8th row 5 lacets.

Rep first-8th rows for length required.

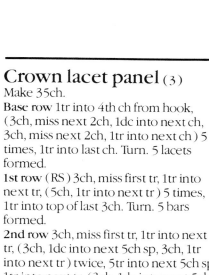

3

5

4

Ribbon lacet panel (4)

Make 30ch.

Base row (2tr, 2ch, 2tr) into 6th ch from hook, *5ch, miss next 7ch, (2tr, 2ch, 2tr) into next ch, rep from * twice more. Turn.

1st row (RS) 5ch, (2tr, 2ch, 2tr) into first 2ch sp, *3ch, 1dc into next 5ch sp, 3ch, (2tr, 2ch, 2tr) into next 2ch sp, rep from * twice more. Turn.

2nd row 5ch, (2tr, 2ch, 2tr) into first 2ch sp, *5ch, (2tr, 2ch, 2tr) into next 2ch sp, rep from * twice more. Turn. Rep first and 2nd rows for length required. Thread ribbon as shown.

Stepped panel (5)

Make 32ch.

Base row (RS) Miss first 5ch, *(1tr into next ch, 1ch, miss next ch) twice, 1tr into each of next 6ch, 1ch, miss next ch, rep from * once more, (1tr into next ch, 1ch, miss next ch) twice, 1tr into last ch. Turn.

1st row 4ch, miss first 1ch sp, 1tr into next sp, 1ch, 1tr into next sp, *5ch, (1tr into next sp, 1ch) twice, 1tr into next sp, rep from * once more. Turn.

2nd row 4ch, 1tr into first 1ch sp, 1ch, 1tr into next sp, 1ch, *6tr into next 5ch sp, (1ch, 1tr into next sp) twice, 1ch, rep from * once more, 1tr into last sp. Turn. Rep first and 2nd rows for length required.

Buttons

Two-colour unfilled button

Drawstring glitter button

Two-colour ball button

Two-colour unfilled button

Use 2 colours, A and B. Using A, make 3ch.

1st round 1ch, 7dc into circle, join with a ss to first ch.

2nd round Working from *left to right* 1ch, miss first dc, 1dc into front loop only of each st to end, join with a ss to first ch. Fasten off.

3rd round Join in B. Working from right to left, 1ch, miss first dc, 2dc into back loop only of each st to end, join with a ss to first ch.

4th round As 2nd round.

5th round 1ch, miss first dc, 1dc into back loop only of each st to end, join with a ss to first ch.

6th round 1ch, miss first dc, *1dc, dec 1dc over next 2 sts, rep from * to end, join with a ss to first ch.

7th round 1ch, miss first dc, *dec 1dc over next 2 sts, rep from * twice, 1dc into next dc. Fasten off.

Drawstring glitter button

Make 3ch. Work as first and 2nd rounds of Drawstring button.

3rd round 1ch, miss first dc, 1dc into each st to end, join with a ss to first ch.

4th round 11ch, miss first dc, *dec 1dc over next 2 sts, 1dc, rep from * to end, join with a ss to first ch. Fasten off, leaving 20cm of yarn. Weave yarn through each st of 4th round and complete as Drawstring button.

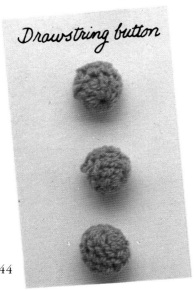

Drawstring button

Drawstring button

Make 3ch, ss to first ch to form a circle.

1st round 3ch, 11tr into circle, join with a ss to 3rd of first 3ch.

2nd round 1ch, miss first tr, 1dc into each st to end, join with a ss to first ch.

3rd round As 2nd round.

Fasten off, leaving 20cm of yarn. Weave yarn through each st of 3rd round. Fill button with small amount of yarn and draw up to secure.

Two-colour ball button

Use 2 colours, A and B.

Using A, make 4ch, ss to first ch to form a circle.

1st round 3ch, 9tr into circle, join with a ss to 3rd of first 3ch. Fasten off.

2nd round Using B, 1ch, miss first tr, *1dc into circle, 1dc into next tr, rep from * to end, 1dc into circle, join with a ss to first ch.

3rd round 1ch, miss first dc, 1dc into each st to end, join with a ss to first ch.

4th round 1ch, miss first dc, *dec 1dc over next 2 sts, rep from * 3 times, 1dc into next dc, join with a ss to first ch. Fasten off leaving 20cm of yarn. Weave yarn through 4th round and complete as Drawstring button.

Cluster button

Before beginning wind off a small ball of yarn for padding.

Make 5ch, ss to first ch to form a circle.

1st round 4ch, leaving last loop of each st on hook, work 2dtr into circle, yrh, draw through 3 loops on hook, (leaving last loop of each st on hook, 3dtr into circle, yrh, draw through 4 loops on hook) 7 times, join with a ss to 4th of first 4ch.

2nd round 1ch, (dec 1dc over next 2 sts) 4 times, inserting small ball of yarn as button closes.

Fasten off tightly.

Cluster button

Chapter 4
Know ~ How

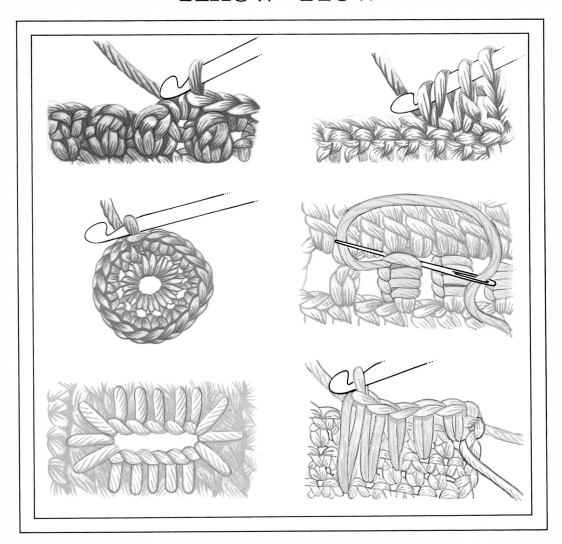

Basic stitches and techniques

Foundation chain (ch)

1 Make a slip loop and place it over the hook. Hold the hook in your right hand as if you were holding a pencil.

2 Thread the yarn as shown between the fingers of the left hand so that it will flow freely and evenly.

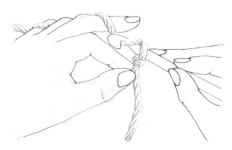

3 Take the yarn round the hook and draw through the loop to make the first chain. After making a few chain, move up your finger and thumb to just below the hook.

Slip stitch (ss)

1 To work slip stitch along a foundation chain, insert the hook from front to back under the top two loops of the second chain from the hook. Take the yarn anti-clockwise round the hook and draw it through the chain and the loop on the hook — one loop remains and one slip stitch has been worked. Continue in this way to the end.

2 Slip stitch is often used when shaping. When the required number of slip stitches has been worked, slip stitch into the next stitch, work the turning chain to count as the first stitch (here we show two, for a half treble fabric) and continue in pattern.

3 Slip stitch is also used when working in rounds to join the last stitch of the round to the first. After the last stitch has been worked, insert the hook into the top of the turning chain, which counts at the first stitch, and work a slip stitch.

Double crochet (dc)

1 To work the base row, miss the first of the foundation chain and insert the hook from front to back under the top two loops of the second chain from the hook. Take the yarn round the hook and draw through a loop — two loops on the hook.

2 Take the yarn round the hook and draw it through the two loops on the hook — one loop remains and one double crochet has been worked. Work one double crochet into the next and every foundation chain, then turn the work so that the hook is once more at the beginning.

3 To begin the next row work one turning chain to count as the first stitch. Miss the last stitch of the previous row and work one double crochet into every following stitch, working the last double crochet into the turning chain of the previous row. Repeat as often as desired to make a double crochet fabric.

Half-treble (htr)

1 To work the base row take the yarn round the hook and insert the hook from front to back under the top two loops of the third chain from the hook. Take the yarn round the hook and draw through a loop — three loops on the hook.

2 Take the yarn round the hook and draw through all three loops — one loop remains and one half treble has been worked. Take the yarn round the hook and work a half treble as before into the next chain. Continue in this way to the last chain. Turn the work.

3 Work two chain to count as the first half treble. Miss the first half treble of the previous row and work into the next stitch.

4 Work one half treble into each half treble to the turning chain. Then work one half treble into the top of the turning chain and turn.

Treble (tr)

1 Make a chain the length needed. Take the yarn anti-clockwise round the hook. Miss the first three chain and insert the hook from front to back under the top two loops of the fourth chain from the hook. (The three chain missed at the beginning should be counted as the first treble.)

2 Take the yarn anti-clockwise over the hook and draw through the chain — three loops on the hook.

3 Take the yarn anti-clockwise over the hook. Draw the yarn through the first two loops on the hook — two loops remain on the hook.

4 Take the yarn anti-clockwise round the hook. Draw the yarn through the remaining two loops on the hook — one treble has been worked and one loop only remains on the hook.

Double treble (dtr)

1 To work the base row, take the yarn anti-clockwise round the hook twice and insert the hook from front to back under the top two loops of the fifth chain from the hook. Take the yarn once round the hook, through the chain and draw yarn over it through the first two loops on the hook — three loops remain on the hook.

2 Take the yarn round the hook and draw it through the first two loops on the hook — two loops remain. Take the yarn round the hook and draw it through the remaining two loops on the hook — one loop remains and one double treble has been worked. Continue working double treble in this way into the next and each chain to the end. Turn.

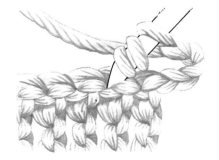

3 At the beginning of the next and every following row work four turning chain to count as the first double treble. At the end of each row work the last double treble into the top of the turning chain.

Triple and quadruple treble (tr tr and qtr)

These long stitches are usually worked as part of a more intricate stitch pattern.

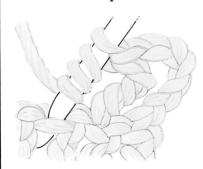

1 Begin a triple treble row with five turning chain. Yarn round hook three times and insert the hook into the next stitch. Yarn round hook and draw through a loop — five loops on hook. * Yarn round hook and draw through first two loops on hook*, repeat from *to* three more times until there is one loop left on the hook. One triple treble has been completed.

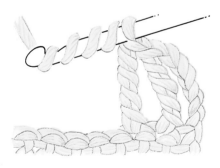

2 Quadruple treble is worked in the same way except that each row begins with six turning chain and the yarn is wound four times round the hook. Insert the hook into the next stitch and work from * to * five times when one loop will remain.

Fastening off

Work the last stitch of the last row in the usual way. Cut the yarn to approximately 5 in. Take the yarn over the hook and draw through the loop on the hook to fasten off.

Joining in new yarn

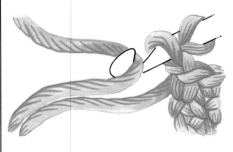

Always join new yarn at the end of a row. Insert hook into turning chain, yarn round hook and draw through a loop — two loops on hook. Cut off old yarn to 5 in. Complete stitch using the new yarn.

Using two colours

1 To change colours on any crochet fabric, work the stitch (treble shown above) as usual until there are two loops on the hook. Drop the old colour and draw the new colour through two loops on hook.

2 When working in stripes, change colour as in step 1 on the last stitch of row, drawing the new colour through the last two loops on the hook. Work the turning chain in the new colour.

3 Use separate balls of yarn when working large areas in one colour. However, when working only a few stitches in each colour, carry the colour not in use loosely on the wrong side at the base of the row working over it with the other colour.

Increasing

1 To increase one stitch in a double crochet, half treble or treble fabric, simply work two stitches into the top of one stitch of the previous row. Although increases are usually worked at the edges of the fabric, they can, if desired, be worked into any stitch of the row.

2 It may be possible (depending on the pattern) to achieve a neater edge when increasing by working all the extra stitches one stitch in from each edge. At the beginning of the row, work the turning chain and miss the first stitch, work two stitches into the next stitch; at the end of the row, work to within the last two stitches (including the turning chain) and work two stitches into the next stitch and one stitch into the top of the turning chain.

3 Occasionally it may be necessary to increase two or more stitches into one stitch of the previous row. To increase two stitches into one stitch, simply work three stitches all into one stitch (i.e. two increased stitches plus the original stitch).

Decreasing

Decreases can be worked into any stitches but are usually worked near the edge.

1 To decrease one double crochet stitch, insert the hook into the next stitch, yarn round hook and draw through a loop — two loops on the hook; insert the hook into the next stitch, yarn round hook and draw through a loop — three loops on the hook; yarn round hook and draw through three loops — one double decreased.

2 To decrease one half-treble stitch, take the yarn round the hook, insert the hook into the next stitch, yarn round hook and draw through a loop — three loops on the hook; yarn round hook, insert the hook into the next stitch and work as before until five loops remain; yarn round hook and draw through all five loops — one half treble decreased.

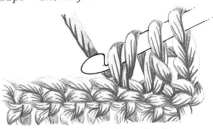

3 To decrease one treble, take the yarn round the hook, insert the hook into the next stitch, yarn round hook and draw through a loop — three loops on the hook, yarn round hook and draw through the first two loops — two loops on the hook. Work the next stitch as before until three loops remain, yarn round hook and draw through all three loops — one treble decreased.

149

Berry stitch

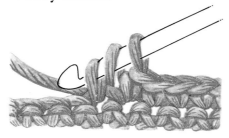

1 With the wrong *side facing, work to the position of the berry stitch. Wind the yarn anti-clockwise round the hook and insert the hook into the next stitch. Wind the yarn round the hook and draw through a loop loosely. Wind the yarn round the hook and draw through the first loop on the hook — three loops remain on the hook.*

2 *Wind the yarn round the hook and insert the hook into the same stitch as in step 1. Wind the yarn round the hook and draw through a loose loop as before — five loops on the hook. Wind the yarn round the hook and draw through the first four loops on the hook — two loops remain.*

3 *Draw the yarn through the remaining two loops — one loop remains and one berry stitch has been formed. When working an all-over berry stitch fabric, keep the work even by slip stitching into the next stitch and by working, on the following right side row, a slip stitch into the top of each berry and a double crochet into the top of each slip stitch.*

Bullion stitches

Bullion stitches are tiny bobbles which are usually combined with other stitches to form a variety of textured patterns.

1 *To work a small bullion stitch, make any number of chain plus three turning chain. Wind the yarn three times only round the shank of the hook.*

2 *Securing the loops on the hook with the third finger of the left hand, insert the hook into the fourth chain from the hook. Wind the yarn round the hook and draw through a loop — five loops are now on the hook.*

3 *Keeping the working yarn taut, wind it round the hook and draw through all loops on the hook to form a smooth, even roll. It may be difficult at first to draw through all loops in one movement; if so, you can either draw the hook through loops one at a time or lift loops off the hook with your fingers.*

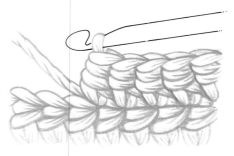

4 *Continue in this way, working a bullion stitch into each chain. On following rows work into the two top horizontal loops of each stitch.*

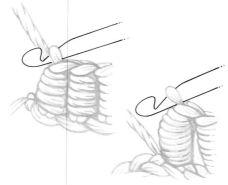

5 *Larger bullion stitches — which require more turning chain — are worked by winding the yarn more times round the hook. The stitches on the left were formed from five loops and the stitches on the right from ten. Using a larger hook than usual will make it easier to draw the hook through the greater number of loops.*

Rice stitches

Rice stitches are worked in much the same way as bullion stitches. Again, practice is necessary for good results.

1 *To work small rice stitch, make an odd number of chain plus three turning chain. Wind the yarn three times round the hook.*

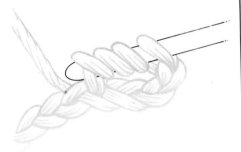

2 *Insert the hook into the fourth chain from the hook and draw a loop through the chain and through the four loops on the hook to complete the first rice stitch.*

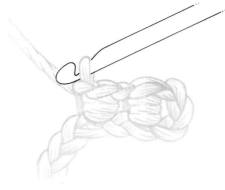

3 *Work one chain, miss the next foundation chain and work a rice stitch into the next stitch. Continue in this way to the end. On following rows work rice stitch into the chain spaces, working one chain after each individual stitch.*

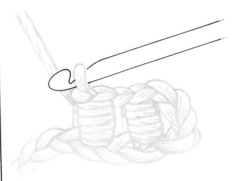

4 *Larger stitches can be worked by winding the yarn more times round the hook. Again, using a larger hook and winding the yarn round the shank will make it easier to draw the hook through the loops. Try to keep an even tension at the same time.*

Graduated-stitch patterns

It is easily possible in crochet to work stitches of different heights – 'graduated stitches' – in the same row. This characteristic of crochet can be used to create interesting wave-like patterns.

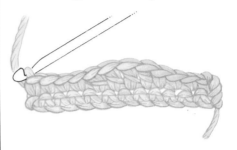

1 *A simple pattern, based on a combination of doubles and trebles illustrates this technique very well. After a base row of double crochet, begin the first row with four double crochet followed by four treble. Work these double and treble crochet alternately along the row to produce a series of tall and short stitches.*

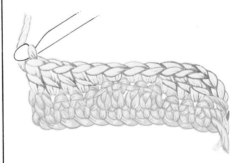

2 *On the next row, to prevent the fabric from wrinkling, compensate for the unevenness of the previous row by working tall stitches into the short stitches and vice versa. So work treble into the double crochet and double crochet into the treble. Note: When working these patterns, emphasize the wavy appearance by using contrasting yarns.*

Elongated stitches

Zigzag effects can be created easily by working double crochet stitches of varying lengths over a double crochet fabric in a contrast colour.

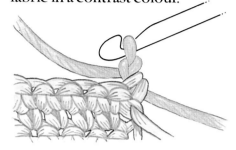

1 Work the required number of double crochet rows in the first colour. Drop this colour and join in a contrast colour. Make one chain and miss the first stitch.

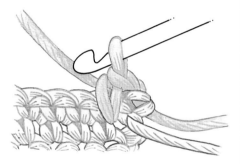

2 Miss the last row in the first colour and insert the hook into the preceding row one stitch to the left. Work a double crochet as usual, extending the yarn so that the fabric is not pulled out of shape.

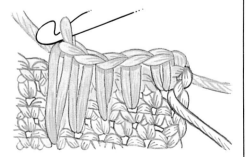

3 Insert the hook one row below and one stitch to the left of the last point. Work a double crochet as usual. Continue in this way until the slope is the desired length.

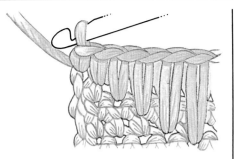

4 Work the second side of the zigzag in the same way, still working one stitch to the left but one row higher each time. Complete the pattern by working one double crochet into the last row in the first colour, then work double crochet into the turning chain.

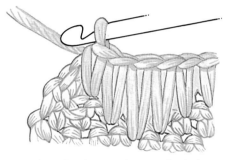

5 When shaping an elongated-stitch fabric, work the decreasing or increasing in the ordinary double crochet rows. Then adjust the zigzag pattern to fit.

Working afghan squares in rounds

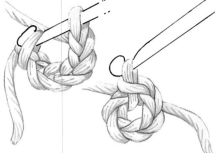

1 Make a small number of chain — usually between four and six — and join them into a ring with a slip stitch; insert hook in first chain, yarn round hook, and draw through chain and through loop on hook.

2 On the first round, work four groups of treble (here there are four stitches in each group) into the ring, separating the groups with two chain. Fasten off.

3 To begin the next round, join the new colour to the next chain space and work three chain to count as the first treble. On this and following rounds, work two treble groups separated by chain spaces at each corner, and one group of treble into each chain space along the sides.

152

Working in continuous rounds

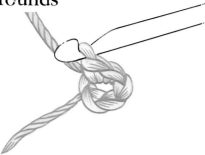

1 Many patterns and motifs are worked in continuous rounds of crochet. At the beginning of the first and following round, omit the one chain that is normal when working rounds of double crochet.

2 To end a round, work one double crochet into the last stitch. Do not join the first and last stitch with a slip stitch as usual, but simply begin the next round by working one double crochet into the first stitch of the round.

3 To change colour when working continuous rounds, work the last double crochet in the old colour. Insert hook into first stitch of round and draw through new colour. Continue in pattern, working into same place as join, using the new colour and working over the end of the old colour.

Lacets

Lacets are two-row patterns, formed from a combination of V-shaped *lacets* and chain *bars*.

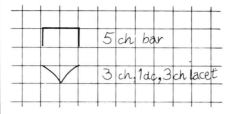

| | 5 ch bar |
| | 3 ch, 1 dc, 3 ch lacet |

1 Patterns may be formed entirely from lacets, but often the lacets are combined with filet spaces and blocks; in this case filet charts and are used. The symbols are given in the diagram above, which also shows the number of chain in the lacet and bar.

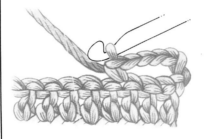

2 Begin with the lacet row. Make six chain to count as the first treble and three chain. Miss the first three stitches and work one double crochet into the next stitch. Make three chain; miss the next two stitches and work one treble into the next stitch

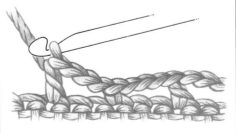

3 Make three chain, miss the next two stitches and work one double crochet into the next stitch. Make three chain, miss the next two stitches and work one treble into the next stitch. This step forms the lacet and is repeated to the end.

4 Work the bar on the next row. Begin with eight chain to count as the first treble and five chains. Miss the first treble and work one treble into the next treble. * Work five chain to form the next bar and work one into the next treble. Repeat from *.

5 To work a lacet over a bar, work the treble into the treble of the bar row and work the double crochet into the third of five chain of each bar.

Irish crochet

Working over a cord

To give a raised effect, Irish motifs may be worked over a cord. For the cord use either three or four strands of cotton twisted together or a thicker cotton in the same colour. When the motif is finished, cut the cord close to the stitches.

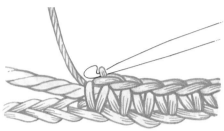

1 Having worked the foundation chain, hold the cord at the back of the work in the left hand. Work into the chain and over the cord at the same time.

2 At the end of the row, turn and work the next row over the cord, still holding the cord at the back of the work.

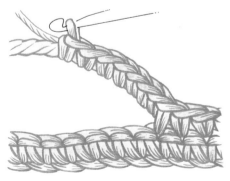

3 To work over the cord alone, hold it away from main body of the crochet, and work along the cord, pushing the stitches together to cover the cord.

Traditional method of working Irish crochet

For the basic outline of the garment, choose a fairly simple dressmaking pattern without elaborate shaping. Make the pattern in a medium-weight interfacing, omitting shoulder seams and cutting away seam or hem allowances on the front, neck and lower edges. Ignore facings and do not seam or set in the sleeves, if any.

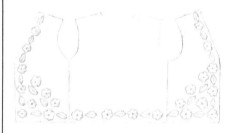

1 Lay the seamed pattern pieces out flat and arrange the motifs on the interfacing as you wish. Pin and tack the motifs firmly to the interfacing.

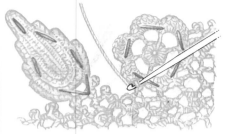

2 Using a matching yarn, fill in the spaces between the pattern motifs with picot mesh. Join the mesh to the edge of the motifs as you work using double crochet or slip stitch. Do not worry if the mesh seems irregular. This is unavoidable, and adds to the beauty of the lace.

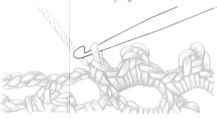

3 Remove the work from the interfacing and, after blocking, join shoulder and sleeve seams and set in sleeves. Work a narrow picot edging along the neck, front and lower edges, or work a separate edging and sew it to the mesh.

Embroidery on crochet

A good way of varying simple crochet fabrics is by embroidering them. For beginners a double crochet fabric, worked with a firm tension in double knitting yarn on a 4.00mm hook, is the ideal fabric. Other stitches, such as treble, can also be decorated, but working the embroidery on the looser fabric produced is more difficult.

Embroidery on double crochet

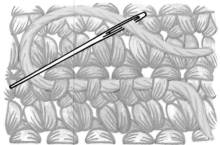

1 Thread the embroidery yarn—double knitting is probably easiest for beginners—into a large-eyed tapestry needle. When working embroidery to cover an area secure the yarn by threading it through the centre of a few stitches on the right side of fabric. Work over the end of yarn when embroidering.

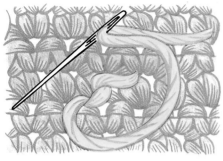

2 *To secure the yarn when working running stitch or stem stitch, work a small backstitch on the wrong side of the crochet fabric, making sure that the fabric is not pulled out of shape and that the backstitch is invisible on the right side.*

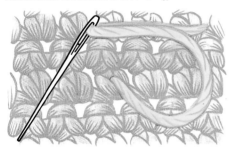

3 *When working the embroidery, try to insert the needle through the centre of the stitches. Working between rows of stitches could easily pull the crochet out of shape, so forming a hole.*

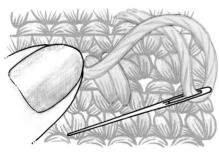

4 *Never pull the embroidery yarn too tightly through crochet, as this could pucker the fabric. Holding the yarn with the thumb and forefinger of the left hand while you draw it through the fabric should help you to keep the tension loose. To fasten off the embroidery yarn, take it to the back of the work and run it through the embroidery stitches. Cut off the end close to the stitches.*

Embroidery on treble crochet

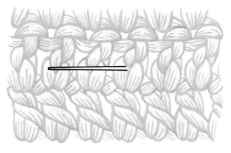

1 *When working an all-over or free-hand embroidery design on treble or mesh fabrics, insert the needle through the centre of the stitches as for double crochet.*

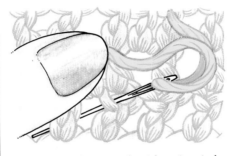

2 *Outline filet motifs with satin stitch. Work the embroidery stitches very loosely, holding the yarn as in step 4 above to avoid puckering the filet and inserting the needle into the top of each treble.*

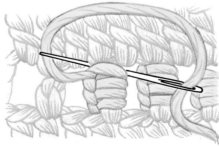

3 *Decorate a treble and chain space fabric by working buttonhole stitch loosely round the treble.*

Surface slip stitch

This resembles embroidered chain stitch, but is worked with a crochet hook.

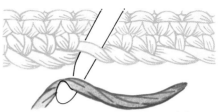

1 *Use either one or two strands of yarn, depending on how raised you want the crochet to be. Hold the yarn at the back (wrong side) of the work and insert the hook from front to back into the foundation chain and draw through a loop to the front.*

2 *Insert the hook from front to back into the first row. Wind the yarn round the hook and draw through a loop to the front of the work to form the first slip stitch and to secure the yarn firmly.*

3 *Continue in this way up the fabric. You can work either a straight line or zigzags or curves. Your instructions will tell you to work into, for example, 'one row above stitch to the right' or the pattern will be shown in chart form.*

155

Jacquard patterns

Working from charts

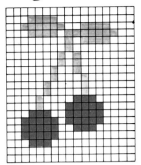

1 Odd-numbered rows are shown on the right-hand side of the chart and even-numbered rows on the left. Read odd-numbered rows from right to left and even-numbered rows from left to right

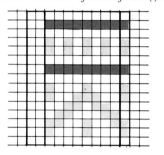

2 On 'Fair Isle' charts the stitches shown within the bold lines are repeated across the row, while those outside these lines are worked at the beginning and end of the rows only.

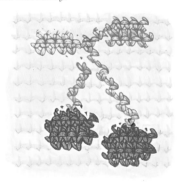

3 Patterns may sometimes instruct you to 'reverse the chart' to produce a mirror image. The illustration above is a mirror image of the chart in step 1. This is done simply by reading the odd-numbered rows from left to right and the even-numbered rows from right to left.

Stranding yarn

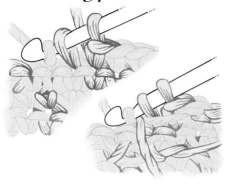

1 When working jacquard patterns, change colours as shown on page 149. In repeating patterns, as in step 2 of 'Working from charts', strand the yarn not in use loosely at the back of the work on right-side rows (above left). On wrong-side rows strand the yarn at the front of work (above right).

2 It is possible to work over the yarn not in use (see page 149) to produce a double fabric. This technique can also be used when introducing a new ball of yarn. Work over the ends as shown to avoid darning in ends when the work is completed.

Working large motifs

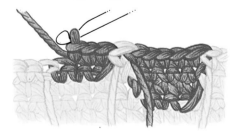

1 When working individual motifs, such as the cherries in step 1 of 'Working from charts', do not waste yarn by stranding. Instead, use a separate ball of yarn for each section of colour. To

prevent tangles, use metre-long pieces of yarn. Although these will tangle, they are fairly short and so it is easy to pull each length free as required.

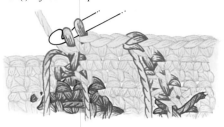

2 Change colour as usual, but leave the old colour hanging on the wrong side of the work, ready for the return row. If necessary, however, strand across a few stitches — for example, across the cherry stems.

Charting motifs

1 Work a tension square in your yarn; for best results work in double crochet. Draw a graph showing the number of stitches and rows required to make the motif the desired size; each square represents one stitch. Sketch the motif on to the graph. Using suitable colours, block in the shape. Where more than half of a square falls within the outline, colour it in; where less than half, leave it blank.

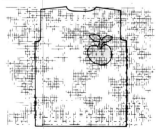

2 To position a motif, draw the outline of the garment on graph paper. Place the motif as required on the graph and follow this chart when making the garment.

Picture jacquard

As a base for the design use an existing pattern for a garment worked in double crochet.

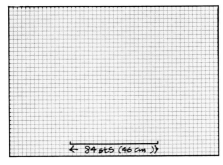

1 Use large sheets of graph paper and a sharp pencil. Count the number of double crochet on the front across the first row after the welt (on a pullover, the same as for the back) plus any increasing.

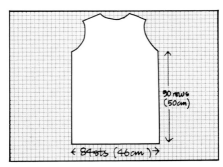

2 Count off and mark the number of rows to the armhole shaping. If the pattern is not specific, multiply the number of rows to 10cm as given under 'Tension' by the length in centimetres to the armholes, then divide by 10. Then draw in any shaping.

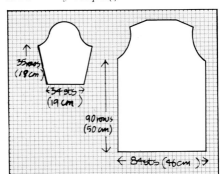

3 If you want to extend the pattern across the back and sleeves, draw these outlines in the same way.

Charting the picture

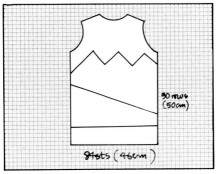

1 Because double crochet — which is best for picture jacquard — often has the same number of stitches and rows to 10cm, a picture can be drawn directly on to the graph. If the stitch is not square, take this into account when transferring the picture.

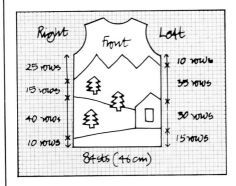

2 Next add finer detail. The amount of this depends on the thickness of the yarn: the finer the yarn, the more detail is possible. Whatever the yarn, however, very fine details, such as those used on the winter sweater on page 52, are best embroidered.

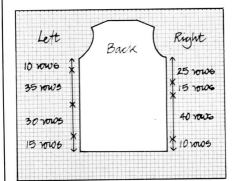

3 If you want to continue the picture on the back, it must match precisely at the side seams. Count the number of rows to the first outline on both edges of the front and mark the corresponding squares at each edge on the back. Continue marking other corresponding outlines in the same way.

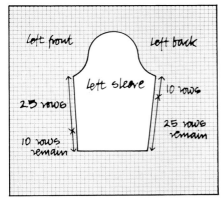

4 To extend the picture on to the left sleeve, count the number of rows on the front from the beginning of the left armhole shaping down to the first outline. Mark the same number of rows on the front edge of the left sleeve from the beginning of the shaping. Draw in the outlines on the back edge of the left sleeve in the same way. Mark outlines on the right sleeve to correspond with the outlines on the right armhole edges of both the front and the back.

5 Finally, colour within the outlines to provide a guide to follow when making the sweater. Use natural colours and introduce areas of textured yarn as appropriate (see page 57).
When working the jacquard, don't waste yarn by stranding; instead use bobbins. Introduce each new colour neatly when completing the last stitch in the old colour (see Special Technique, page 54).

Left-handed crochet

Because right-handed people are in the majority most instructions and tools are designed with them in mind. Crochet patterns are no exception, since it would be very costly to print two sets of instructions. Some left-handed people can learn right-handed crochet and, with practice, they become as proficient as the naturally right-handed. If you find this impossible, don't be discouraged; it is perfectly possible to crochet with the left hand.

Beginning

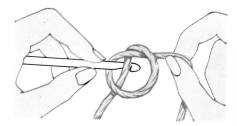

1 Hold the hook lightly but firmly in your left hand. Make a slip knot on the hook and pull the short end of yarn to tighten the loop.

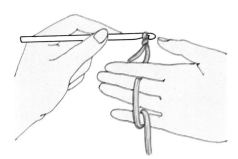

2 To maintain even tension, wind the working yarn round the fingers of your right hand: loop the yarn round your little finger, across your palm and behind your first finger. Pull the yarn gently so that it lies firmly round your fingers.

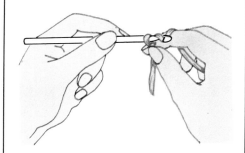

3 To work the foundation chain: hold the short end of yarn in your right hand to secure the loop. Take the hook under the taut working yarn and catch the yarn with the hook. Draw the yarn through the loop on the hook to form the first chain. Continue in this way.

Basic stitches

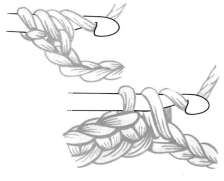

1 Although left-handers crochet from left to right the instructions for basic stitches in this 'Know-how' section can usually be used by left- or right-handed people, though the illustrations are 'right handed'. The illustrations above show the first two steps of double crochet as worked by a left-handed person.

2 The drawings in step 1 are the same as those on page 146, but they have been reversed and so are 'left-handed'. To reverse other drawings in this book, simply hold a mirror at the side of the drawing at a right angle to the page. The resulting mirror image will be left-handed.

Following patterns

Practice the basic crochet stitches until you are ready to tackle a pattern. For your first attempt choose a simple garment in a basic stitch.

Many crochet patterns do not mention left or right. When they do, read 'left' for 'right' and vice versa. With practice and common sense you will learn when to apply this rule.

Interesting textures and motifs

Working around the stem

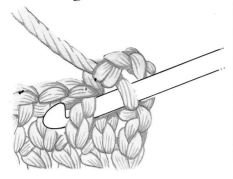

1 To work a treble from the front — known as "1tr front" — round the stem of a stitch, take the yarn round the hook, and insert the hook from front to back into the space between two stitches. Bring the hook to the front of the work between the second and the next stitch. Complete the stitch in the usual way.

2 Work a treble from the back — known as a "1tr back" — round the stem of a stitch in the same way, but insert the hook between stitches from back to front and then from front to back.

3 A neat crochet rib pattern can be formed by working treble round the stem from the front and back alternately along the row.

Working between stitches

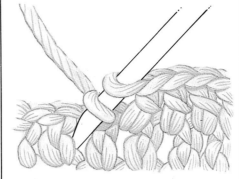

Take the yarn round the hook and insert the hook from front to back into the space between two stitches beneath the small connecting loop at the top of the stitch. Complete the stitch in the usual way.

Working into a single loop

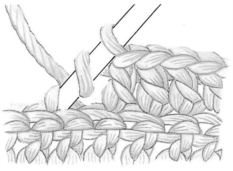

1 To work a treble into the back loop of a stitch, take the yarn round the hook and insert the hook into the back loop of the two loops lying at the top of the stitch. Complete the stitch in the usual way.

2 A treble worked into the front loop of a stitch is formed in the same way, except that the hook is inserted into the front loop of the two loops lying at the top of the stitch.

Double treble bobbles

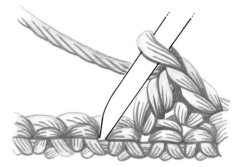

1 Small bobbles can be worked on a double crochet fabric by bending double treble in half. With the wrong side facing, work a double treble in the usual way. Work a double crochet into the next stitch, bending the double treble in half to form a small bobble on the front of the work. If the bobble seems flat after it has been bent in half, push it through to the right side of the work with the fingers.

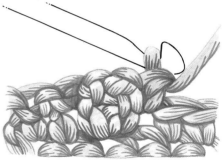

2 Larger bobbles may be formed by working two or more double treble into the next stitch, but leaving the last loop of each double treble on the hook. Take the yarn round the hook and draw through all loops. Secure the bobbles as in step 1. (Wrong side is shown above.)

Working filet crochet

Filet charts

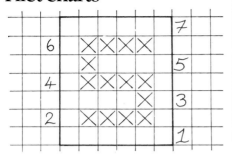

1 Filet crochet is usually worked by following graphed charts, in which blocks of treble and spaces, formed by working chain across a given number of stitches, are shown as crosses and blank squares respectively. In the chart above, each blank square represents a two-chain space plus a connecting treble, and each cross represents two treble plus a connecting treble.

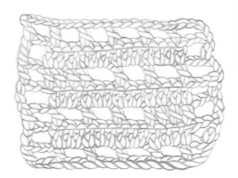

2 The sample above has been worked following the chart in step 1. Read the odd-numbered rows from right to left and the even-numbered rows from left to right.

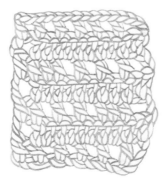

3 Sometimes filet patterns are worked so that each space is formed from one chain plus a connecting treble and each block is formed from one treble plus one

connecting treble, thus producing a narrower fabric. The same chart can thus be interpreted in different ways. The sample above has been worked from the chart in step 1.

Mesh background

1 Make a multiple of three chain plus two extra. Work one treble into the eighth chain from the hook. * Make two chain. Miss the next two foundation chain and work one treble into the next foundation chain. Continue from * to the last foundation chain.

2 On following rows, begin by working five chain to count as the first treble and two chain space. Work one treble into the next treble. * Work two chain and then one treble into the next treble. Continue from * to the end, working the last treble into the turning chain.

Beginning with a block

1 To begin a piece of filet with a block of treble, make enough foundation chain for the spaces and blocks on first row. Work two more chain and then work one treble into the fourth chain from the hook; the first three chain count as the first treble. Complete the first block by working one treble into each of the next two foundation chain.

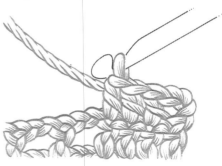

2 On following rows, to begin with a block work three chain to count as the first treble. Miss the first treble and work one treble into each of the next three double crochet.

Working a block above a space

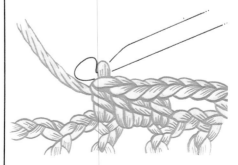

Work one treble into the next connecting treble. Then work two treble into the space, followed by one treble into the next connecting treble.

Working a space above a block

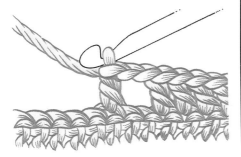

Work one treble into the next connecting treble. Work two chain. Miss the next two treble and work one treble into the next treble.

Shaping filet crochet

The methods of shaping given here are for a two-treble, two-chain mesh; for a wider or denser mesh, work more or fewer chain at the beginning or end of the rows.

Increasing a space

1 *To increase a space at the end of a row, work seven chain at the beginning of the previous row. Miss the first chain from the hook and slip stitch into each of the next three chain. (The remaining three chain count as the first treble of the row.)*

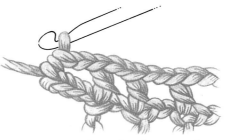

2 *Pattern to the end and turn. Work to the end of the increase row, working the last treble into the turning chain. Make two chain and work one treble into the first slip stitch as shown to form the new space.*

3 *To increase a space at the beginning of a row, work seven chain at the end of the previous row. Turn. Begin the increase row by working one treble into the first stitch to form the new space.*

4 *To increase two spaces at either end of a row, work ten chain at the beginning or end of the previous row, as appropriate. At the beginning of the row below the increase, slip stitch into the second to seventh chain from the hook. Work two chain and one treble into the top of the second treble of the previous row. When increasing over chains made at the end of a row, work one treble into the eighth chain from the hook, make two chain, and work one treble into the first treble of the previous row.*

Increasing a block

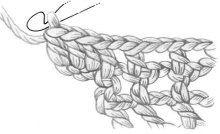

1 *To increase at the end of a row, follow step 1 of 'increasing a space'. Pattern to the end of the row and turn. Work to the end of the row, working one treble into the turning chain. Work one chain into each of the additional slip stitches to form the new block. To increase two blocks, work ten chain as in either of the two methods in step 4 of 'Increasing a space'.*

2 *To increase a block at the beginning of a row, work five chain at the end of the previous row and turn. Work one treble into the fourth chain from the hook (the first three chain count as the first treble). Work one treble into the next chain and one treble into the first treble of the previous row to form the new block. Work ten chain as before to increase two blocks.*

Decreasing a space

1 *At the beginning of a row, work one chain and miss the first treble. Slip stitch into each of the next two chain and into the next treble. Work five chain to count as the first treble and two-chain space. Work one treble into the next treble and pattern to end. Decrease two spaces by slip stitching over an extra two chain and a treble.*

Padded work

2 At the end of a row, leave the last space unworked. To decrease two spaces, miss an extra space.

Decreasing a block

1 At the beginning of a row, make one chain and miss the first treble. Slip stitch into each of the next three treble to decrease one block. Begin the row with five chain to count as the first treble and two-chain space. Decrease two blocks by slip stitching across two blocks of the previous row.

2 To decrease at the end of a row, pattern to the last four treble, work one treble into the next treble. Turn, leaving the remaining treble unworked. Decrease two blocks by leaving six treble unworked.

By padding or quilting with synthetic wadding you can add more texture and warmth to your designs.

Simple padding

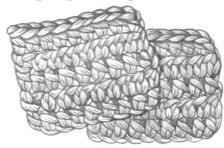

1 Almost any shape can be padded, but rectangular pieces are best. Work two pieces of crochet with the same number of stitches and rows. The right-side piece could be decorated, though any fancy stitches should be closely textured to conceal the wadding.

2 Use lightweight or medium-weight wadding. Cut it 5mm smaller all round than the crochet. Place the wadding on the wrong side of one piece of crochet and place the wrong side of the other piece on top. Pin through all three layers to hold them together.

3 Either join the pieces with double crochet (see page 124) or work a stitch-by-stitch oversewn seam. For the latter, secure the yarn at the corner.

Holding the two edges together, insert the needle under corresponding top single loops of the both pieces and draw the yarn through.

4 Continue in this way to the end. This method produces a neat seam, which is almost invisible on the right side.

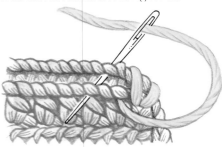

5 To join the padded pieces, place them together with right sides facing. Use stitch-by-stitch oversewing as before, inserting the needle under the loops seamed in steps 3 and 4.

Quilting

Quilting crochet is easier if you use your pattern as a guide – geometric designs are simplest.

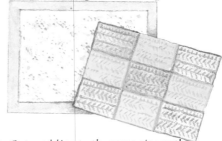

1 Cut wadding to the same size as the crochet. Cut out lining approximately 1cm larger all round than the crochet to provide a seam allowance. Place the wadding on the wrong side of the lining and then place the wrong side of the crochet on top of the wadding.

Finishing techniques

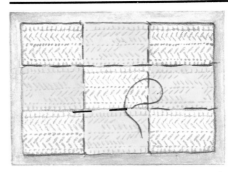

2 Using contrasting sewing thread, tack through all three layers along the quilting lines. Stitch along quilting lines. Experiment to find the best stitch length and foot pressure. Remove the tacking stitches.

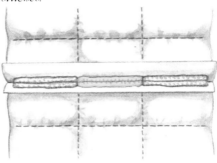

3 To seam quilted crochet, place the quilted pieces together with right sides facing. Machine stitch approximately 1.5cm in from the edge, catching the edge of the crochet. Trim the lining seam allowance on one side only.

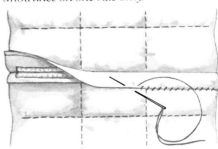

4 Turn under the raw edge of the other lining seam allowance; slipstitch it to the lining on the other side, as shown, to hide the raw edges. Bind the outer raw edges either with strips of crochet or with bias strips of lining fabric.

Buttonholes

Buttonholes keep their shape best when worked in fabrics made of firm, close-textured stitches such as double crochet. They can be worked either in the main fabric or in a separate band.

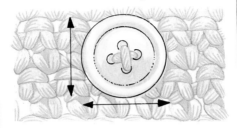

1 Before beginning, place the button on the crochet. Count the number of rows or stitches covered by the diameter of the button, then subtract one. This will give a rough idea of the number of chain or rows needed to form the buttonhole; but check as you work to make sure this is correct.

2 Crochet buttonholes should look very neat, but they will keep their shape better if reinforced with buttonhole stitch. Use a tapestry needle and matching yarn to work the stitches.

Horizontal buttonholes

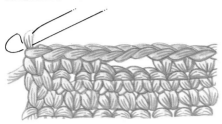

1 Beginning at the edge nearest to the buttonhole, work to the position of the buttonhole. Make the number of chains needed to form the buttonhole. Skip the same number of stitches and work into the next stitch.

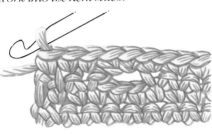

2 On the return row, work one stitch into each chain of the previous row. Work to the end of the row. One horizontal buttonhole has been formed.

Vertical buttonholes

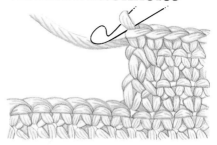

1 Beginning at the edge nearest the buttonhole, work to the position of the buttonhole. Turn, leaving the remaining stitches unworked. Work the number of rows needed for the buttonhole, ending at the buttonhole edge.

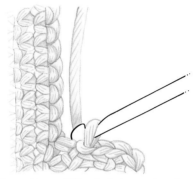

2 Do not turn. Slip stitch down the edge of the buttonhole, working the last slip stitch into the same place as the first stitch on the side of the buttonhole.

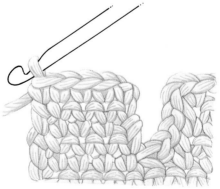

3 Miss one stitch and work into each of the stitches left unworked in step 1. Pattern on these stitches until the second edge of the buttonhole is the same number of rows as the first, ending at the side edge.

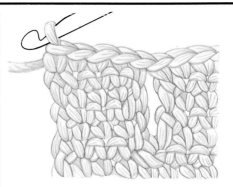

4 Turn and work to the buttonhole. Work one stitch into the edge stitch on the other side of the buttonhole to join the two sides together. Pattern to the end of the row. Count the stitches to make sure none have been accidentally missed. Turn and continue in pattern, working over the top stitches of the buttonhole very carefully. Repeat steps 1 to 4 for each buttonhole.

Button loops

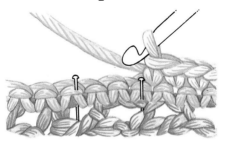

1 With the wrong side facing, work one row of double crochet into the side edge of the work. Mark the position of the loops with pins. Turn and work to the first pin.

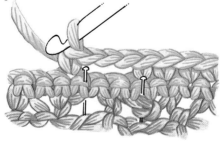

2 Make enough chain to slip easily, but not loosely, over the button. Miss the same number of stitches. Work a double crochet into the next stitch. Continue in this way until all loops have been worked.

Making a twisted cord

1 A twisted cord can be made of various numbers of strands, to produce different thicknesses of cord. The number is usually specified in the pattern. Take the required number of strands, cut to three times the length of the finished cord, and knot each end.

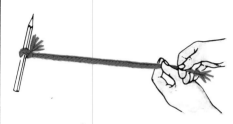

2 Fasten one end of the cord around a door handle, or knot it over a pencil and anchor in a convenient place. Holding the strands taut, rotate them until they are tightly twisted.

3 Fold the strands in half at the centre and knot the ends together. Holding the knot, give the cord a sharp shake and even out the twists by smoothing the cord from the knotted end. Re-knot at the fold and cut both ends to make neat tassels.

Working an invisible seam

1 *This flat seam is ideal for baby clothes and other delicate garments, especially those made of lace, since it does not produce a hard ridge. It also has the advantage of enabling patterns to be matched easily. First place the pieces edge to edge, right side upwards, matching patterns.*

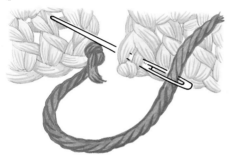

2 *Using a matching yarn (here a contrast colour is used for clarity) and a tapestry needle, secure the yarn to one lower edge. Take the needle over to the other side edge and pass it under one stitch.*

3 *Take the needle back to the first side edge and under the next stitch. Pull the yarn through firmly to make the stitch invisible, but not so tightly that the fabric puckers.*
Continue catching one stitch on each edge until the seam is complete.

Picking up stitches

Picking up stitches is a technique used more often in knitted than in crocheted garments, but it is required wherever knitted rib is added to a crocheted fabric edge. The pattern will specify the size needles to be used and the number of stitches to picked up. The instructions are written: 'Knit up [K up]' followed by the number of stitches.

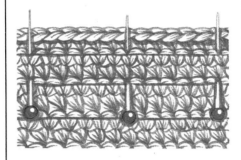

1 *To ensure that the stitches are picked up evenly, divide the edge into equal sections and mark the sections with pins.*

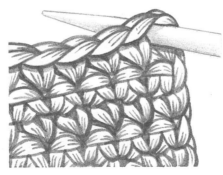

2 *Divide the number of sections into the number of stitches specified in the pattern and start picking up an equal number of stitches per section. Insert the tip of the needle into a row end on vertical edges or into a stitch on horizontal edges.*

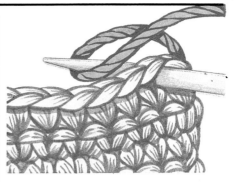

3 *With yarn at the back of the work, take it under and over the point of the needle, and draw a loop through.*

4 *Insert the tip of the needle into the next stitch or row end. Take the yarn under and over the point of the needle and draw a loop through. Continue in this way until the correct number of stitches have been picked up.*

INDEX

Crochet hook sizes

Old UK sizes		Metric (I.S.R.)
7		0.60mm
6½		0.75
5½		1.00
4½	cotton	1.25
3½		1.50
2½		1.75
1½		
		2.00
14		
13		2.25
12		2.50
10		3.00
9	wool	3.50
8		4.00
7		4.50
6		5.00
5		5.50
4		6.00
2		7.00

Care of yarns

To make sure that your crocheted garment maintains its fresh new look as long as possible, pay careful attention to the information given on the ball band regarding the proper care of the yarn. This information is normally given in the form of the internationally-understood symbols which are explained in this chart.

5 / 40°	MACHINE Warm Medium wash (40°C)
HAND WASH	HAND WASH Warm (40°C)
6 / 40°	Warm Maximum wash (40°C) Cold rinse. Short spin.
	Warm (40°C) Do not wring.
(hand)	HAND WASH ONLY WARM (40°C)
(machine)	MACHINE WASHABLE
(machine crossed)	DO NOT MACHINE WASH
P	DRY CLEANABLE
P crossed	DO NOT DRY CLEAN
triangle crossed	DO NOT BLEACH
iron •	COOL
iron ••	WARM
iron •••	HOT
iron crossed	DO NOT IRON
hand in basin crossed	DRY CLEAN ONLY